AF506127

The Future of Development Financing

Knowledge is essential in an increasingly complex world. In order to contribute to a better understanding of global development and an increased effectiveness of development cooperation, the EGDI secretariat of the Swedish Ministry for Foreign Affairs manages the Global Development Studies series. The studies in this series are initiated by the ministry, but written by independent researchers.

The current study builds on a previous project, the Development Finance 2000-initiative. Leading up to the UN conference on development finance in Monterrey, March 2002, Sweden published studies on issues about the financing of multilateral aid, and of global public goods. The current study pulls threads together in an attempt at looking at all the components in the international *system* for development finance, and where that is likely to go in the near future.

The arguments and positions expressed in this study are those of the authors, and do not necessarily reflect the views of the Swedish government.

Another task of the secretariat is to serve the EGDI (Expert Group on Development Issues), in its task of channelling research findings into the heart of policy making. The EGDI is an independent group of internationally renowned researchers and policy makers.

For further information, please contact:
The EGDI Secretariat
Ministry for Foreign Affairs
Department for Global Development
SE-103 39 Stockholm, Sweden

Phone + 46 8 405 10 00
Fax + 46 8 723 11 76

egdi.secretariat@foreign.ministry.se
www.egdi.gov.se

The Future of Development Financing

Challenges and Strategic Choices

Francisco Sagasti, Keith Bezanson and Fernando Prada

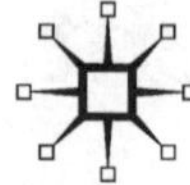

First published 2005 by
PALGRAVE MACMILLAN
Houndmills, Basingstoke, Hampshire RG21 6XS and
175 Fifth Avenue, New York, N. Y. 10010
Companies and representatives throughout the world

PALGRAVE MACMILLAN is the global academic imprint of the Palgrave Macmillan division of St. Martin's Press, LLC and of Palgrave Macmillan Ltd. Macmillan® is a registered trademark in the United States, United Kingdom and other countries. Palgrave is a registered trademark in the European Union and other countries.

ISBN-13: 978–1–4039–4951–6 hardback
ISBN-10: 1–4039–4951–4 hardback

This book is printed on paper suitable for recycling and made from fully managed and sustained forest sources.

A catalogue record for this book is available from the British Library.

Library of Congress Cataloging-in-Publication Data
Sagasti, Francisco R.
   The future of development financing : challenges and strategic choices / Francisco Sagasti, Keith Bezanson, and Fernando Prada.
      p. cm.
   Includes bibliographical references and index.
   ISBN 1–4039–4951–4
      1. Finance–Developing countries. 2. Economic development–Finance. 3. International finance. 4. Economic assistance–Developing countries. I. Bezanson, Keith. II. Prada, Fernando. III. Title.

HG195.S24 2005
332¢.09172¢4–dc22   2005040542

10   9   8   7   6   5   4   3   2   1
14   13 12 09 08 07 06 05 04 03

Printed and bound in Great Britain by
Antony Rowe Ltd, Chippenham and Eastbourne

Contents

List of Tables, Figures and Boxes

Boxes

List of Acronyms

ACC	Administrative Committee on Co-ordination
ACP	African Caribbean and Pacific countries
ADRs	American Depositary Receipts
AfDB	African Development Bank
AfDF	African Development Fund
AFESD	Arab Fund for Economic and Social Development
AIDS	Acquired Immune Deficiency Syndrome
APEC	Asia Pacific Economic Forum
AsDB	Asian Development Bank
AsDF	Asian Development Fund
ASEAN	Association of Southeast Asian Nations
BADEA	Arab Bank for Economic Development In Africa
BASU	Business As Usual
BCIE	Central American Bank for Economic Integration
BOAD	West African Development Bank
BWI	Bretton Woods Institutions
CABEI	Central American Bank for Economic Integration
CAC	Collective Action Clauses
CAF	Andean Finance Corporation
CAS	Country Assessment Strategy
CCA	Common Country Assessment
CDB	Caribbean Development Bank
CDF	Comprehensive Development Framework
CFF	Compensatory Financing Facility
CLAC	Collective Action Clauses
CORE	Comprehensive Reform
CPIA	Country Policy and Institutional Assessment
DAC	Development Assistance Committee
DFID	Department for International Development
EADB	East African Development Bank
EBA	Everything But Arms
EBRD	European Bank for Reconstruction and Development
EC	European Community
ECLAC	Economic Commission for Latin America and the Caribbean
ECOSOC	Economic and Social Council (UN)

EDF	European Development Fund
EEC	European Economic Community
EFF	Extended Fund Facility
EIB	European Investment Bank
EMP	Emerging Markets Partnership
ESAF	Enhanced Structural Adjustment Facility
EU	European Union
FAO	Food and Agricultural Organization
FDI	Foreign direct investment
FLAR	Latin American Reserve Fund
FONPLATA	Fund for the development of the Rio de la Plata Basin
FSAP	Financial Sector Assessment Program
FSO	Fund for Special Operations
FTAA	Free Trade Agreement of the Americas
GAVI	Global Alliance for Vaccines and Immunisation
GDP	Gross Domestic Product
GEF	Global Environment Facility
GMO	Genetically Modified Organisms
GNP	Gross National Product
GPG	Global Public Good
HIPC	Highly Indebted Poor Countries
IADB	Inter-American Development Bank
IAEA	International Atomic Energy Agency
IBCA	Intervest Bancshares Corporation
IBRD	International Bank for Reconstruction and Development
ICAO	International Civil Aviation Organization
ICSID	International Centre for the Settlement of Investment Disputes
IDA	International Development Assistance (World Bank)
IDB	Islamic Development Bank
IDRC	International Development Research Centre
IEO	Independent Evaluation Office (IMF)
IFAD	International Fund for Agricultural and Rural Development
IFC	International Finance Corporation
IFF	International Finance Facility
IFIs	international financial institutions
IFS	International Foundation for Science
IIC	Inter-American Investment Corporation
ILO	International Labour Organization

IMDIS	Integrated Monitoring and Documentation System
IMF	International Monetary Fund
IMO	International Maritime Organization
IsDB	Islamic Development Bank
ITU	International Telecommunication Union
LDCs	least developed countries
LICUS	Low Income Countries Under Stress
LILs	learning and innovation loans
MCA	Millennium Challenge Account (US)
MDBs	Multilateral Development Banks
MDGs	Millennium Development Goals
MERCOSUR	Common Market of South America
MIF	Multilateral Investment Fund
MIGA	Multilateral Investment Guarantee Agency
MTP	Medium Term Plan
MYFF	Multi-year Financial Frameworks
NADB	North American Development Bank
NAFTA	North American Free Trade Agreement
NDF	Nordic Development Fund
NEADB	North East Asian Development Bank
NEPAD	New Partnership for African Development
NGOs	non-governmental organisations
NIB	Nordic Investment Bank
NIEO	New International Economic Order
NPV	net present value
ODA	Overseas Development Assistance
OECD	Organisation for Economic Co-operation and Development
OPEC	Organization of Petroleum Exporting Countries
OPEC Fund	Organization of Petroleum Exporting Countries Fund
OPIC	Overseas Private Investment Corporation
PRGF	Poverty Reduction and Growth Facility (IMF)
PRSPs	Poverty Reduction Strategy Papers
R&D	research and development
RBB	Results-Based Budget
RBM	Results-Based Management
RDBs	regional development banks
ROSC	Reports on Standard and Codes
RPG	Regional Public Good
SADC	South African Development community
SDDS	Special Data Dissemination Standard

SDRM	Sovereign Debt Restructuring Mechanisms
SDRs	Special Drawing Rights
SRDBs	Sub-Regional Development Banks
SRF	Supplemental Reserve Facility
SRI	socially responsible investment
SWAps	sector-wide approaches
TOKTEN	Transfer of Knowledge through Expatriate Nationals
UK	United Kingdom
UN	United Nations
UNCDF	UN Capital Development Fund
UNCHS	UN Centre for Human Settlements
UNCTAD	UN Conference on Trade and Development
UNDAF	UN Development Assistance Framework
UNDG	United Nations Development Group
UNDP	United Nations Development Programme
UNEP	UN Environment Programme
UNESCO	United Nations Educational, Scientific and Cultural Organization
UNFIP	UN Fund for International Partnerships
UNFPA	UN Population Fund
UNHCR	UN High Commissioner for Refugees
UNICEF	UN Children's Fund
UNIDO	UN Industrial Development Organization
UNITAR	UN Institute for Training and Research
UNRWA	UN Relief & Works Agency for Palestinian Refugees in the Near East
UNU	United Nations University
UPU	Universal Postal Union
US	United States
USAID	United States Agency for International Development
WB	World Bank
WEF	World Economic Forum
WFP	World Food Programme
WHO	World Health Organization
WIPO	World Intellectual Property Organization
WMO	World Meteorological Organization
WTO	World Trade Organization
WWII	World War II

Preface

International development emerged as a field of activity and of scholarship in its own right during the second half of the twentieth century. More than five decades later, it is generally acknowledged that adequate and sustained levels of investment in all its forms are essential for economic growth and for improving living standards in poor countries. There is also, however, widespread realization that financial resources are a necessary but not a sufficient condition for development: on their own, and in the absence of strong institutions, good governance, sensible policies and the capacity to generate and utilize knowledge, they are of little help. One consequence of this realization has been a steady growth in the number and reach of entities that provide financial and development resources assistance to developing countries. These now comprise a large network of public and private national, regional and international organizations that are usually referred to as the 'international development financing system'.

This 'system', however, is really not much of a *system*. It is rather a collection of disjointed entities that lack coherence, often work at cross-purposes and are not up to the task of mobilizing finance in the amounts and ways required to assist a growing diversity of developing countries in their efforts to reduce poverty and improve living standards.

In spite of this – and also because of it – the early years of the twenty-first century have brought about an unprecedented 'window of opportunity' for a conscientious re-examination and re-alignment of the institutions and organizations that configure the international development architecture. There is a renewed impetus for reform, partly because global communications have increased awareness of the plight of the poor in developing countries, partly because criticisms about the effectiveness of the development financing system have multiplied, and partly because of increased awareness that the haphazard approaches to reforms of the past have not been successful. In addition, the specific and time-bounded nature of the Millennium Development Goals (MDGs) has helped to focus attention on the inadequacies of current international development financing arrangements. There is also evidence that the terrorist attacks of September 11 2001 have caused political leaders concern that deeper international security crises may be looming (and perhaps imminent) unless the widespread poverty, marginalization and growing inequalities that lead to frustration and despair are significantly reduced.

Whatever the relative weights one assigns to these factors, the first years of the twenty-first century are characterized by a much greater international focus on development financing issues than in the previous three decades. Current attempts to reform the international development financing system appear to be serious and far-reaching, to have engaged a wide constituency and to have generated substantial political momentum.

Sustaining this momentum will require exceptional political will and leadership. The inertias in the 'system' are formidable and there is also a considerable risk that the current sense of crisis and fear could divert development thinking and practice towards narrow and short-term security concerns – such as the 'war on terrorism'. This could hijack the development enterprise in a manner reminiscent of the impact of the Cold War from the 1950s to the 1980s. Political realities dictate that efforts to reform the international development financing system cannot be on an 'all or nothing' or 'anything goes' basis. If meaningful and sustained reforms are to occur, they will need to be guided by a long-term vision, to focus on clearly articulated strategic choices, and to identify practical and politically viable short-term actions – what we term in this study a 'radical incrementalism' perspective.

This perspective informs the approach and theme of this book. It leads to a 'framework for strategic choices' and to the identification of the key actors that will make such choices. This is pursued through the construction of scenarios that combine institutional arrangements, financing instruments, categories of countries and political viability, and through an analysis of the policy implications of alternative scenarios. This study, therefore, does not offer a 'blueprint' for change, but rather a set of options from which to choose in order to reform international development finance.

The first chapter outlines the legacy of more than five decades of growth and change in the international development financing system, and ends with a critical assessment of its main defining characteristics at the end of the twentieth century. Chapter 2 reviews and summarizes the main recent attempts to reform the international development architecture, focusing on actions undertaken by United Nations bodies, international financial institutions, bilateral aid agencies and the European Union, and also on initiatives to establish new sources and mechanisms for development finance.

Chapter 3 begins by suggesting the attributes of an effective international development financing system. It then describes the components of four scenarios that portray alternative futures for development financing in or about 2015 (the established target date for achieving the Millennium Development Goals). The first component, institutional arrangements, posits two extreme hypothetical situations: one in which there are few and mostly inconsequential changes in institutional arrangements ('business as usual', or BASU), and another in which the impetus for reform has carried the day and has led to a major restructuring of institutional arrangements including the creation of new entities ('comprehensive reform', or CORE). A broad range of possible intermediate situations between these two extremes is then briefly discussed. The second component introduces considerations regarding the range of existing and proposed financial instruments to channel resources to developing countries. The third component explores the ways in which developing countries are classified – usually according to their income per capita levels – and concludes that this is not very useful for development financing purposes. A new approach to categorize countries in terms of their capacity to mobilize external and domestic financial resources is then proposed. Chapter 3 closes with a discussion of political viability, the fourth and final component of the scenarios, outlining trends in international relations and identifying the main actors that could bring about change in the international development architecture.

Chapter 4 starts with a brief account of the interactions between the scenario components, showing the correspondence between different sets of financing instruments and categories of developing countries. It then describes four scenarios for the future of the international development financing system: *Inertia, Limited Reforms, Major Reforms* and *Transformation*. These scenarios should be seen both as heuristic devices to explore how development financing may evolve over the next decade, and as a projection of the outcomes that may result if certain sequences of critical decisions are taken. *Inertia* corresponds to a 2015 situation similar or slightly worse than the one prevailing at the end of the twentieth century, while *Transformation* describes a situation in which a critical mass of reform efforts have succeeded in making the international development financing system much more effective and efficient. *Limited Reforms* refers to a situation in which minor and piecemeal improvements, focusing exclusively on the poorest countries, are put in place, while in the *Major Reforms* scenario there are significant and visible improvements reaching all types of developing countries, but without their achieving fundamental and sustained aggregate changes for the better.

Chapter 5 derives the policy implications of the four scenarios, articulating them into a framework for strategic choices. Several questions and answers are put forward to assist policy and decision makers in taking stock of the current situation and assessing alternative pathways to reform. Some concluding remarks close the last chapter of the book.

This book is the product of an extended association between the authors, the Institute of Development Studies (IDS) at the University of Sussex and the Ministry for Foreign Affairs of Sweden. It began in 2000 with the preparation of a report on the multilateral development banks as part of the Swedish 'Development Financing 2000' initiative, continued with another study on the provision and financing of global public goods, and culminated with the preparation of the present book as part of the work carried out on Global Development Studies by the Expert Group on Development Initiatives (EGDI) at the Swedish Ministry for Foreign Affairs.

Keith Bezanson, Director of the IDS to July 2004, led the overall project. Francisco Sagasti, Director of Agenda: PERÚ and IDS Senior Associate, was lead researcher and principal author of this report with the collaboration of Fernando Prada as associate researcher. Kristine Blockus and Ursula Casabonne provided research assistance, and Ana Teresa Lima and Joanne Salop contributed research papers on specific issues.

The authors are grateful to Andreas Earshammar, who steered the initial phases of the project, and to Mats Hårsmar and Torgny Holmgren of EGDI, who provided the project team with unflinching support. Valuable comments were received at various stages of the project, especially from the participants in a seminar held in Stockholm in February 2004 to discuss the interim report and a second seminar in the same city in July 2004 to review the draft final version. Additional suggestions were received in presentations in Washington at the World Bank and the International Monetary Fund in November 2004, and in Paris at an event organized by the United Nations Development Programme and the French Ministry for Foreign Affairs in January 2005. The authors are also grateful to Zoe Mars for her help in editing and structuring the book, and to Amanda Hamilton at Palgrave Macmillan for shepherding the manuscript with extraordinary patience.

1
The Inheritance: Evolution of the International Development System and of Development Financing

1.1 The evolution of the concept of development

The period from the end of the Second World War can be called the 'age of international development'. Initial emphasis on the reconstruction of Europe through the Marshall Plan was quickly transformed into a bold, new political campaign on a global scale. Its stated aim was to make 'the benefits of (Western) scientific advances and industrial progress available for the improvement and growth of underdeveloped areas'.[1]

The idea of development was initially interpreted as being more or less synonymous with economic growth and the early conception of how to bring about development assumed a direct relationship between capital investment and economic growth. The dominant development models of the 1940s and 1950s held that, as developing countries usually had an abundant supply of labour, it was a lack of investment that constrained economic growth and development. This thinking was embodied in the writings of W. Arthur Lewis (1955), for example, who focused attention on investment ratios and insisted on 'growth and not distribution' as the essential path to development. A similar emphasis is found in the works of Walter Rostow (1960) who defined a path to development consisting of five stages of economic growth and in Ragnar Nurske's (1953) theories of massive investment in the urban-industrial sector as essential to capital formation and structural transformation.

During the 1950s and 1960s, therefore, mainstream development theory assigned nearly exclusive importance to finance and investment. Making international finance available was accorded the central role and prescriptions focused on providing a 'big push' of investment to initiate self-sustaining growth. In essence, an adequate level of finance was held to be a sufficient condition to bring about development. Yet, in spite of the pre-eminence awarded to capital investment during this period, there were at the same time early estimates for the US economy that placed the contribution of the rate of growth of inputs (capital, labour, land) to the rate of growth of output at between 10 and 15 per cent, suggesting that other factors such as productivity, innovation, technological change, institutions, education and human capital played a key role in growth (Abramovitz 1956; Solow 1957; Denison 1964).[2] More recent estimates (Baier, Dwyer and Tamura 2002) for a large number of developed and developing countries indicate that the contribution of total factor productivity to the rate of growth of output could be around 40–50 per cent, if weighted estimates considering the relative size of the countries and the number observations available, and up to 80–90 per cent if unweighted data are used.

The development experience of the 1960s and 1970s brought about a major transformation in development thinking from a singular emphasis on finance and investment towards a much more complex mosaic of factors that included the quality of the labour force, the technological capabilities of firms and government policies. These changes derived in part from a growing realization that economic growth had some undesirable effects and that it did not lead directly and unambiguously to improvements in social conditions. They were also driven by larger philosophical concerns about the conflation of the meaning of development with the idea of economic growth (Seers 1969). These concerns were institutionalized in the World Bank under the presidency of Robert McNamara who insisted that new thinking was required that would 'dethrone GNP' as the measure of development. Thus, concepts such as marginalization and exclusion, together with an emerging concern about the environmental consequences of growth, led to broader views about the factors influencing development and crystallized in approaches that emphasized the satisfaction of basic human needs, redistribution with growth and human-scale development. Starting in the 1980s, increased attention was paid to the role of macroeconomic stability, market-oriented policy reforms, the role of the private sector, and to the interactions between the public and private sectors and their relations with civil society organizations. This was followed in the 1990s by a focus on institutions and governance, knowledge and technological innovation, and social capital. Thus, at the beginning of the twenty-first century the availability of capital came to be seen as only one of many factors contributing to successful development.

The development efforts of the past five decades have been neither a great success nor a dismal failure. On the positive side, several low-income countries, particularly in Asia, have in one generation achieved the standards of living of the industrialized nations; life expectancy and educational levels have increased in most developing countries, and income per capita has doubled in countries like Brazil, China, South Korea and Turkey in less than a third of the time this took in the United Kingdom or the United States a century or more earlier. On the negative side, the absolute number of poor people has increased in the world, income disparities between rich and poor nations (and between the rich and the poor in many nations) have become more pronounced, the environment has been subjected to severe stress, and unsatisfied social demands have grown many times over throughout the developing world.

What has been the role of international development assistance in this process? Aid, and, in particular, financial and technical assistance, have been characterized by a combination of unrealistic expectations, confusing or conflicting goals, and inadequate instruments. For example, since at least the 1970s it has been generally accepted that the main drivers of development are factors internal to individual countries and the external factors that matter most are access to markets, capital, and technology, and supportive security, economic, sociopolitical and environmental conditions for development. Yet most attention has focused on resources provided through official development assistance (ODA) and not directly on these main drivers of development, in spite of the widely accepted fact that the role of ODA is quite limited and that it can at best only act as a catalyst – and not as a substitute – for other forms of cooperation, and for domestic resource mobilization and internal development efforts.

Compared with the first two or three decades following the Second World War, development thinking today is far less exclusively concerned with the role of capital investment as the engine of growth and development. Yet it is also clear that financial resources, whether mobilized from domestic or international sources, are essential: they remain a necessary, but not sufficient, condition for development. Thus, whatever the other factors and requirements to bring about development, establishing an adequate international development financing system remains a matter of high priority.

1.2 Institutional changes in the international development system

Fifty years ago, a small handful of institutions comprised the organizational arrangements of the international development system. Today that system is made up of a bewildering array of bilateral, multilateral, non-governmental, private and hybrid institutions characterized by overlapping functions, duplication and a confused or non-existent division of labour. Recent efforts notwithstanding, mechanisms aimed at systemic co-ordination and improved cost-effectiveness have been mostly frustrated by two powerful and pervasive factors. The first is that there is no accepted authority or 'consortium of owners' that can make decisions for the system as a whole. The absence of an overall authority means that development finance issues are generally settled by yielding to politically powerful interests, or are subject to only partial and inadequate responses.

Secondly, even where widespread consensus exists that some institutions have little impact or have outlived their usefulness, closures and/or mergers have not occurred. New institutions continue to be created to rectify perceived deficiencies in existing ones and institutions that are ineffective and marginalized continue to exist because of political patronage ties, inertia and non-transparent funding formulas. In 50 years of aid there has been no closure or merger of a major international institution.

The combination of these two factors ensures a system that Rogerson (2004: 7) has described as:

> riddled with imperfections, inertia and bureaucratic 'intrapreneurship' (with) a distinct, sheltered bureaucratic culture, outside the mainstream of donor (and sometimes recipient) government administrations. These factors also tend to neutralise sporadic top-down reform initiatives, which have mostly been limited in scope and time.

Between the late 1940s and the early 1960s, almost all development assistance was provided on an exclusively bilateral (i.e. country to country) basis[3] with the United States as the dominant source of international development financing, accounting for more than 50 per cent of total ODA during the 1950s.

The balance between bilateral and multilateral channels for ODA underwent a major shift starting in the mid-1960s. From an average of 8 per cent of the total during the 1950s, the multilateral share had reached nearly 25 per cent by 1975. In part, the explosive growth in multilateral assistance during this period was a matter of necessity. At that time bilateral agencies simply did not have the capacities and experience needed to programme the increasing levels of official financing that were being made available. In addition, multilateral development institutions had been strengthening their administrative and technical capacities and were thus able to attract strong support from bilateral donors. Particularly notable were the major changes brought about in the World Bank under the McNamara presidency (1968–81), including a significant reorientation toward antipoverty projects and the strengthening of the World Bank's research capacity. The UNDP also had expanded its in-house technical and administrative capabilities and had established a strong network of resident representatives in most developing countries. The share of ODA provided through multilateral channels continued to grow until the 1980s when it stabilized at about 28–30 per cent of the total (including contributions to the EEC).

Potentially explosive imbalances in the global economy in the 1980s, most notably Japan's large and accelerating current account surpluses and a corresponding United States deficit, led to a large expansion in Japanese development assistance programmes. The extent of this change becomes clear when it is recalled that until the early 1960s Japan was a recipient of foreign aid for reconstruction and by the late 1980s it had become the largest ODA donor. Also, during the 1980s, Japan's operations in the field shifted from rather narrow bilateral economic interests, such as promoting exports and investments in the Asian region, to broader multilateral considerations related to international economic and political stability. Multilateral institutions were major beneficiaries of Japan's expanded ODA, particularly the concessional loan windows of the World Bank and of the Asian Development Bank. The munificence of Japan towards multilateral institutions, however, also concealed a trend towards the 'bilateralization of multilateralism' through an array of special parallel funding, co-financing and trust fund arrangements that later spread to other donors.

The 1980s also witnessed an international debt crisis that was, in large measure, a consequence of the lending practices of commercial banks eager to recycle the huge amount of petrodollars deposited following the dramatic increase in the price of oil brought about by OPEC during the 1970s. This crisis began in 1982 with Mexico's default on its commercial loans, and led to major changes in the international development financing system. The traditional role differentiation in multilateral development finance between the IMF and the World Bank was abandoned when the IMF moved closer to development financing and structural reform and the World Bank increased its role in balance-of-payment support to manage liquidity crises in developing countries. The net result was that the activities and policy instruments of the two institutions assumed a more overlapping than complementary character.[4]

This blurring of traditional division of labour boundaries was not limited to the IMF and World Bank. A similar blurring occurred between the World Bank and the development agencies of the United Nations. The roots of this may be traced back to the 1960s when, under the 'Kennedy Compromise', it was decided to channel soft financial aid through the World Bank (i.e. IDA), while technical assistance and food aid were to be provided principally by UN agencies. Initially, the application of this division involved World Bank concessional loans going mainly into infrastructure, including social infrastructure such as the building of schools and hospitals, while the United Nations agencies concentrated more on the 'soft' parts of development (i.e. poverty reduction, employment, vulnerable groups, health and education delivery systems). This is no longer the case (Singer 1995). The change was gradual and started in the 1970s, but over the past decade World Bank financing for infrastructure has declined sharply and there has been a wholesale migration of Bank lending activities into those same 'soft' areas that were previously the purview of the United Nations. Today the World Bank provides as much technical assistance as the UNDP and the IMF is rapidly expanding its technical assistance operations.

By the end of the 1980s, the 'golden age' of rapid growth for the multilateral agencies of international development had come to an end. This was due, in the first instance, to an ending of the age of high year-on-year growth in ODA. It also resulted from a sharp erosion of confidence in multilateral channels for development. A widely held perception had emerged of multilateralism as an unwieldy set of organizational arrangements characterized by turf battles, diminishing accountability, a lack of focus and a proliferation of costly and overlapping organizations. In this context, open and aggressive criticisms of the Bretton Woods Institutions and United Nations agencies multiplied. Yet as companions to the erosion of confidence in their capabilities and mounting criticism of their effectiveness, new agendas and new roles were simultaneously being thrust onto multilateral development agencies. The already overcrowded international development agenda became even more so during the 1990s with the addition of new items such as good governance, environmental sustainability, culture and ethnic issues, post-conflict reconstruction, humanitarian assistance and global public goods.

This complexity was increased yet further by an explosion in the number of actors and agents of international development that occurred during the 1990s. The size, diversity and spread of the non-profit non-governmental organization (NGO) sector is especially noteworthy, as this took on an increasingly significant role in channelling development assistance and as the annual budgets of some of these organizations grew to rival those of several of the bilateral development institutions (Salamon 1994). But this new complexity was not due to NGOs alone. Transnational corporations and international banks also became increasingly significant development actors as a consequence of the surge of private capital flows to developing countries (both foreign direct investment and more volatile shorter-term flows), increased trade liberalization and privatizations.

An entirely new stage in the evolution of the architecture of international development financing accompanied the end of the Cold War, which ushered in a radically different era in international affairs. The disappearance of residual Cold War justifications for development assistance did not produce a 'peace dividend' for international development. On the contrary, throughout almost all of the 1990s publicly financed international development assistance declined, both in absolute terms and relative to the economic output of most industrialized countries. At the same time, a diversity of policy studies emerged that focused on fundamental reforms to the system of international institutions, the future of the UN system and wider issues of global governance. These included the Nordic UN reform project (1991 and 1996), the Commission of Global Governance (1995), the Urquhart and Childers reports (1990), the South Commission (1990), and the Bretton Woods Commission (1994), among many others. The latest addition is the Report to the Secretary-General of the High-level Panel on Threats, Challenges and Change (2004).

The two major geopolitical crises of the late 1990s and early twenty-first century produced further significant changes to the international development system. The system was shaken to its foundations in 1997–8 by the Asian financial crisis followed by the implosion of Russia's economy. This produced a change in the division of labour between the IMF and the World Bank (1998–2000) and prudential instruments such as the Financial Sector Assessment Programmes

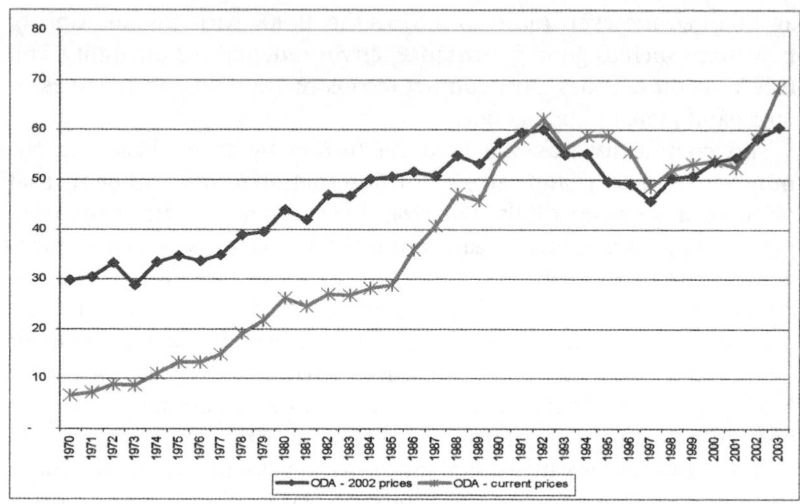

Figure 1.1   Official Development Assistance (US$ billion in nominal and real terms)
Source: OECD DAC (2004b).

(FSAP) and the Reports on the Observance of Standards and Codes (ROSC). Of far greater impact and significance, the terrorist attacks in September 2001 and the wars in Afghanistan and Iraq have shifted the development system's concepts and definitions of human security in substantial, although still incomplete ways. They are also providing new – and still quite opaque – reasons for reforming the international development financing system. These factors have also contributed to a recent reversal in the annual decline of ODA. In real terms, ODA to developing countries increased by 7 per cent between 2002 and by 3.9 per cent in 2003. Yet while the 2003 figure of US$60.5 billion (2002 prices) represents an apex in nominal terms, in real terms it still remains at the level reached in 1992 (Figure 1.1). Moreover, if the percentage of ODA in relation to the size of the economies of donor countries that prevailed in 1992 had been maintained throughout the decade, in 2003 the total volume of aid in real terms would be about 30 per cent higher, which implies that, notwithstanding the good performance of a few donors, as a whole rich countries reduced the size of their aid efforts in relation to their economic might. The increases are also tightly linked to new concerns for and definitions of human security, with very high percentages earmarked to the Iraq reconstruction account and an additional US$1 billion allocated to Afghanistan and Pakistan (OECD DAC 2004).

But however inadequate the responses to date, these recent crises have also generated new opportunities for and a fresh momentum in international development. This is being driven by a deep and amorphous unease that a more secure world will not be possible unless vast global inequalities and the marginalization of large sections of the world are significantly reduced. The fear of a major, looming crisis has set in motion actions aimed at renewing development cooperation and forging a new global partnership compact, building on the OECD/Development Assistance Committee (DAC) proposals of 1996 (Shaping the 21st Century), the UN's Millennium Development Goals of 2000, the 'Monterrey Consensus' of 2002 on Financing for Development, the Johannesburg Review Summit on Sustainable Development (2002) and the New Partnership for Africa's Development (NEPAD). The resulting combination of efforts now underway for a revitalized international development assistance effort is arguably larger and more serious than anything that preceded it over the past several decades.

The international development system is at present composed of the IMF, the World Bank, more than 20 regional and sub-regional development banks, over 40 bilateral development agencies, the UN family of organizations and thousands of large and small NGOs, and private foundations. As never before in its sixty-year history, the international development system is now bringing together the state, the private sector and civil society in complex and myriad interactions that will determine the success or failure of future development efforts and is engaged in a new dynamic that pulls simultaneously in two directions: towards collaboration and towards conflict.

1.3 The evolution of development financing mechanisms

Since the 1950s, external capital flows to developing countries have undergone a succession of modifications in size, composition and distribution. These can be divided into four distinct periods: (i) 1950 to 1972 – a pre-eminence of official flows (loans and aid), with a stable pattern of FDI (around 20 to 30 per cent of external financing) and some modest expansion in export credits; (ii) 1973 to 1981 – a rapid expansion of private financing to almost two thirds of total external inflows, mainly in the form of loans from international private banks recycling the surpluses of major oil-exporting nations; (iii) 1982 to 1991 – a major and sudden contraction in private inflows brought on by deflationary macroeconomic policies in the industrialized world which triggered a deep global recession and debt crisis for much of the developing world; (iv) 1992 to the present – an unprecedented expansion in private capital inflows to developing countries to between 80 and 90 per cent of total capital inflows. Table 1.1 shows aggregate data for the last 35 years from which three central patterns are apparent:

- *Shift of financing sources. In the aggregate, the balance between public and private net capital inflows to developing countries has undergone a profound shift towards reliance on private capital inflows.* Net official capital flows increased from an annual average of US$15 billion in the 1970s to US$51 billion in the 1990s, but over the same periods net private capital flows increased from an average of US$37 to US$185 billion. Although the financial crisis in 1998 slightly reversed the growing trend of private capital inflows, the resilience of FDI ensured the continuing relative importance of private capital inflows and these remain by far the largest single source of financial flows to developing countries taken as a whole.
- *A downward trend and higher volatility in net official flows.* Net official flows to developing countries increased steadily from the 1970s through to the early 1990s, but the trend since then has been sharply downwards from an annual average of US$54 billion during the period 1990–1994 to US$35 billion during the period 2000–2003. In addition, unpredictable year-to-year swings in bilateral flows and in IMF-led debt rescue packages produced high levels of volatility in net official flows. For example, these stood at US$32 billion in 1996, rose to US$62 billion in 1998 and dropped to US$23 billion in 2000.
- *Shift in the type of private financial flows: from debt to equity.* Over the two decades of the 1970s and 1980s, the annual average of private loans (or private debt inflows) to all developing countries was US$43 billion. This has subsequently declined to an average net private debt flow to developing countries of only about US$10 billion over the period 2000–3. The decline is usually attributed to the cumulative effects of the East Asian crisis of 1997–8, the turmoil in global fixed income markets in the summer of 1998, and, most recently, the problems in global high yield markets in the aftermath of the 2001 slowdown. It would seem highly unlikely that levels of net debt inflows will recover in the medium term as a large percentage of developing countries will be paying off previous debts at least until the end of this decade. The steep decline in private debt inflows has been accompanied by an even steeper increase in annual net equity flows (FDI and portfolio equity). These have increased tenfold from only US$13 billion over the period 1970–89 to US$135 billion between 1990 and 2003.

Table 1.1   Net capital flows to developing countries, 1970–2003 (annual average US$ billion)

		1970–1974	1975–1979	1980–1984	1985–1989	1990–1994	1995–1999	2000–2003
1.	**Net private flows**[a]	**11.36**	**47.15**	**59.10**	**39.66**	**126.60**	**238.71**	**169.41**
2.	**Net official flows**[b]	**7.67**	**17.72**	**31.56**	**33.61**	**53.78**	**48.70**	**35.18**
3.	**Net equity flows**	**2.26**	**6.89**	**15.84**	**15.22**	**72.26**	**170.66**	**163.95**
3.1.	Foreign direct investment[c]	2.26	6.89	15.82	14.31	52.10	152.26	154.87
3.2.	Portfolio equity flows	0.00	0.00	0.02	0.91	20.16	18.40	9.08
4.	**Net flows on debt**	**13.57**	**50.56**	**63.34**	**41.46**	**77.90**	**88.96**	**10.10**
4.1.	Official creditors (a+b)	4.46	10.29	20.09	17.01	23.55	20.91	4.64
a.	*Multilateral creditors*	*1.10*	*3.05*	*6.59*	*7.90*	*13.93*	*23.21*	*14.11*
	– World Bank	1.10	3.05	6.59	7.90	7.00	8.06	3.33
	IBRD	0.63	1.88	4.42	4.57	2.35	3.00	–1.52
	IDA	0.47	1.16	2.17	3.32	4.65	5.06	4.84
	– IMF	n.d.	n.d.	n.d.	n.d.	1.50	6.63	7.71
	Non-concessional	n.d.	n.d.	n.d.	n.d.	0.71	0.55	0.43
	Concessional	n.d.	n.d.	n.d.	n.d.	1.16	6.08	7.18
	– Major RDBs	n.d.	n.d.	n.d.	n.d.	4.11	6.73	4.18
	non-concessional	n.d.	n.d.	n.d.	n.d.	1.65	1.72	1.38
	Concessional	n.d.	n.d.	n.d.	n.d.	3.48	5.01	2.80
	– Others[d]	n.d.	n.d.	n.d.	n.d.	1.66	1.79	–0.09
b.	*Bilateral creditors*	*3.36*	*7.25*	*13.50*	*9.12*	*9.62*	*–2.30*	*–9.47*
	Non-concessional	0.45	2.18	4.84	0.58	1.91	–5.40	–9.34
	Concessional	2.91	5.07	8.66	8.54	7.71	3.11	–0.13

Table 1.1 Net capital flows to developing countries, 1970–2003 (annual average US$ billion) (*continued*)

		1970–1974	*1975–1979*	*1980–1984*	*1985–1989*	*1990–1994*	*1995–1999*	*2000–2003*
4.2.	Private creditors (a+b)	9.11	40.26	43.25	24.44	54.35	68.05	5.46
a.	*Net short-term debt flows*	*1.72*	*13.31*	*6.56*	*9.08*	*22.74*	*2.23*	*0.37*
b.	*Net L-M term debt flows*	*7.38*	*26.96*	*36.69*	*15.36*	*31.61*	*65.82*	*5.09*
	– Bonds	0.12	1.68	1.57	2.10	15.96	36.14	18.63
	– Banks	5.98	20.50	26.82	6.47	7.04	30.08	–6.63
	– Others[e]	1.28	4.78	8.30	6.78	8.61	–0.40	–6.91
	Memo							
5.	**Changes in reserves**	n.d.	n.d.	–5.39	3.30	46.23	58.04	145.27
6.	**Grants[f]**	3.21	7.42	11.47	16.59	30.23	27.78	30.54
7.	**Workers' remittances**	0.40	7.33	19.17	21.76	36.45	60.75	81.63

Source: Global Development Finance 2004, CD-ROM.
[a] Private debt plus equity; [b] Bilateral aid grants plus debt; [c] Net inflows; [d] Other multilateral sources (e.g. export credit); [e] Other private credits from manufacturers, exporters, and other suppliers of goods, and bank credits covered by a guarantee of an export credit agency; [f] Excluding technical cooperation grants.

These trends configure a new pattern of external financing for developing countries. Further trends in financial flows appear when the data are disaggregated according to the source of financing, the type of creditor (official multilateral and bilateral, or private sources), the type of equity flow (foreign portfolio investment or foreign direct investment), the term of the financial instruments (short or long term), the lending window type (concessional or non-concessional) and so on. We now turn to an overview of some the main factors and trends that emerge from a more detailed examination of the data.

Private sources of development finance

Inflows from private sources are composed of equity and debt, provided in the form of FDI and portfolio equity flows (Table 1.1, lines 3.1 and 3.2), and net flows of debt by private creditors (line 4.2), respectively. The explosive growth in private flows, especially equity flows, that occurred in the 1990s was, in substantial measure at least, a response to policy changes in developing countries. Policies of earlier decades that reflected previously widespread nationalistic or autarkic attitudes (e.g. ownership restrictions) were repealed and replaced with new policies to encourage foreign investment (e.g. protection of property rights, tax stability guarantees, fewer capital controls). Even with such measures, however, the levels of private equity flows reached in the 1990s do not necessarily presage a general trend. Indeed, much of this is probably attributable to one-off privatizations of public enterprises, which became quite common in the developing world during the 1990s, but which cannot be repeated as the stock of publicly owned assets for much of the world has now been greatly reduced.

As we have already seen, the balance between private debt and equity inflows has also varied markedly – an important 'supply-side' distinction. International bank lending amounted to more than 60 per cent for all private capital flows to developing countries in 1971, rising with the recycling of oil wealth to a peak of 96 per cent at the close of that decade. By contrast, FDI and portfolio investment (bonds and equity) were relatively unimportant in the 1970s but rose by the end of the 1990s to account for about 85 per cent of equity inflows.

The decline in net private debt inflows at the close of the last decade was as dramatic as it was sudden, falling from an annual average of US$68 billion in 1995–9 to US$5 billion in 2000–3. Commercial bank debt, supplier's credit and export credits all moved into negative net inflows over the past three years.[5] The aggregated data on private flows present a highly skewed and unrepresentative picture for, in general, private flows have been and remain highly concentrated in only a few countries, and in the energy, minerals and telecommunications sectors. Moreover, the data show that the degree of concentration has been increasing. Between 1975 and 1995, 20 developing countries accounted for roughly 40 per cent of total private net capital inflows, but by 1999, this figure had doubled to approximately 80 per cent and this high level of concentration has continued in more recent years.[6] The regional distribution of private capital flows also shifted significantly between the 1980s and the 1990s. A roughly balanced distribution between developing regions in the 1980s gave way to a concentration in East Asia and a few countries in Latin America, which in 1990 accounted for 42 and 32 per cent of total net private capital inflows, respectively.

Foreign portfolio investment (FPI) comprised only a small fraction of equity inflows at less than one per cent during the 1970s and early 1980s and less than 12 per cent on average since then. FPI inflows have been heavily concentrated in a few developing countries. By contrast, following the Mexican crisis in 1994, developing country equity issues fell from US$6 billion to US$0.6 billion between the last quarter of 1994 and the first quarter of 1995. Likewise, total FPI plummeted from US$27 billion in 1997 to US$7 billion in 1998, following the Asian crisis, and returned in 2003 to US$14 billion.

In general, FDI is held to be of greater development value for developing countries than portfolio capital on the grounds that it does not add to a country's debt burden, is far less volatile than portfolio capital and tends to involve longer-term commitments and to bring with it technology, know-how and management skills. Certainly, FDI flows have been demonstrably more stable than portfolio flows and have remained resilient over the past several years, in spite of the Asian financial crisis and the subsequent global recession. One of the reasons for this stability is that large volumes of stock of FDI cannot be moved in the way that portfolio flows can be shifted quickly from one country to another. This is especially so when FDI is intertwined in international production networks or where 'sunk costs' are high. But patterns of FDI flows also show responsiveness to uncertainties and that economic downturns cause FDI investors to reduce new commitments, accelerate affiliates' repayments of debt to home offices, or take offsetting positions through derivatives. The data also suggest a further need for considerable prudence in claiming or interpreting the benefits of FDI as profit remittances could offset some of these benefits in the medium term. These have soared from US$18 billion in 1991 to

US$55 billion in 2001. Also the US Congress is considering a temporary break on repatriation taxes (the Homeland Investment Act), which could mean that a great portion of the US$500 billion investment earnings of the major US companies in developing countries would return in the form of dividends (J.P. Morgan 2003).[7]

Official capital flows

However great the developmental potential of private financing, for the foreseeable future there will simply be no substitute for ODA, particularly for the poorest countries. The future for ODA, however, is highly uncertain. On the one hand, and as noted earlier, the initiatives now underway for a revitalized international development assistance effort are arguably larger and more serious than any of the previous efforts over the past several decades. In addition to the pledges of increased finance made in Monterrey and the priority accorded to NEPAD, the international political profile of development has moved to a twenty-year apex with the recent launching of the 'Commission for Africa' by the British prime minister, Tony Blair. The mandate of the Commission is to go beyond yet another study and to come up with an action plan to be proposed to the G8 in 2005.

The magnitude of these efforts to revitalize ODA and the emergence of at least some political focus on development by the large industrial nations should not be underestimated. They follow a period of severe decline in ODA by over 25 per cent in real terms (from US$59.9 billion in 1992 to US$45 billion in 1997). Although nominal growth in ODA has returned since 1998, the level in 2003 of US$60 billion remains in real terms close to the 1992 level.

ODA as a percentage of GDP in OECD countries declined steadily between 1992 and 2001 from 0.34 per cent to 0.22 per cent before increasing slightly to 0.25 per cent in 2003. There have been numerous recent announcements and pledges[8] to increase the percentage further. Nevertheless, even if all the pledges and announcements made in Monterrey were to be met, ODA would rise only to 0.26 per cent by the end of 2006. Moreover, the history of donor ODA pledges over the past three decades does not give cause for optimism that all pledges will be met. In addition, substantial fiscal deficits are now a defining characteristic of most OECD countries.[9]

From a developing country perspective, net flows are usually considered of greater importance than gross inflows alone. Net official flows are composed of multilateral and bilateral net debt flows (see

Table 1.1, line 4.1) and grants excluding technical cooperation (Table 1.1, line 6). Over the period 1970–89, net debt flows averaged US$4.5 billion with multilateral institutions and US$8.5 with bilateral creditors. In other words, for almost two decades the average net flows of both bilateral and multilateral agencies to developing countries were positive with the bilateral balance roughly twice that of the multilaterals. This situation changed dramatically over the next 13 years (1990–2003) as net bilateral flows turned negative while the annual positive balance of those from multilateral sources increased to approximately US$20 billion. Moreover, the debt net flows gap between bilateral and multilateral channels has remained very large since the mid-1990s, and negative bilateral net flows increased from US$2.3 billion in 1995–9 to US$9.5 billion in 2000–3. This is mostly attributable to past non-concessional bilateral debt to export guarantee agencies for which payment is required under Paris Club debt-restructuring agreements.

Two further factors are important to note with regard to official capital flows from multilateral sources. The first is that the major year-on-year fluctuations that these show between 1994 and 2002 result mainly from the 'bulkiness' of IMF rescue packages and do not indicate a trend in the overall availability of multilateral financing. The second is that most of the comparisons of the relative roles of the World Bank and other development banks do not take adequate (if any) account of the role played by the sub-regional development banks. If these were taken into account, particularly those in the Latin American and Caribbean regions, the relative importance of the combined regional and sub-regional banks relative to the World Bank would increase substantially, as most sub-regionals maintain large positive net flows to their borrowing countries.

Workers' remittances

Arguably, the most dramatic shift in development financing over the last two decades has been in the area of workers' remittances. From relative insignificance in the 1970s, these have become the second largest source, behind FDI, of external funding for developing countries (Table 1.1, line 7). This is attributable to the combined effects of the greater mobility of international labour and the relaxation of capital controls that began throughout most of the developing world beginning in the 1980s and that accelerated through the 1990s. In 2003, workers' remittance receipts of developing countries were estimated at US$93 billion, substantially higher than total official flows and private non-FDI flows, and 68 per cent of total FDI flows to developing countries. Remittances to low-income countries are reported as having been larger as a share of GDP and imports than were those to middle-income countries. According to one study, low-income countries as a whole now receive 2.7 per cent of annual GDP in remittances (Ratha 2003 a, b).

Given that their magnitude and importance is a quite recent phenomenon, remittances have not yet been subject to extensive, systematic study. As a result, much remains to be learned about their characteristics. The evidence to date, however, indicates not only that remittances have a reasonably predictable character but also that they may even rise in response to downward economic cycles in recipient countries. Among the positive characteristics of remittances is the fact that they do not create liabilities for recipient countries and that they can be directed, at least in part, to small investment projects, education services or to improve rural infrastructure. Remittances, however, are not without certain risks. Depending on the volume, they could exert exchange rate pressures in the wrong direction and, as they are person-to-person flows, they may be used exclusively for consumption purposes, thus not contributing directly to economic growth. These risk factors suggest that it would be desirable, at least in certain cases, to establish institutional arrangements to support and channel remittance flows. Some efforts in this regard are already underway, although currently on a modest scale.[10]

One factor that emerges clearly from the studies that are available on remittances (see, for example, World Bank 2004) is that the costs involved in the actual transfers can be very high (the World Bank calculates that the average cost of transferring remittances to Central and South America is in the range of 13 per cent, and often exceeds 20 per cent). It follows that there is an urgent requirement to establish international mechanisms, norms and standards that will reduce these transactions costs and act as an incentive to the increased flow of remittances.

1.4 Main defining characteristics of the international development system at the end of the twentieth century

Today's international development architecture is considerably less than 'systemic', resembling more closely a collection of rather inarticulate components, efforts and initiatives that have shaped and reshaped themselves in the face of renewed challenges and issues over more than half a century. New institutional arrangements are regularly created in order to bypass or rectify perceived deficiencies in existing institutions but inertial forces remain dominant, and reform efforts are usually frustrated by the pervasiveness and magnitude of a combination of structural characteristics, including the following:

- *Lack of global governance of the system.* The present international development system is composed of a plethora of organizations and none of them plays the pivotal and coordination role needed to address global economic and social issues. The consequences of this lacuna are that some issues are left without any form of international governance and others are solved only on an ad hoc basis. The United Nations was originally intended to ensure coherence, consistency and the design of overall policy over the international development system, but this has never been possible because the governance structures of other institutions, notably the World Bank and IMF, accord them virtually full autonomy from the UN.
- *Lack of overall coherence and delineation of mandates and roles.* The international development system can be currently viewed as a 'dysfunctional family' of different organizations and agencies with confusion and conflict over mandates, roles and comparative advantage. Attempts at 'harmonization' rarely, if ever, acknowledge asymmetries and the vast differences that exist between different actors in power, influence, capabilities and experience. The dominant discourse of 'partnerships, inclusion and equality' reinforces the rhetoric of cooperation and collaboration, but until now it has failed to introduce greater overall coherence to the system.
- *Inappropriate governance structures: inadequate representation, lack of accountability and transparency.* The governing structures of the institutions within the international development system are asymmetrical and unequal. A very large proportion of the voting rights in some of them, mainly the Bretton Woods Institutions, are vested in a very small number of industrialized countries, as they are the principal shareholders in terms of paid-in capital. Such imbalances are perceived increasingly by developing and some developed countries, by advocacy organizations and by political analysts, as a major defect that produces decisions that do not adequately take account of the interests of the developing countries they are intended to serve, and do not reflect the real nature of burden sharing in the international financial institutions. It is further noted by many observers that the balance of power in decision making has not evolved to match the growing economic importance of countries such as China, India and Brazil, thus perpetuating outdated patterns of representation, weak

accountability and interests that do not focus sufficiently on the real needs of a very large number of countries or even on collective good issues in the world economy (Nayyar and Court 2002).

- *Lack of predictable funding to international development system institutions and stable funding to developing countries.* The report of the High-Level Panel on Financing for Development (United Nations 2001b – the Zedillo Report) of 2001 estimated that an additional US$50 million annually would be required if the Millennium Development Goals (MDGs) were to be achieved by 2015 and that this would also require that developing financing be made available on a predictable and stable basis. As we have already seen, however, the patterns of development financing over the past three decades have been characterized by large swings, and a high degree of uncertainty and instability. It will clearly require unprecedented world action if this situation is to be modified in accord with both the qualitative and quantitative recommendations of the Zedillo Report.

    Problems of unpredictability and instability in development financing have been particularly acute for the development agencies of the UN. Core financing has declined precipitously since the 1980s, with a small number of donors now providing a disproportionate share of the core operating funds required by agencies such as UNDP, UNICEF and UNFPA.[11] Non-core or voluntary contributions have become the dominant financial instrument for many UN agencies, amounting to over two-thirds of total financing for both UNDP and UNICEF (Bezanson and Sagasti 2002). This raises the key question of whether it makes a difference if resources are core or non-core. Resources after all are still being made available. The answer depends on the nature of the non-core resources and merits careful study. Even though non-core or trust fund resources may broadly conform to the programme structure of an agency, many of these funds are of a 'tied aid' nature, responding to the domestic priorities, policies and preferences of the donor country. There is the additional factor that joint and participatory decision making is a cornerstone of multilateralism. If member states shift increasingly from core to earmarked funds, this defining feature of multilateralism will be compromised. Programme development and strategic decisions will shift away from the boards and governing bodies of UN organizations to bilateral donors, thus eroding the legitimacy of these institutions. The shift from core to non-core resources, therefore, holds implications outside the realm of financing and raises fundamental questions of multilateral governance.

With regard to the soft loan windows of the multilateral development banks, the pattern of replenishments on a three- or four-year basis represents a much more predictable and stable financing formula than the annual pledging model of the UN. In addition, the lending programmes of the banks generate income (net income), a significant percentage of which is transferred to soft lending windows for concessional lending to the poorest countries.[12] The financing demands of HIPC over the past few years have placed this use of net income under considerable strain. More worrying in terms of the predictability and stability of development financing, however, has been the introduction of a full grant element into the concessional financing of the banks, beginning with IDA 13. As a result of strong pressure from the United States, about 20 per cent of funds available through IDA 13 are being provided to developing countries on a 100 per cent grant basis. There will, of course, be no future repayments on this amount, reducing thereby the stable annual income stream of the concessional lending window of the World Bank. This would pose no problems of predictability or stability if the resulting gap were to be guaranteed through future replenishments by donor countries, but that is not the case. The result is that a considerably higher future uncertainty and possible instability has been introduced into the pattern of development financing for the poorest countries, precisely at the very moment when the rhetoric of donors is calling for the opposite (section 2.3).

- *Imbalances between the financing requirements of developing countries and those for the provision of global public goods.* The stagnation of ODA in the 1990s coincided with the emergence of major new demands requiring financing, including post-conflict reconstruction, humanitarian relief, assistance to refugees, debt forgiveness, support for democratic institutions, improvement of governance structures, assistance to transition economies, efforts to fight drug traffic, crime and more recently 'terrorism', many of which are considered as 'global public goods'. The results of this are seen in an ever- increasing competition for funding and a squeezing out of resources allocated to fields that once were the main focus of development assistance, such as health and population, food and nutrition, education and training, small and medium-sized enterprises, technical assistance and balance-of-payments support. A further result is seen in mounting pressures on ODA for allocations to 'global public goods' and on developing countries themselves to contribute more to 'global efforts'. According to some recent estimates, as much as 15 per cent of total annual ODA is now assigned to international public goods related purposes (United Nations 2001d). This raises the question of whether taking active part in the provision of global public goods could place an unfair burden on poor countries struggling to improve the living standards of their people. This would occur if such countries, and the institutions, firms and organizations in them, were required to divert resources from domestic development tasks to share the cost of production of an international public good from which they would receive marginal relative benefit. This would result in an 'inverse Robin Hood effect' (Stalgren 2000: 34), which would worsen inequalities between rich and poor countries. A similar outcome would be observed, if scarce development assistance resources were reallocated away from domestic development activities to the provision of international public goods.

Taking into account the above considerations, it is clear that the structure is now skewed more in favour of highly concentrated and mobile private investments and less towards the long-term needs of development finance. Moreover, the vastly increased mobility of international capital limits the capacity of most developing country governments to tax capital flows and profits. This makes it difficult to maintain a level of public expenditure commensurate with the growth of social demands, especially in the poorest countries. From this perspective, a possible additional motivation for official development assistance may be to compensate for the negative impact that financial globalization has had on the economy of many developing countries.

This suggests that a systematic re-examination and re-alignment of the international development architecture is urgently called for. The international development architecture is driven more by historical inertias than by current needs and demands. Most international organizations were created half a century ago to address an entirely different set of problems and are now struggling with today's complex realities and changing demands. Several proposals for systematic and comprehensive reform have emerged recently, motivated in considerable measure by the crisis of September 11 and a fear that a larger crisis of insecurity may be imminent unless vast global inequalities and the marginalization of large sections of the world are tackled successfully. The resulting initiatives now underway for a revitalized international development assistance effort are arguably larger and more serious than their predecessors. Yet it remains unclear and uncertain that these will generate the broad consensus and political support that will be imperative if the efforts are to succeed.

2
Attempted Change: Recent Attempts to Transform the International Development Financing Architecture

The previous chapter has outlined an international development system defined by continuous transformation and by growing complexity. Its institutional architecture, constructed in an earlier era when international aid policies were a straightforward matter of project identification, financing and management, has evolved into a dense and at times almost impenetrable forest of development assistance organizations. The demands on these organizations have expanded in a virtually exponential manner such that today they are challenged to operate simultaneously at global, regional and grassroots levels; to function in new and ever-expanding partnership arrangements with decentralized authorities, the private sector, bilateral, multilateral and NGO agencies; to decentralize and increase operational strengths 'on the ground', while simultaneously reducing operating expenses and administrative costs; and to embrace and operationalize a myriad of often incompatible or conflicting priorities. Many are simultaneously criticized for 'mission creep' and urged to assume larger roles in new areas and respond to a greater variety of concerns.

At the same time, the past decade has called into public question, as never before, the purposes, means and impact of development assistance. The combination of diminishing resources for development assistance and growing demands from both developing countries and transitional economies has catalysed such questioning and led to numerous studies and reports on the subject. The perceived ineffectiveness of international development cooperation has been seen as an important contributing factor to donor fatigue, expressed during much of the 1990s in declining public support for government spending on foreign aid and in reductions in ODA.

Criticisms of development assistance can be grouped into three categories:[1] (i) radical critiques that consider aid harmful; (ii) criticisms that see development assistance as beneficial but rather inefficient; and (iii) those that view it as appropriate only for the poorest countries, arguing that it crowds out private investment in all other developing countries and transition economies.

The *radical critiques of development assistance* in all its forms, whether bilateral, multilateral or private, are voiced mostly by some academics and representatives of NGOs. These critics argue that development assistance is harmful, has nothing to show for the billions of dollars provided to poor countries, and that the whole aid enterprise is a waste of taxpayers' money. An extreme example of such critiques is provided by Graham Hancock (1992), who argues that 'aid is not bad, however, because it is sometimes misused, corrupt or crass; rather, it is *inherently* bad, bad to the bone, and utterly beyond reform' and that it is 'the most formidable obstacle to the productive endeavours of the poor'.

The *critics who focus on how to improve the effectiveness of development assistance* see it as beneficial but riddled with delivery and efficiency problems. For these critics 'aid works' but could be made to work better. Some of them focus on the shortcomings of international development institutions, while others stress the problems and difficulties at the recipient country level. Recent studies have placed emphasis on the importance of good domestic policies and institutions, arguing that they are a condition for development financing, in all its forms, to have a positive impact. However, the Asian and Russian financial crises of 1997 and 1998 have served to create extensive and lingering scepticism about the 'good policies' advocated by international development organizations.

A third group of criticisms focuses more specifically on the role of multilateral development banks, and argues that they *should restrict their activities to those areas where the private sector shows no interest.* They see the regular lending operations of these institutions as 'crowding out' and reducing opportunities for private investment. Accordingly, they propose to limit the functions of the MDBs to the provision of grants, concessional assistance and project finance in countries and sectors that are unattractive to the private sector.[2]

As a result and in response to all of this, the international development system is undergoing what has been described as 'an arduous transition' (Sagasti and Alcalde 1999). Decades-old habits of thought and practice are being discarded while new ones are still in the making. Organizations are struggling to adapt to a vastly changed international context and new policies, partnership arrangements and instruments are constantly emerging. Many of the principal institutions that make up the international development system now acknowledge their defects and deficiencies openly and much official discourse is centred on the need for fundamental and sweeping architectural reform of the system itself. Numerous attempts have recently been made by major institutions to transform themselves from within. New strategic and programmatic initiatives have been launched to improve efficiency and to enhance development effectiveness. Several OECD governments have pledged greater amounts of financing to institutional reform efforts that are successful.

This combination of exogenous and endogenous factors presents an unusual and probably unprecedented opportunity for more systemic approaches to basic architectural reform of the international development system than had previously been possible. In this chapter, therefore, we examine and briefly assess the nature and possible implications of shifts that have been occurring and some of the main and recent efforts at basic reform in some of the principal international development agencies, including the United Nations, the IFIs, a selection of bilateral donor agencies, and the EU. We also provide a very short preview of chapter 3 with an outline of emerging new initiatives in development financing.

2.1 Reforms in the United Nations

Since the 1960s, the United Nations development system has experienced a succession of top-down reform efforts aimed at bringing a greater degree of strategic coherence into being, together with more effective control over an institutional configuration made up of multiple uncoordinated entities with no overall management and inclined to inter-agency squabbling. The consensus is that prior efforts proved unable to contend with the inertial forces within the system and were frustrated by combinations of narrow institutional interests, political indifference and nepotism. The current effort, underway since 1997, is based on approaches that are quite distinct from those of earlier years. The essential character of previous efforts was that they shared a 'big bang' approach based on a single prescriptive study or set of measures and aimed at integrating highly disparate institutions under central managerial and governance structures. In sharp contrast, the current effort is patient and incremental. At first blush, it appears far less ambitious than its predecessors, but its multiple measures and its focus on detail and the political dynamics of change may amount to the most ambitious and comprehensive package yet attempted.[3]

Among the main systemic components of the current reform programme are the elements summarized in Box 2.1.

As part of the package of incremental reforms, efforts are also underway to modify substantially the role and activities of the UN in peacekeeping and post-conflict reconstruction. These are guided by the recommendations set out in the 'Brahimi Report' (UN 2000b) and predicated on the explicit recognition of soaring demands for peace-keeping and humanitarian assistance in a post-Cold War era.[4] It was estimated that full implementation of the Brahimi recommendations for humanitarian programmes and post-conflict reconstruction could require in the order of US$70 billion annually by 2003 (UN 2000c).

A further component of current reform efforts aims to achieve greater coherence and complementarity between the development efforts of the United Nations and those of the Bretton Woods Institutions. To this end starting in 1998, the Economic and Social Council (ECOSOC) has hosted a series of annual meetings with BWI finance ministers and the World Trade Organization (WTO). This model of inter-agency engagement has no precedent and is clearly intended to introduce a better division of labour and improvements in inter-secretariat and inter-governmental aspects of the financing for development.

The current efforts are by no means limited to a focus only on inter-governmental organizations. They also recognize the extensive range of new international development actors (see section 1.3) and include measures aimed at building and strengthening UN partnerships with civil society organizations and the private sector (UN 2001c). Under the Secretary-General's 'Global Compact', for example, the normative role of the United Nations is being strengthened through collaboration with participating multinational corporations and civil society organizations in establishing and implementing core UN values, norms and standards in the areas of human rights, labour standards and the environment.[5]

Finally, building on the gains of the incremental approach launched in 1997, in November 2003 the Secretary-General convened a high-level international panel and tasked it to undertake a root-and-branch re-examination of current challenges to peace and security, to suggest collective action measures to address these and to recommend further reforms to the roles, processes and institutional architecture of the

BOX 2.1. **Some main components of the United Nations reform programme**

A Cabinet System of Management. A cabinet system of management has been introduced that has no precedent in the five-decade history of the United Nations. This includes numerous initiatives aimed at achieving improved coordination and cooperation across UN agencies.

The Resident Co-ordinator System. The changes recently implemented in the selection and evaluation of the RC seem nothing short of revolutionary. All agencies are now invited to submit candidates who are processed through a Competency Assessment Programme. By 2000, 148 positions (42 per cent occupied by women) had been staffed following the new procedures, with 50 per cent of candidates coming from agencies other than the UNDP.

UN House. This initiative seeks to achieve effective coordination by bringing UN agencies at field level together under a single roof. In 1997, a common UN country facility was almost unknown (only one existed), but 40 had been established by 2001.

Common Programming Approaches. The UN Development Assistance Framework (UNDAF) and the Common Country Assessment (CCA) are instruments that aim to assist the Resident Co-ordinator System to translate the broad objectives of the UN into operational results. The Executive Boards of all the major UN voluntarily funded programmes have agreed that their own country programmes must be based on the CCA/UNDAF. The World Bank is an invited participant. As of November 2001, 93 CCAs and 49 UNDAFs had been prepared, all of which are posted on the UNDG website.

Partnership with the Bretton Woods Institutions. A UNDG-led working group known as the UN-World Bank Learning Group on CDF/PRSP (co-chaired by UNDG and the Bank) was established in 1999 in order to integrate the various planning frameworks of the UN and the Bretton Woods Institutions. In April 2000, 14 pilot countries were selected for more intensive joint monitoring of the linkages between the frameworks with summaries of lessons learned being disseminated.

Adoption of New and Standardized Management Tools. All major funds and programmes in the UN system have adopted the core management tools of most bilateral aid agencies, including Results Based Management (RBM) and Multi-year Financial Frameworks (MYFF). This should increase accountability and also allow bilateral donors to establish clear objectives and to monitor their achievement. In addition, the major UN agencies have all adopted common methods of presenting financial and programme information, a vastly different situation to the multiplicity of highly divergent reporting systems that applied until only recently.

United Nations. The panel's final report was submitted to the Secretary-General in December 2004 and strongly reinforces the call for reform of the international development architecture.[6]

Overall, there would appear to be ground for optimism for successful outcomes from the UN reform programme launched in 1997. There is already evidence of coherency gains to the work of the United Nations and indications of improved collaboration and cooperation between disparate elements of the system (Bezanson, Sagasti *et al.* 2002; COWI, in association with Oxford International Associates 2000). Matters are still at a relatively early stage, however, and the history of failure of previous efforts recommends caution in judgement at this time. There are also assessments that the UN will, in the end, prove incapable of meaningful reform (Schlesinger 1997) and even anecdotal reports suggesting that many reforms may involve more matters of central intent than changes that actually penetrate operations (Flint 2002). Finally there is the inescapable fact that there are yet to be any closures or mergers from a highly diverse range of institutions, at least some of which are widely held to be – at best – of limited effectiveness.

2.2 Reform of the international financial institutions

Major reform efforts were undertaken by the main international financial institutions (IFIs) during the 1990s. To some extent these were the result of strategic assessments undertaken from within the institutions themselves or following the arrival of new leadership, such as occurred in the World Bank in 1996. The main drivers, however, were exogenous: on the one hand, dramatic changes in the context for development efforts, including the frequency and magnitude of recurrent financial, humanitarian and political crises in developing countries, and on the other hand stinging criticisms of institutional weakness and failures[7] (see Bezanson and Sagasti 2002 for a review of these drivers).

Whatever the drivers, there is little doubt that the extent and pace of change in the IFIs over the 1990s has been more extensive and more dramatic than those of the preceding four decades. In what follows, we review briefly some of the main changes in product lines, procedures and focus that have taken place and are ongoing.

2.2.1 The World Bank and IMF

In March 1997, the World Bank launched its Strategic Compact 1998–2000, with the stated aim of equipping the Bank Group to meet the development challenges of the twenty-first century.[8] This led to a major internal reorganization and restructuring that transformed the highly centralized *modus operandi* of the Bank into one that is now country-based and heavily decentralized. Measures were also initiated by the Bank to harmonize approaches and procedures with other development agencies, most notably the IMF and bilateral donors. New programme instruments were adopted (such as sector-wide approaches (SWAps), strategic selectivity in the Bank's programme, the Comprehensive Development Framework (CDF), Poverty Reduction Strategy Papers (PRSP), and the Enhanced-HIPC initiative). In addition, Bank programming underwent a wholesale shift away from individual projects in economic infrastructure and towards the social areas of health, basic education and social instruments aimed directly at poverty reduction. In making the latter shifts, Bank activities moved increasingly into the areas that had been the purview of the United Nations development agencies, thus producing a blurring of what had been a traditional division of labour.

The adoption of the PRSP by the Bank is intended both to exert an especially widespread impact on all aspects of its operations and to increase the dominance of the Bank's international leadership. The goals of the PRSP are to provide the functional framework for all aspects of the organization, structuring and relationships of development cooperation, and to shift the general approach away from individual projects and programmes and into strategies that take a comprehensive long-term perspective, focus on results, facilitate collaborative efforts, streamline conditionality and achieve overall greater coherence and consistency of effort across institutions (see IMF-World Bank 2004b). To the extent that these goals are achieved, the defining characteristic of most development financing since the 1960s – projects and programmes financed by a single institution – will have been replaced by large partnership frameworks linking development financing partners in coalitions of effort and with funds provided essentially on the basis of more predictable transfers. There are also, however, undeniable factors of influence and power that are at play in the transition that is occurring and the World Bank clearly sees itself, and has been taking steps to ensure that it becomes, the dominant institution and undisputed intellectual leader in the emerging new calculus of development cooperation.

A recent reform in the structure of the World Bank concessional window (IDA) has major and potentially very worrying implications for the future of development financing and of development cooperation in general. This has been alluded to in section 1.4. In July 2002, it was agreed that 18–21 per cent of IDA 13 (to cover the period 2003–2005) would be provided to least developed countries in the form of outright grants. At the same time, the US Treasury announced that this would be a permanent feature and would be incorporated into future IDA replenishments. The preliminary plans for IDA 14 prepared by the management of the World Bank include provisions for a grant programme, indicating that the arrangement reached in 2002 is likely to be of a permanent nature. When this new arrangement is combined with the impact of HIPC debt reduction programmes,[9] however, the flow of repayments into IDA will decrease sharply. In IDA 10 (1994–96), reflows accounted for roughly 19 per cent of the total (US$16.3 billion). Reflows in IDA 11 amounted to US$9.86 billion, equivalent to 40 per cent of the full replenishment amount of US$16.36 billion. In IDA 12, reflows accounted for US$6.4 billion (34 per cent) of a total replenishment of US$18.84 billion. The reflows in IDA 13 will amount to almost 39 per cent of the total. The importance of reflows to the availability of IDA financing for poor countries has clearly increased in recent years to around 34–40 per cent of the total. Moreover, a recent study estimates from current trends that by 2030 up to 73 per cent of the money needed to fund IDA loans will need to come from reflows (Sanford 2004). The same study includes projections to 2020 based on two assumptions, first that the 20 per cent grant component does in fact become permanent and second that donor countries do not increase their future contributions to IDA in real terms. Under these assumptions, IDA's cash balance turns negative in 2012, the year it first begins losing reflows because of grants approved in 2002. The plan submitted by Bank management in 2001 for IDA's future aid programmes assumed that IDA would be reimbursed in full by donor countries for the decline in reflows caused by IDA grants and HIPC cancellation, but no such provision has thus far been made by the donors. Moreover, given the history of fickle donor 'commitments' to future funding levels, the net effect of these recent reforms may add up to both the collapse of IDA and a net decline in the overall future availability of ODA funding for poorer countries.

In parallel with the World Bank, the IMF has been conducting its own programme of institutional transformation. Compared with the World Bank, however, the reform programme of the IMF appears more as a series of incremental adjustments than as major shifts in strategic direction or of relative power and influence. For the IMF, the emphasis has been on measures to enhance existing instruments by streamlining conditionality,[10] improving codes and standards of international financial practice,[11] making room for greater national ownership of reform programmes, increasing accountability and ensuring greater transparency principally through the establishment of an independent evaluation office.[12]

Beginning in the late 1980s with the introduction of the Extended Structural Adjustment Facility (ESAF) and accelerating thereafter through a number of measures and the introduction of new instruments, the IMF has also been taking steps to strengthen its role in support of low-income countries. External and internal assessments of the ESAF in 1997 and 1998 highlighted several weaknesses that hindered its effectiveness,[13] including the lack of country ownership, analytical and empirical weaknesses in the underlying empirical base with regard to social aspects, and insufficient attention to trade-offs for alternative paths to growth and poverty reduction. This resulted in a decision in 1999 to replace the ESAF with the Poverty Reduction and Growth Facility (PRGF), a new instrument aimed specifically at allowing the IMF to provide low-income countries with longer-term, concessional interest rate financing in support of approved poverty reduction programmes. Although the PRGF has remained since its introduction a relatively modest component of overall IMF activity, its significance lies in the modification it introduced to the traditional role of the IMF as the provider of temporary financial support to remedy short-term current account imbalances. The resulting blurring of role definition and of the traditional division of labour between different international institutions has been acknowledged. The IMF has attempted to deal with this in policy pronouncements by underscoring that, while it has an important role to play in support of poverty reduction and growth in low-income countries, it is not primarily a provider of long-term financial assistance (IMF 2003c).

Other significant reforms to the framework of IMF activities have been proposed but have not been approved. Until 1997, for example, there had been considerable momentum towards a modification of the IMF Articles of Agreement to require full capital convertibility as a condition of IMF membership. Proposals in this regard disappeared quickly and completely from the agenda as a result of the East Asian and then the Russian financial crises of 1997 and 1998. Had the crises not intervened, however, and had the IMF Articles been modified along lines that had been formally proposed, the change would have represented a shift of seismic proportions from the original purposes for which the IMF had been established. More recently, Argentina's default on its sovereign debt produced proposals for a new IMF role through the establishment of a Sovereign Debt Restructuring Mechanism (SDRM) for orderly debt defaults, especially for middle-income countries. This proposal remains technically under review, but as concern over the Argentine default has receded so also has any momentum that the proposal might have had (IMFC 2003). In addition, however, significant problems were seen to be associated with the proposal in that its application would be involuntary and *ex post*, hence imposing a decision after the fact on creditors who have not agreed to abide by the will of the 'major majority' in restructuring and other matters. In contrast, proposals for IMF stewardship of a new framework of Collective Action Clauses (CACs) based on voluntary *ex ante* agreements have been welcomed and encouraged for their further voluntary use by countries (IMFC 2002).

Overall, the recent reforms of the World Bank and IMF have been assessed as increasing country focus and ownership, results orientation of operations, commitment for the Millennium Development Goals (MDGs) and partnerships (IMF-WB 2004a). The same report also underscores, however, the need for further and more intensive reforms in order to: (i) strengthen institutional roles in low-income countries, including the deepening of the PRSP process, harmonizing operational programmes and practices around national strategies and systems, while also continuing to adapt approaches and instruments to the evolving needs of middle-income countries; (ii) increase emphasis and progress on the results agenda, including implementation of the action plan endorsed by the sponsoring agencies at the Marrakech Roundtable; (iii) address the needs of middle-income countries, some of which perceive they have been squeezed out by the emphasis on the poorest countries and on the mobilization of large rescue packages for emerging economies; and (iv) improve selectivity and coordination of agency programmes in line with comparative advantage and the mandate to achieve greater systemic coherence and effectiveness (IMF-WB 2004a).

2.2.2 Regional and sub-regional development banks

Viewed as a whole, a dramatic pattern of shifts and reforms was experienced during the 1990s by the regional and sub-regional development banks. In general, the financial base of these institutions grew substantially, allowing them to expand their lending activities and increase their weight, influence and importance with many borrowing countries relative to the World Bank. At the same time the range and diversity of their 'development toolkits' were greatly expanded and with this the scope of their operations. They became an important source of financial innovation, creating new financial instruments, particularly to support private sector activities. This expanded role and influence of regional and sub-regional banks has had paradoxical impacts on inter-agency relationships, including with the World Bank, involving both enhanced cooperation and partnerships, on the one hand, and a marked increase in rivalry, jealousy and competition, on the other (Culpeper 1997; Kapur, Lewis and Webb 1997; Rwegasira and Kifle 1994; Bezanson *et al.* 2000).

The Inter-American Development Bank (IADB), for the tenth consecutive year in 2003 eclipsed the World Bank as the largest source of multilateral financing for Latin America and the Caribbean, both in absolute and in net-transfer terms. The extent of the change that has occurred here is clear when one considers that prior to 1992 World Bank lending to the area was two to four times greater than of the IADB. The IADB has also ventured into 'soft' areas of development, such as the provision of technical assistance and lending to improve the functioning of judiciaries and congresses in Latin American countries, and has committed itself to major increases in lending for social development, and in particular to education.[14] In addition, an increasing component of the IADB portfolio focuses on catalysing private sector investment. For example, in 1995 the IADB began lending up to 5 per cent of its total outstanding loans and guarantees directly to the private sector and increased this to 10 per cent in 2002. Latin America, where the MDBs network includes several sub-regional banks, such as CAF, CDB, BCIE, FONPLATA and NADB,[15] is the region with the highest number of multilateral development banks (Sagasti 2002a).

In the mid-1990s, the *African Development Bank (AfDB)* was in a deep crisis that threatened the continued existence of the institution. Non-regional members had lost confidence in its lending policies and management practices and in 1995 Standard and Poor's lowered the Bank's credit rating from AAA to AA+, because of the increasing politicization of the Bank's corporate governance and management. As a result, the African Development Fund, AfDF (the main concessional financial window of the Bank) experienced a dramatic decline of over 45 per cent during the period 1996–8 (AfDB 2004a).

In response to this, in 1994 the Bank began a root-and-branch reform programme of sweeping changes to structures, organization, policies and programme instruments. A recent independent external evaluation assessed as 'exceptional' the extent of the reforms over the decade from

1994 to 2004 (AfDB 2004a). Standard and Poor's restored the Bank's AAA bond rating in 2003. The reform programme and its successes were recently accorded formal recognition by the Bank's shareholders who increased the finances for its concessional window by over 40 per cent.

The Asian Development Bank (AsDB) encountered controversy in the negotiations to increase its capital base during the 1990s, primarily because of differences between shareholders over the role it should play in the Asian region – in issues such as the balance of lending between public and private sectors, concessional lending to India and China, and the provision of loans to Vietnam. The key role played by the AsDB in helping to defuse the 1997 East Asian financial crisis served to mollify criticism and to reduce the controversy. Also, attention has recently been drawn to the privileged position that the AsDB may occupy, given that the region it serves has accumulated a staggering US$705 billion in international reserves (2003 figure) and has by far the highest internal savings rates in the world. These factors have raised the possibility of dramatic increases in the range of AsDB operations and for major resource expansions through the establishment of a new assessed contribution framework and capital market operations.

Since the mid-1990s, significant expansion has taken place in the activities of both the *European Bank for Reconstruction and Development* (EBRD) and the *European Investment Bank* (EIB) with the result that they have grown to become the dominant sources of development finance for Eastern Europe. Regarding the countries that have joined the European Union in May 2004, the EIB has been the largest single provider of long term funding and the EBRD the single largest investor in the private sectors of those countries. Accession to the European Union has opened up new sources of financing to those countries and EBRD operations are beginning to decline. In 1999 the EBRD disbursed €1.6 billion, €1.3 billion in 2002 and €1 billion in 2003. Nevertheless, the amount of capital investment that will be needed for new EU members if they are to catch up with longer-term members suggests that EBRD and EIB financing will continue to play an important role.[16]

Sub-regional development banks have recently acquired a major importance in Latin America, where several of these institutions have been in operation for many years. They have become an important source of finance and have also focused on the areas that the regional bank (IADB) and the World Bank have progressively given less emphasis to, such as infrastructure projects. Moreover, because their portfolios are less mature than those of the IADB or the World Bank, they provide a much larger level of positive net transfers to member countries. For example, from 1990 to 1998 the Andean Finance Corporation (CAF) consistently had a larger positive net flow of resources to its members – Bolivia, Colombia, Ecuador, Peru and Venezuela – than the IADB, which has had a small positive net flow during these years, and also than the World Bank, which has had a large aggregate negative net flow in the same period. A similar situation prevails in the Caribbean region with regard to the relation net transfer relationship between the Caribbean Development Bank, the IADB and the World Bank. In addition, conditionality appears to be less severe in the sub-regional development banks, which makes them more attractive to borrowing countries.

Overall, regional and sub-regional development banks are assuming an increasing relative importance in development financing. Net inflows from RDBs surpassed those of the World Bank in the 2000s (section 1.3), and sub-regional development banks account for 41 per cent of total MDBs' disbursements in 2002 (approximately US$40.5 billion). A strong case can be made, therefore, for building on these factors and enhancing the role of regional and sub-regional development banks. Among others, regional institutions are able to provide financing on better than sovereign terms, are more flexible due to their relatively small scope of operations; have closer relations with and better knowledge of the countries of the region than do global agencies; and they can promote competition between public agencies to increase development effectiveness (ECLAC 2002).

2.3 Reforms and recent developments in bilateral agencies

During the 1990s, OECD's Development Assistance Committee (DAC) launched new efforts to adapt and transform bilateral development cooperation to respond to changed development imperatives in a period of rapid global change, and also to restore public confidence in and support for international development. The 1996 publication *Shaping the 21st Century: The Contribution of Development Co-operation* continues to serve as the official road map to this transformation. It covers a vast range of social, economic and political dimensions of development and sets out a vision of development cooperation based on partnership around development strategies owned and led by developing country governments and civil societies (OECD DAC 1996). Drawing on this, specific proposals have been formulated by the OECD's DAC Secretariat for greater selectivity in aid allocation to least developed countries, increased focus on poverty reduction, reducing tied aid, achieving greater policy coherence, and enhancing aid coordination between donor countries. These efforts converged into the February 2003 Rome Declaration, where 18 bilateral donors and 16 multilateral institutions committed themselves to adopt common criteria on aid harmonization, programme-based alignment of budget support with budget year cycles and initiatives aimed at continuous and shared learning (Rome Declaration 2003). The follow-up work to Rome is being coordinated via a new structure (the OECD DAC Working Party on Aid Effectiveness and Donor Practices – WP-EFF) which has been given the task of developing specific action proposals to increase collective aid efficiency and effectiveness, taking into account issues such as alignment and harmonization, public financial management, procurement, and managing for development results (OECD 2004a).

The extent to which these reform efforts may be expected to succeed is moot. With regard to the objective of greater concentration and focus of effort, for example, bilateral aid became progressively less concentrated over the period 1960–90 (see Table 2.1 on aid-giving patterns). Also, concerning the objective of increased flexibility, the most recent Global Monitoring Report notes that in 2002 only about 30 per cent of total bilateral assistance was available 'flexibly' for project and programme expenditures in developing countries. The remaining 70 per cent had been 'earmarked' for special purpose grants such as technical assistance, debt relief, food aid, emergency and disaster relief and the cost of aid administration. Moreover this proportion between flexible and earmarked bilateral funding has been increasing in the wrong direction; it was 60:40 in the early 1980s (IMF-WB 2004a). Recently, there have also been indications of the increased earmarking of bilateral development financing to issues of conflict, humanitarian assistance and global public goods, among others.

To illustrate the extent to which some of the main bilateral development agencies are attempting to contribute to OECD's transformation framework, we will review briefly some of the main reform efforts recently undertaken by four of the most important donors in terms of ODA volume (the United States, United Kingdom, France and Japan) and/or recent policy initiatives (Sweden).

In 1993 *the United States* launched the Government Performance and Results Act, requiring that every government agency implement a coordinated strategic planning, implementation and monitoring system. In this regard, the United States Agency for International Development (USAID) was requested to implement a performance-based and results-oriented approach in its operations. The USAID response is reflected in a policy statement on 'A New Compact for Development', which

Table 2.1   Aid-giving patterns of individual bilateral donors

Donors	Number of countries aided by the donor					Number of countries receiving less than 1% of total aid*	Percentage of total portfolio received by the top 10 recipients (2002)
	1966–1969	*1970–1979*	*1980–1989*	*1990–1999*	*2000–2002*		
Australia	37	80	116	137	104	127	81.3
Austria	71	71	114	144	127	104	68.1
Belgium	5	69	109	148	120	85	44.1
Canada	82	104	133	165	151	110	44.4
Denmark	42	90	71	97	75	62	58.9
Finland		72	104	129	104	79	48.7
France	42	76	137	173	167	145	51.2
Germany	95	125	139	177	166	126	34.2
Greece				100	77	69	90.0
Ireland		25	59	127	97	81	76.7
Italy	69	103	117	141	131	117	52.9
Japan	23	124	145	177	168	151	67.8
Luxembourg				93	76	53	59.4

Table 2.1   Aid-giving patterns of individual bilateral donors (*continued*)

Donors	Number of countries aided by the donor					Number of countries receiving less than 1% of total aid*	Percentage of total portfolio received by the top 10 recipients (2002)
	1966–1969	*1970–1979*	*1980–1989*	*1990–1999*	*2000–2002*		
Netherlands	18	122	129	159	139	106	45.4
New Zealand		54	64	111	100	78	60.9
Norway	20	77	100	132	122	93	50.1
Portugal				34	56	49	98.5
Spain				120	123	97	60.4
Sweden	40	56	90	129	120	90	45.2
Switzerland	68	85	107	136	118	83	42.0
UK	112	133	133	168	150	125	58.6
USA	101	112	113	156	158	126	55.7

*Percentage of recipients receiving less than one per cent of the total aid disbursed by the donor (1999–2002 average).

advocates collaboration among development actors, increased national ownership and results-based management, and which should also promote a 'Global Development Alliance'. Yet, in contrast to some of the central tenets of these policy statements, the 'Millennium Challenge Account' initiative of the United States, which has been expected to provide an additional US$5 billion in annual aid by 2006, aims to target a small group of low-income countries on the basis of governance criteria that have raised concerns about US unilateralism and the use of ODA resources to promote its strategic interests (section 3.4).

The official development assistance (ODA) of *France* increased to US$7.3 billion in 2003, from US$4.2 billion in 2001 (an increase in nominal terms of 43 per cent over only two years), with the result that France has become the G7 country with the highest ODA/GNI ratio (0.41 per cent). Moreover, France has pledged to increase its official development assistance (ODA) to 0.5 per cent of GNI by 2007, equivalent to around US$9 billion, and then to 0.7 per cent by 2012, with at least half of the money going to Africa in support of efforts to achieve the MDGs. A recent DAC review (May 2004) indicated, however, that achieving these targets will not be a straightforward task, given the current budgetary deficit situation of France and fiscal pressures that are expected to persist for many years (OECD DAC 2004a).

In 1997, *the United Kingdom* embarked on a wholesale transformation of its bilateral development policy. A separate government department, the Department for International Development (DFID), was established at that time under a senior minister and with a commitment to reverse the long decline in British ODA levels. This was followed by the launching of two white papers, *Eliminating World Poverty: A Challenge for the 21st Century*, issued in November 1997; and *Eliminating World Poverty: Making Globalisation Work for the Poor*, released in December 2000. These papers announced the government's intention to end the tying of its development assistance to the procurement of British goods and services.[17] It also included the pledge to increase the United Kingdom's ODA as a proportion of GNP to 0.33 per cent by the 2003/04 financial year, and to continue to make progress towards the 0.7 per cent UN target. Finally, it committed the government to introduce a new International Development Bill into Parliament which would consolidate poverty reduction as the objective for Britain's ODA, except in the case of assistance provided to United Kingdom overseas territories.

In *Japan*, the country's mounting fiscal deficit in the late 1990s reversed the lengthy upward trend in Japanese ODA and led to a decline in real terms of almost 20 per cent. This downward trend shows no sign of diminishing. For the fiscal year beginning in April 2005. Japanese ODA will be cut by a further 4 per cent.

Among OECD countries, *Sweden* has been one of the most consistent and strongest supporters of international development and of multilateralism. Three recent initiatives taken by Sweden have reaffirmed its national commitment both to improvements and reform of the overall system and to updating and strengthening its own national capabilities for development effectiveness. The three initiatives are: the *Development Financing 2000* project, the catalysing and financing of an *International Task Force on Global Public Goods*, and the launching of its own new policy framework under the title *Shared Responsibility: Sweden's Policy for Global Development.*

The Development Financing 2000 initiative involved a series of in-depth studies which were aimed specifically at strengthening and re-orienting development financing in ways that would ensure a strong, efficient and well-funded multilateral system for development. The studies themselves are reviewed and summarized individually in Annex A. Taken as a whole, these underscore the severity of structural weaknesses within the overall system of development financing and the imperative for more comprehensive and systemic thinking and approaches to improve the level and to achieve a more effective division of labour. The studies contain numerous specific recommendations on key areas requiring multilateral reform and on how these might be approached.

Establishing an *International Task Force on Global Public Goods* was a specific recommendation made in one of the studies conducted under the Development Financing 2000 initiative (*Financing and Providing Global Public Goods: Expectations and Prospects*). The study underscored the point that inherent in claims and debates of global public goods is a range of dangers to the interests of development and developing countries including: an absence of an agreed framework for priority-setting or for determining the arrangements required for the provision and financing of a global public good, and an accelerating number of claims on development in the name of global public goods based more on 'fuzzy thinking' than on precision on what part of any good is global and what part is not. Accordingly, the report recommended that a time-bound task force be set up to try to introduce some order into this situation. Sweden, in partnership with France, established such a task force in 2003[18] with a mandate to assess and define priorities for international (global and regional) public goods, and to recommend to policy makers and other stakeholders measures to improve and expand their provision. The Task Force will report in 2005.

Shared Responsibility: Sweden's Policy for Global Development In 2003, following an extensive process of study and consultations, both nationally and internationally, Sweden became the first country in the world to present to its parliament an integrated policy for global development. The specific aim of the policy is to mobilize and align all national instruments at Sweden's disposal in support of a global effort to reduce poverty and to achieve the MDGs. The policy aims to enhance the coherence of Sweden's approach to development issues by requiring the coordination of international development policies with public policies in other fields, including security and defence, trade and business investment, migration, social welfare and public health, education, economic and finance, agriculture and fisheries, culture, environment, and industry and employment.

At the international level, the policy commits Sweden to continue to support multilateral development organizations and press for improvements in their operations and for achieving a better division of labour. In particular, it will seek to strengthen the development cooperation activities of the European Union and foster greater country-level coordination between EU member states, the European Commission and other actors to enhance policy coherence.

Going beyond the Swedish case, overall, bilateral donors have been making serious attempts to increase aid levels in the last five years. However, less visible results are perceived in the case of aid quality, though several diagnostics have been addressing these deficiencies. The Rome Declaration and the Marrakech Roundtable on Development Effectiveness are positive signals for future changes, although strategic considerations and fiscal imbalances in developed countries could slow down the reform effort.

2.4 The EU aid reforms

The EU[19] taken as a whole is by far the largest single source of ODA. For example, in 2002 it amounted to slightly over 51 per cent of the total, and over 20 per cent of this was transferred from individual EU member states through the Union's multilateral programmes, which are administered by the European Commission headquartered in Brussels. This makes the EU multilateral programme one of the largest single sources of ODA.

EU programmes, however, have been subject to serious criticism in recent years. The criticism has come mainly from without but also from within the Commission of the EU itself. For example, the EU's former Commissioner responsible for external aid, Chris Patten, was publicly outspoken about 'gross inefficiencies' and 'limited impact' of EU aid (*The Economist*, 16 August 2001 and 25 October 2001). Externally, criticism has often been far more scathing (Cox, Folke, Schulpen and Webster 2001; Van Reisen 2002). Britain's former International Development Secretary, Clare Short, told a House of Commons committee that EU aid was simply 'appalling', that it was 'skewed quite dreadfully against the poorest countries' (Hansard, House of Commons, Column 305W, Wednesday 22 January 2003), and that if major improvements were not forthcoming she would reduce greatly Britain's ODA contributions through the EU. These concerns were also reflected in a 2002 peer review report of the Development Assistance Committee of the OECD (The Courier ACP-EU no. 194) that pointed to severe shortcomings due, *inter alia*, to a fall in EU aid to LDCs from 70 per cent in 1990 to 39 per cent in 2000, the large number of budget lines and instruments, the proliferation in the number of procedures, and a lack of flexibility for moving funds from non-performing programmes areas.

In addition to the criticisms over its aid performance, many aspects of EU trade policy have been the object of consistent and savage attacks for their pernicious effects on developing countries. This has been especially evident with regard to agricultural trade policy under the Common Agricultural Policy (CAP). The OECD calculated that in 2002 each farmer in the member countries of the EU would receive a subsidy of about US$14,000 (European Commission, 15 May 2002).[20] EU support to agriculture in 2003 amounted to almost exactly double the combined aid budgets of EU multilateral programmes and those of all 15 of the countries that were member states at that time (i.e. before enlargement).

These criticisms of the policies and practices of the EU in aid and trade with developing countries have been major drivers of EU reform efforts in recent years. It is important to recall that EU development aid policy was originally aimed unequivocally at a trade-focused relationship with the former colonies of France and the UK (known as the ACP, or African Caribbean and Pacific countries). This shifted gradually throughout the 1970s and 1980s to embrace the wider concerns of other donor agencies, such as human rights, good governance and conflict prevention. Geographically, the EU's focus has also shifted over time beyond ex-colonial relationships and towards political dialogue and support to areas including the Middle East, the Balkans, and, increasingly, its neighbours in Eastern Europe.

But the more sweeping and far-reaching reforms to the EU have been quite recent. In 2000, a radical shift in trade and aid linkage policy occurred with the signing of the Cotonou agreement, which for the first time afforded ACP countries trade negotiations with the EU in order to establish free trade agreements. In addition, the agreement envisaged over the subsequent eight to ten years the phasing out completely of EU policy based on similar trade treatment of all ACP countries, to be replaced by regional arrangements based on levels of development. In February 2001, the EU approved the so-called 'EBA (Everything But Arms) Regulation' (Regulation (EC) 416/2001), granting duty-free access to imports of all products from least developed countries without any quantitative restrictions, except to arms and munitions. For agricultural imports into the EU from LDCs, only fresh bananas, rice and sugar have not now been fully liberalized and duties on these exempted products are to be gradually reduced with duty-free access for all products to apply by 2009.

In the specific area of aid policy, a major and formal change occurred in EU development aid policy in 2000, which established poverty reduction as the overarching aim and the MDGs as the means through which to achieve it. A new department, the EuropeAid Cooperation Office, was created to harmonize the management of all development assistance, and approximately half the staff of EuropeAid have been or are being moved to country offices in a massive organizational reform in favour of 'deconcentration'.

The implications of the enlargement of the EU and of growing fiscal pressures as a result of the demographic transitions now occurring in European states are likely to be the main drivers of future and further major reforms in EU development policy and practice. Some of the pressures inherent in these drivers are likely to be in the opposite direction to recent trends in EU aid policy.

On 1 May 2004, 10 additional countries acceded to the Union, increasing the total to 25. Preparations are ongoing for the next enlargement. Bulgaria and Romania hope to join by 2007. With regard to development assistance and development financing, only half the countries that joined in 2004 had policy frameworks defining the principles and objectives of their foreign aid. The most immediate implications for development policy and financing of the recent enlargement are twofold. First, the accession has increased the gap between the current level of ODA provided by Europe and the target of 0.39 per cent of GDP promised by the EU at the Monterrey summit of 2002 – this pledge was made it was before enlargement occurred. At that time, a few EU states such as Denmark, Sweden and the Netherlands were well above this percentage, but most were below and some very significantly so (e.g. Germany at 0.27 per cent, Italy at 0.15 per cent and Greece at 0.17 per cent). Thus, it was agreed at that time that each member state would contribute to the achievement of a collective average of 0.39 per cent by contributing not less than 0.33 per cent individually. For the new members of the EU, the fiscal implications of this commitment are daunting. They imply an annual growth rate of non–EU ODA of 18 per cent for Poland, Hungary and the Baltic countries, and a growth of 11 per cent for Cyprus, the Czech Republic, Malta, the Slovak Republic, and Slovenia (Migliorisi 2003: 61).

Pressures towards a major shift in the political and programmatic focus of development assistance may also result from enlargement. To the extent that the newly acceded states have produced development policy frameworks, these appear to place emphasis on regional integration, global security and 'cross-cutting' issues such as environment and human rights and to assign little importance to poverty reduction and the MDGs. In the new member states, current ODA is for the most part directed towards neighbouring countries, in terms of both public opinion and official development frameworks. Eastern Europe is a region characterized by imposed postwar borders and support for diasporas in the area is often a significant part of official aid. For example, Hungary's bilateral aid is mainly targeted at supporting the approximately three million Hungarians living in bordering countries, particularly Romania. While this is clearly a legitimate and important focus, it is likely to contribute to a shift away from ODA to LDCs. There is also at least some evidence of possible trends towards this emphasis in some of the original member states, evidenced in the volume of ODA commitments to large-scale humanitarian operations as in Iraq and Afghanistan, proposals to link aid to issues of regional security and stability and concerns to align aid policies to a tightening of immigration and asylum legislation (Maxwell and Engel 2003).

The second major driver of future EU development policy will probably be fiscal pressure resulting from profound shifts in Europe's demography. The 'European Model' of a high degree of state provision for social security is already under great strain. The inertial forces of Europe's demographic profile make much greater stress inevitable over the next several decades. In several European states birth rates have fallen below the levels required for stable population size and, as a result, these countries are already de-populating. They are also rapidly aging and the ratio of working age population to the total is fast declining. By 2050, on present trends, there will be 75 pensioners for every

100 workers; in Spain and Italy the ratio of pensioners to workers is projected to be one-to-one. These demographic trends are being exacerbated by cautious to hostile views of immigration and populist pressures to maintain tough anti-immigration policies. The consequences of these factors are already apparent in fiscal deficits in several countries that either have already become, or risk becoming, structural. The overall implications for the flexibility of the EU to increase financing for international development are probably strongly negative.

2.5 Emerging initiatives in development financing[21]

The foregoing outline of reform efforts shows unquestionably that attention to development and to developing countries has been increasing over the past few years. It also demonstrates that the international development system is struggling to deal with the fact that its overall architecture remains considerably less than systemic, that it lacks adequate governance structures and that its level of financing falls far short both of adequacy and of predictability. The reform efforts demonstrate further that ODA and development financing in general will continue to carry a disproportionate burden in attempting to satisfy the expectations of the international development community, and that (excepting the case of Sweden) far less attention is being accorded to the policies of rich and powerful countries with regard, *inter alia*, to trade, investment, intellectual property, access to technology and migration that are far more potent than ODA as drivers of development.

Yet some of this is changing nonetheless and development assistance concerns will receive increased and more responsive attention in the current decade than was generally the case during the period 1973–2000. The momentum has been building in the many lessons that have been learned from prior development efforts, and has been strongly reinforced by a heightened political awareness of linkages between new concerns about global security and development. As part of this, much more serious efforts than in previous years are being invested in seeking new ways and new mechanisms to generate increased financial resources for development, including market-based instruments to enhance ODA, trade revenues, private capital inflows, and domestic resource mobilization.

The quest for additional resources (*additionality*) for development is thus more central today than ever before to the international geopolitical agenda. It is promoting the emergence of new proposals for financing instruments and a renewed interest in previously proposed ones.[22]

We will examine in section 3.3 of the following chapter the main characteristics and potential of these which may be classified into the following five broad categories according to their main objectives and orientation: (i) performance-linked financial mechanisms; (ii) financing instruments to promote private flows to developing countries; (iii) global and regional partnerships for specific purposes; (iv) direct support for public finances; and (v) global taxes.

Performance-linked financial mechanisms. These are financial instruments that seek to link resource disbursements with recipient country performance. One example would be GDP-indexed bonds, which are simply a standard sovereign bond with an indexation clause. They have already been issued by a handful of emerging economies. For example, Mexico has issued bonds indexed to oil prices, some private Chilean firms have issued bonds indexed to the price of copper, and Costa Rica, Bulgaria, Bosnia and Herzegovina have issued bonds containing an element of indexation to GDP growth rates as part of their Brady restructuring agreements (Borensztein and Paolo 2004). More recently, at the Atlanta G7-G8 Summit, the United States floated the idea of launching 'democracy bonds', which would be bonds indexed to growth in developing countries with good policies and which would be enhanced by some sort of official guarantee scheme (Basu 2004). Another, quite different, example is the US Millennium Challenge Account (MCA), which consists in selecting aid recipients based on ratings of their policy environment and governance practices, and not necessarily on their need. The MCA raises important questions of 'need vs. performance' criteria in bilateral aid allocations to poor countries. The first group of countries eligible for MCA funds was announced on 10 May 2004 and includes Armenia, Benin, Bolivia, Cape Verde, Georgia, Ghana, Honduras, Lesotho, Madagascar, Mali, Mongolia, Mozambique, Nicaragua, Senegal, Sri Lanka and Vanuatu. The US Congress appropriated $1 billion for the programme in 2004, the Administration has requested US$2.5 billion for 2005 and hopes to reach US$5 billion in 2006.

Increasing private flows to developing countries. The second group of innovative financing instruments comprises those aimed at increasing private flows to developing countries. These include loan guarantees, liquidity facilities and derivatives to mitigate poor creditworthiness, political and commercial risks, and high foreign currency exposure of investors, all of which are mostly used in project finance transactions.

This group also comprises Social Responsible Investment (SRI) initiatives. At present, SRI assets in developing countries are estimated to be US$2.7 billion, an important figure but still only about one-tenth of one per cent of SRI worldwide (IFC 2003). The third group of mechanisms that promote private flows to developing countries are workers' remittances, which have become an increasingly important source of financing in several developing countries. Although these transfers currently provide support essentially to families and individuals, they could, in principle, be leveraged to larger development efforts.

Issue-based global and regional partnerships. These constitute a third group of proposals for innovative financing mechanisms. An earlier example of this would be the Global Environment Facility (GEF), which came into being through the collaboration of international agencies and multilateral and bilateral agencies. The GEF began to operate in the early 1990s, and provides grants to finance the incremental cost of reducing the negative environmental impact of developing country projects, thus acting as a catalyser of financing resources for the protection of the environment. More recently, other special purpose arrangements have been proposed, such as the Global Issues Network and the Sustainable Energy Finance Facility, and at least one, the Global Fund for AIDS, Tuberculosis and Malaria (which has committed US$2.1 billion since its creation in 2000), has become fully operational. The proposed International Finance Facility (IFF) could become a partnership involving capital markets, bilateral and multilateral agencies, to provide a medium-term source of financing for the MDGs.

Direct support for public finance. The fourth group of innovative financing mechanisms are those oriented to providing *direct support for public finances* (in effect, predictable and stable fiscal transfers to developing countries). Concerns over tied aid and the excessive use of conditionality have promoted the search for more flexible ways to support developing countries' public sector finances. The possibility of issuing SDRs to increase the resource availability for balance of payments distress or for development purposes would fall into this category.

Global taxes. A variety of global taxes have been proposed for quite some time and there is currently renewed and heightened interest in them. Some, such as the 'Tobin tax', have been the subject of detailed study and have resulted in quite specific proposals that have gained at least some important support from senior international political leadership.[23] These developments and current interest notwith-standing, indications are that agreements will not soon materialize on any of the more significant proposals for global taxes.

Accompanying these new initiatives and the search for additional financial resources for development are some continuing concerns over the old issue of the absorptive capacity of poor countries. The consensus view that seems recently to have emerged, however, is that while absorptive limitations may pose problems there is little doubt that increased financial resources are imperative. A related component of the consensus view is increasingly that absorptive constraints should be approached as challenges to be overcome expeditiously rather than as excuses to limit financial flows. Diverse studies on the topic show varying results, but a growing body of evidence supports the consensus position. For example, Devarajan, Miller and Swanson (2002) found that if US$40–60 billion of additional aid is allocated only to those countries with 'good' policies and institutions, the saturation point – where the level of aid starts to have a negative impact on economic growth – will only be reached in four of the 65 countries of the sample. Goldin, Rogers and Stern (2002) provide further evidence that aid is becoming more effective: better results and development impact is being achieved with less money allocated. In conclusion, the impetus towards financing instrument innovation should not be slowed down due to concerns over absorptive capacity, although efforts should continue to increase developing countries' capacity to absorb more aid.

2.6 Major opportunities and threats for the future of international development financing

The magnitude and intensity of recent reform efforts in both bilateral and multilateral development agencies, coupled with a range of new financing initiatives, demonstrate a renewed concern for development effectiveness. It is important to bear in mind, however, that this is far from unprecedented, as we saw in chapter 1. The general pattern of prior efforts provides little encouragement. It informs us that these were initiated in response to major crises (e.g. the sharp decline in relative commodity prices in the 1960s, the oil shocks and 'stagflation' of the 1970s, the debt crisis of the 1980s, and so on), but also that reform efforts were not sustained and that, after varying periods, they were quietly and unceremoniously abandoned. The most notable example would be the New International Economic Order (NIEO) of the 1970s. Yet the current effort towards aid effectiveness would appear to have greater momentum and a broader constituency than its predecessors. The current thrust is serious, far-reaching, and widely shared among donors and partner-countries. If conscientiously applied, this reform agenda is likely to upgrade substantially the value of development cooperation and the importance of development financing in their particular areas of comparative advantage. At the same time, however, it needs to be recognized that there is a high probability (almost a certainty) that the reform agenda will really only be fully applied to a part of total ODA expenditure, although this part should be substantial. ODA allocations will also be determined by new geopolitical imperatives, particularly the 'war on terrorism', and continuing strains will also result from the allocation of ODA funding to an increasing range of global public goods, including those defined in terms of global security and, again, the 'war on terrorism'.

Chapters 3 and 4 will examine scenarios for the future of development financing and chapter 5 will derive their implications. At this stage, it is sufficient to note from the foregoing analysis that the early years of this decade have ushered in a period of a possibly unprecedented international disposition towards major reforms in the international development system. There is also at least a reasonable prospect that international thinking in the coming years will advance on the ways and means of strengthening the provision of global public goods reflecting the demands of interdependence and globalization. At a minimum, it should be reasonable to anticipate that much greater clarification will have been achieved through the work currently underway in relation to different types of international public goods and which of these needs are appropriate for 'core' development assistance funding, or for funding from other sources.

The sense of cumulative unease that currently characterizes thinking about the 'system' has established a moment of new opportunities for a fundamental rethinking of the international development architecture, and of development financing mechanisms. The criticisms about the effectiveness of the development financing system have multiplied in the last decade, and the patchwork-like approaches of the past have not been successful in addressing them. The UN agencies, the IMF and the WB have launched numerous panels and round-table discussions to bring forward proposals to better coordinate their interventions. However, their implementation could take several years and may be counteracted by the 'go-it-alone' attitudes of individual institutions.

Major shocks and upheavals have always been the most important drivers – both positive and negative – for changes in the international development architecture, and reforms within multilateral and bilateral institutions. Whether the world economy today is at the precipice of a new major shock and upheaval is a matter of deep contestation. There is little dispute over the 'hard facts' of the extent and severity of the structural imbalances in the global economy (e.g. the current and fiscal account deficits of the United States, the fiscal deficit of Japan, the fiscal implications of Europe's demographic transition, the overheated and unsustainable growth levels of China's economy, increasing instability in global energy supply, and so on). The dispute is over whether these factors now make inevitable a major upheaval within the very near term. What is probable is that if one should occur it would bring widespread misery to a highly interconnected world and would result in some combinations of a resurgence of inflation, a period of 'stagflation' and a new round of trade protectionism. It would also almost certainly impact in highly negative ways on the international development system, its current reform agenda and any prospects for advances or breakthroughs in development financing.

3
Building Scenarios for International Development Finance

3.1 Introduction

3.1.1 Key attributes of an effective international development financing system

As indicated in the preceding chapter, the current international development architecture and the development financing system associated with it have evolved over the past six decades in an incremental and haphazard manner. For example, one of the most important elements of the system – ODA – comprises more than 80 bilateral, multilateral and international agencies. In spite of a surge of multilateral flows in the 1970s and 1980s, official aid remains heavily dominated by bilateral flows, which accounted for about 70 per cent of ODA in 2003, and particularly for European countries, which were responsible for more than 50 per cent of these flows in the same year. At the same time, as mentioned in chapter 1, private capital inflows, comprising primarily direct foreign and portfolio investments, have increased greatly, although they tend to be concentrated in a few emerging and middle-income countries and focus on specific sectors (mining, energy, telecommunications, finance and some manufacturing activities). Finally, there have been impressive increases in other private flows, especially over the past decade, including remittances, grants from private foundations, and donations from NGOs and individuals.

The previous two chapters have drawn attention to the fact that, although over time the number of institutions has grown and the volume of resources has expanded, there have been very few modifications to the basic institutional development architecture that was established six decades ago. Some adjustments and fine-tuning have occurred, but no major institution has disappeared through merger or closure. New institutions have been created mainly in response to emerging needs and the perceived deficiencies of existing development assistance organizations, and have grown in parallel with these (Rogerson 2004). As a consequence there is a bewildering array of development assistance organizations with no clear delineation of roles or division of labour between them. When the various private agents that provide financing to developing countries are added to the picture, a quite incoherent picture emerges that can hardly qualify as an international development financing 'system' in the proper sense of the word.

The previous analysis has also shown that, by the 1990s, rising and spreading disillusionment in donor countries had begun to undermine public and political support for development cooperation, aid budgets had declined and residual Cold War justifications for development assistance had disappeared. This raised questions about the nature and effectiveness of the 'system'. Impetus to address these questions increased with the advent of the MDGs and of post-September 11 security concerns linked to development. Some of these key questions include:

- Is it possible to advance towards a more coherent and effective international development financing system in the current political climate?
- What possible paths for the evolution of the institutional and financing architecture could be charted that could better serve the needs of international development?

This chapter explores these questions. It describes the components that will be used to construct scenarios for the possible evolution of the international development financing system with a ten- to fifteen-year horizon. The following chapter describes the scenarios and derives some of their key policy implications.

A first task is to define the attributes of an effective, or at least much better, set of institutional and financial arrangements to mobilize and channel resources to the growing variety of developing countries. These attributes provide a yardstick to compare outcomes of different paths that the international development financing system could take. A starting point in identifying these attributes is the debates that took place before and during the United Nations International Conference on Development Financing of 2002 (United Nations 2002b), which suggest widespread agreement that the main attributes of an effective financing system would include the following:

- *Adequacy.* This refers both to the total amount of development financing and to the match between financial instruments and the needs of developing countries. With regard to amounts, there have been many attempts to estimate the financing requirements of developing countries under various assumptions for rates of growth and poverty reduction, among other variables. Calculations presented at the Monterrey Summit and exercises carried out after it have addressed this question by estimating the amounts required to achieve the MDGs. While there is wide variation in these estimates, a general consensus is that it would be necessary to at least double the current annual level of ODA. Regarding the fit between financial instruments and the needs of different types of developing countries, the criterion of adequacy suggests there should be a wide range of instruments, tailored to specific domestic situations and conditions, and in particular to a country's capacity to mobilize external and domestic resources.
- *Predictability.* The lack of predictability in financial flows to developing countries creates significant problems for macroeconomic management, public expenditure planning, and institutional development, and may also undermine the confidence of private investors. The questions of predictability are different according to the type of instrument and developing country, with private portfolio flows for middle-income and emerging countries being most volatile, bilateral assistance to some low-income countries showing greater stability, and multilateral lending occupying an intermediate place. In addition to factors such as resource availability, developing country policies and investor's appetite for risk, the predictability of financial flows is also affected by the type of conditionality adopted by bilateral and multilateral agencies and the range of financial instruments at their disposal.
- *Responsiveness.* An effective development financing system should respond and balance adequately allocation criteria based on developing country needs and on performance. The current multilateral and, to a lesser extent, bilateral emphasis on directing aid towards countries with good policies and institutional arrangements begs two important questions. First, recourse primarily to performance criteria will exclude low-performing countries that could benefit from

development assistance to improve their institutional and policy capabilities, and could lead to some sort of 'Matthew effect' whereby resources are provided to those countries that already receive them. Second, beyond some basic requirements (e.g. transparency, the rule of law and lack of corruption) what are considered 'good policies' as defined by the international financial institutions is subject to change over time – as shown by the debates on the impact of financial liberalization in the wake of the Asian crisis of the late 1990s. Also, while it is almost axiomatic that 'good policies' (as opposed to 'bad policies') are important to development, it is not at all clear that these are reasonable predictors of either performance or effective resource utilization. There are clearly trade-offs involved, but an effective development financing system should be responsive to both need and performance in a diversity of developing countries, tailoring the financial instruments and institutional arrangements to their specific conditions and in particular to their absorption capacities.

- *Diversity and choice.* Recognizing the vast diversity that exists between developing countries and their needs, an effective financing system should allow a reasonable degree of choice regarding financial institutions, instruments, and policies. This implies both a willingness to accept divergence from preconceived ideas on the part of financing institutions and donor countries,[1] and a greater degree of responsibility on the part of recipient countries that must exercise choice and live with the consequences.

- *Capacity to absorb shocks.* This refers to the capacity of the development financing system to respond rapidly and effectively to external shocks – financial crisis, violent conflicts, natural disasters, sudden surges and collapses of commodity prices. To eliminate or reduce the pernicious effects of such shocks, financial instruments and institutional arrangements should be capable of anti-cyclical responses – anticipating shocks (to the extent possible) and of timely and adequate responses to them. In sharp contrast to this, recent work (Griffith-Jones and Ocampo 2004) has found that both multilateral and bilateral aid for the poorest countries is overwhelmingly pro-cyclical. Similarly, the lack of resources available for rapid deployment in conflict prevention activities has been considered to be a major shortcoming of the international system (Malloch Brown 2003).

- *Complementarity to domestic resource mobilization.* While developing countries differ widely in their resource mobilization capacities, in general external sources of finance should be seen as a complement to domestic resource mobilization. They should help to create the institutional framework, the policy environment and the habits that promote domestic savings and investment. This may take time in the poorest countries, and particularly in those that lack a properly functioning state apparatus (e.g. post-conflict countries). But domestic resource mobilization is essential to avoid the dangers of recurrent bouts of aid dependency, which are likely to lead to episodes of donor aid fatigue. In addition to fostering greater reliance on domestic resources, an effective international development financing system should allow and stimulate countries to shift from asymmetric official aid to a more balanced relation with the international financial institutions and private sources of capital. Over a period of several decades, this would imply a transition from heavy reliance on concessional loans and grants to obtaining regular loans from multilateral development banks, and to an active presence in international bond markets and to receiving significant amounts of direct foreign investment, while at the same time strengthening domestic resource mobilization and avoiding capital flight.

- *Voice, representation and accountability.* An effective development financing system should accommodate and give voice and representation in decision making to all relevant stakeholders. This implies that, in addition to being accountable to their main donors (or shareholders), financial institutions should also be accountable to their borrowers. A long-standing concern of developing countries and of advocacy groups has been asymmetry of representation and voice in decisions regarding the financial and development policies and practices of the World Bank, the IMF, bilateral agencies and the Paris Club of official creditors. Such concern extends to the DAC, which generally does not include developing countries officially in the formulation of key policies.

- *Flexibility, efficiency and learning.* An effective international development financing system needs the flexibility to alter established practices in response to changing needs, to alterations in the international and regional contexts, and to emerging issues and events. This should include the possibility of closing or merging some organizations that have outlived their usefulness, and, where justified, the establishment of new ones. Institutional administrative and transaction costs should be reasonably low, but without their being reduced to the point where there is a danger of impairing the ability to plan, manage, coordinate and to engage developing countries in meaningful dialogue. Management procedures and incentives should be structured to foster innovation and judicious risk taking, and also to learn from past failures and from the mistakes of others. Institutions should be able to grow, shrink and even disappear as a function of changing priorities and demands.

Each of these characteristics of what may be considered an ideal international development financing system implies trade-offs and choices, both within attributes and between them. For example, greater predictability may entail a lower level of external resources and may also lead to less flexibility to reallocate resources. Increasing the capacity to absorb shocks may require keeping resources idle for certain periods in order to respond quickly to a sudden deterioration in international financial markets. Moreover, the characteristics outlined above are not intended to be exhaustive, although they are deemed sufficient for the purposes of the present study.

3.1.2 Scenarios for development financing and their components

Four scenarios for the possible evolution of development financing over the next decade and a half will be explored. Two of these comprise extreme cases and two represent intermediate situations. The scenarios are a heuristic tool to derive and highlight the range of strategies and policies that could be pursued to improve the alignment of the international development financing system with the characteristics that have been outlined in the preceding section.

Each of the scenarios is examined against combinations of four components: *institutional arrangements, financing instruments, developing country capacity to mobilize financial resources,* and *political viability.*

Institutional arrangements. This refers to the organizational architecture of the various entities involved in mobilizing and channelling financial resources to developing countries, as well as the rules and procedures that regulate their interactions. In a sense, institutional arrangements provide the scaffolding on which to place financial instruments and to link these to different types of developing countries. As indicated in the preceding chapters, the international development system has evolved in a haphazard manner during the last six decades and is now in need of major restructuring, not only in terms of the number, size and functions of the institutions and organizations that comprise it, but also in the way they operate, interact with each other and relate to developing countries. The design and implementation of new financial instruments is likely to require major institutional adjustments and may even demand the creation of new organizations.

Financing instruments. This component refers to the various mechanisms and operational procedures used to obtain, process and provide financial resources to developing countries. They link sources of funds – government allocations, capital markets, bank deposits, endowments, donations, among others – with the public, private and civil society entities that make use of these funds in the recipient countries. There are numerous financial instruments, many of them developed during the last two decades as a result of innovations in finance (partly linked to advances in information technologies), and also several proposals for new ones. This makes development finance a rather open-ended and fluid field, in which it is difficult to keep abreast of new developments.

The diversity of developing countries and their needs indicates that the richer the array of development financing instruments, the greater should be the opportunities for channelling resources in the amount and in ways that are appropriate to them. Eight categories have been used to group existing and proposed instruments, most of which are appropriate to one or two types of developing countries. For this reason, it is important to link specific financial instruments to the types of countries that can make use of them – which depends, among other things, on their capacity to mobilize external and domestic finance.

Developing country capacity to mobilize financial resources. This component of the scenarios refers to the ability of countries to attract external financing and to generate internal resources to finance development programmes, projects and initiatives. Classifications of developing countries based on aggregate indicators such as income per capita or level of indebtedness may not serve to identify how well various financial instruments match the needs of different groups of developing countries. Thus, several approaches to define categories of developing countries were explored in this study, including the development of a quantitative index of resource mobilization.[2] It was found more appropriate to rank countries along two axes, which correspond to the capacity to mobilize external and domestic finance, and to define categories combining these two to form a matrix. Excluding a category that comprises four outlier countries with unusually high levels of FDI, each of the two axes was divided into three segments to yield nine groups of developing countries. In the first section of the next chapter, these are put together with financial instruments in order to assess the degree to which the range of instruments corresponds to the needs of different types of developing countries.

Political viability. This final component of the scenarios describes some key features of the current international political situation and international power relations, as well as the trajectories they may possibly follow during the next decade, in so far as they affect development finance. It takes into account the risks and also the opportunities for intervention that could shape movement towards a more effective international development financing system. The perspectives arrived at are based on assessments of underlying political inertia, trends and motivations, and on the driving forces that may condition the decisions of key actors regarding the structure and functioning of the international development financing system. In a conventional scenario exercise alternative outcomes should be equally plausible and for this reason viability considerations are usually not included in such an exercise. The centrality of issues of political viability to the purposes of this study, however, make it desirable that these be integrated into the scenarios and this is what has been done.

These components will be combined to define four scenarios for the future of the international development financing system around 2015, and each scenario will be evaluated in terms of the attributes of a desired financing system as described above.

3.2 Institutional arrangements

The first component of the scenarios refers to the set of institutions and organizations involved in the development finance system, and considers two extreme hypothetical situations viewed from the vantage point of 2015 and looking back over the preceding decade. The first is one in which there are few and mostly inconsequential changes in institutional arrangements over the next decade ('business as usual', or BASU), and the second assumes the impetus for reform has carried the day and has led to a major restructuring of institutional arrangements including the creation of new entities ('comprehensive reform', or CORE). There is a broad range of possible intermediate situations between these two extremes, but these can be inferred from a description of BASU and CORE and will be mentioned at the end of this section.

Official institutions (bilateral, multilateral, international) constitute the majority of entities now involved in development financing, so they are the natural starting point for describing the evolution of institutional arrangements. These are addressed in the following order: bilateral agencies, multilateral financial institutions, international and regional agencies, organizations linked to the private and civil society sectors. Some remarks on the interactions between these entities and on their overall effectiveness complement the description of the two extreme cases. As this component focuses on institutional arrangements, wider considerations – such as political will and power relations that affect development finance organizations – are dealt with in section 3.5.

3.2.1 Business as usual (BASU): a view from 2015

A description of the institutional arrangements in 2015 in this scenario would read as follows:

By 2015 there have not been fundamental changes in the structure or the composition of the agencies involved in development financing, or in the ways they interact with each other and with the developing countries. The only institutional innovations during the decade 2005–15 have been the creation of bilateral agencies in the ten countries that joined the EU in 2004, which are very small and have had little impact, and the establishment of a handful of issue-oriented (vertical) global funds, which bypass existing institutional structures and whose effectiveness has been under discussion.

Leadership failures, special interests and bureaucratic inertia have combined to maintain the quite incoherent set of institutional arrangements that obtained a decade ago, albeit with minor and cosmetic changes. Programmes and agencies that have outlived their usefulness (e.g. conventional technical assistance) or are seriously under-funded (e.g. some international and regional bodies) are still in existence; any efforts to close these have failed. Reactive behaviour, inadequate accountability and the lack of flexibility have prevented learning from past mistakes and have not allowed most development financing organizations to respond adequately to new challenges. As a result, their credibility has been seriously eroded. Attempts to build constituencies for development assistance have led some donor countries to place excessive emphasis on short-term 'results' – which are almost impossible to measure adequately – to demonstrate the 'success' of aid. One consequence has been the neglect of long-term, complex and more difficult programmes and interventions that have an impact in the medium and long term. Given the difficulty of showing unambiguous short-term success, this has had the unintended effect of fostering further doubts about the effectiveness of aid.

Following a brief period of enhanced coordination and collaboration among some of the major bilateral agencies in the early and mid-2000s (most notably, through the Utstein Group), by the mid-2010s the impetus and the will to coordinate waned. Lack of cooperation, high transactions costs (affecting mostly developing countries), overlap and duplication, unfair burden sharing, and 'raise-the-flag' attitudes have characterized a rather discordant set of bilateral assistance agencies. In addition, the problems of internal donor country coordination between aid agencies, ministries of finance and ministries of foreign affairs have compounded the difficulties in achieving even a minimum degree of coherence in bilateral development assistance. Donor countries have increased their use of multilateral and international institutions as vehicles for their programmes and projects through trust funds and other special purpose funds. As a result, the proportion of non-core resources in these institutions has continued to expand and multilateral financing has been increasingly bilateralized.

The EU has been locked in an impasse regarding the reform of its development financing activities, which enlargement has made more difficult to resolve. Relations between the bilateral programmes and EU development assistance have remained strained and, as a result, the potential role that Europe could have played in revitalizing development finance has failed to materialise.

Among the international financial institutions, the World Bank has been in a negative net transfer situation for several years, particularly with its middle-income borrowers. Regional development banks find themselves in the same situation with some of their most important clients. In Latin America, and in some parts of the Middle East and Africa, increased resources from sub-regional development banks (e.g. the Andean Finance Corporation, the Arab Development Fund) have in part compensated these negative transfers. The loss of appeal of the World Bank to middle-income countries led in the mid-2000s to anxious but ineffective attempts to devise new financial instruments that would be attractive to them, aimed particularly at mobilizing private capital and reducing vulnerability to financial shocks. Discouraging assessments of the impact of fast disbursing policy-based loans has led to a partial return to programme and project lending, although regional and sub-regional development banks still have the lead in the use of these instruments.

Notwithstanding a protracted debate on the relative merits of grants and loans, the proportion of grants in the International Development Association (IDA) has remained at about 25–30 per cent during the decade, a slight increase in the level of the mid-2000s. These debates have negatively affected replenishment negotiations and burden-sharing arrangements, have not allowed for significant increases in the volume of IDA resources, and may even threaten the existence of IDA in the medium to long run. Something similar, although to a much lesser extent, happened with the soft loan windows of regional development banks. Beyond producing studies on debt sustainability, little progress was made in resolving outstanding multilateral (and bilateral) debt issues, especially in low-income countries. The Poverty Reduction Strategy process continued to provide a framework for coordinating development assistance, but in many cases its ritual character became more evident and developing country ownership claims were seen as exaggerated.

After a period of detente, rivalries between the Bretton Woods Institutions (BWI) and the United Nations agencies re-emerged, especially as the World Bank continued to expand its technical assistance and grant-making activities. Bilateral agencies have usually aligned themselves with the World Bank and the IMF, which they have found easier to interact with – even though this has not prevented bickering between bilateral agencies and the Bretton Woods Institutions on issues such as debt relief. The fact that the World Bank and the IMF do most of the analytical work on the levels and types of debt relief needed by developing countries whilst they are also large creditors has created the perception of conflict of interest.

UN attempts to reform its development functions and activities continued haltingly, and all but ground to a halt during the complex political negotiations to elect a new Secretary-General. While a degree of improved coordination was maintained in the field between UN agencies and, to a lesser extent, with bilateral agencies and IFIs, the same did not happen at headquarters level. Resource constraints – and particularly the decline in core funds – exacerbated rivalries, fostered competition, intensified overlap and duplication, and blurred mandates. Confusion between the normative, policy and operational roles of international agencies has persisted, and there has been little intellectual renewal in most of these agencies.

With the exception of one or two years, the hollowing out of core resources of UN agencies and some regional organizations continued during most of the decade. As the number of trust funds multiplied and non-core resources increased, a handful of donor countries continued to dominate the provision of core resources in some international agencies. This accentuated the bilateralization of multilateral and international assistance, to the extent that some agencies fell virtual hostage to one or another donor country. Notwithstanding the modest but significant successes of the New Partnership for African Development (NEPAD), regional development organizations remained marginal in the institutional arrangements for development financing.

There have been no new large private foundations established during the decade, and most of the existing ones have had to reduce their grant-making activities due to weak capital markets, which has negatively affected their endowments. While many foundations and non-governmental organizations have remained actively engaged in development finance, they have primarily focused on some specific areas (humanitarian assistance, environmental conservation, prevention and treatment of certain diseases) to fill obvious gaps left by official assistance and private flows. Foundations and civil society organizations lack the clout and resources to significantly influence other institutions in the development finance scene, yet they have been very active in leveraging funds and creating partnerships to address specific developing country needs – which has led to a proliferation of relatively small and narrowly focused partnerships. Determined opposition by some large donor countries has succeeded in stifling research and studies on automatic development financing mechanisms (e.g. fees, taxes, market creation), and discussion of these matters has been confined to a few academic centres and international organizations without much influence.

Finally, no forward movement has taken place with regard to improved institutional arrangements for global governance. Despite wide acknowledgment that the existing international governance architecture – centred around the G7-G8, the UN system and in particular the Security Council, the Bretton Woods Institutions, various regional organizations and a large number of ad hoc bodies (e.g. International Panel on Climate Change, Convention on Biodiversity) – is incapable of dealing with the challenges of vastly increased interdependence, it has not been possible for the key players on the international scene to agree on more effective ways of mobilizing collective will to address global concerns. Notwithstanding the moderate success of international trade negotiations, in other fields developed countries and leading developing countries remain highly polarized and unable to reach agreement. A particularly vexing issue is the lack of voice and inadequate representation of developing countries in most governance fora, and particularly those that deal with development financing.

* * *

These enduring features of the main organizations involved in development finance are what could be expected in the absence of any significant and sustained efforts at institutional reform. They are the logical outcome of the failure of the international community, and of leading donor countries in particular, to improve institutional arrangements for international development during the decade leading to 2015.

3.2.2 Comprehensive reform (CORE): a view from 2015

A description of the institutional arrangements in 2015 in this scenario would read as follows:

> *By 2015 there have been significant changes and progress in articulating a set of institutional arrangements that respond to the needs of different types of developing countries, and that also allow them to participate actively in the design of international development policies and programmes. A spirit of collaboration between the major donor countries, international institutions, private foundations and other organizations has generated a series of incremental but lasting organizational and procedural reforms, all of which have restored credibility to the international development effort and visibly improved the effectiveness of international development initiatives. This was greatly helped by the expansion and consolidation of constituencies for development assistance in donor countries, particularly among young people. A number of highly visible and impending crises around 2010 – more frequent humanitarian catastrophes, episodes of severe water scarcity, the proliferation of terrorist acts, extreme weather conditions as a result climate change, the spread of contagious diseases – has prompted international collaboration to face these threats, to promote the cause of development and to revamp the international development financing system. Crucial to this has been the presence of active and forward-looking developed and developing country leaders willing to work in concert, supported by leading academic, intellectual and mass media opinion makers.*
>
> *Institutional changes that were put in place during the decade comprise: an amalgamation of special purpose or 'vertical' funds (including those that finance the provision of global public goods), which retain their own technical profiles but share operational and administrative support functions; the creation of new large time-bound programmes for specific functions and regions, which have explicit sunset clauses and avoid the creation of additional bureaucracies; a restructuring of EU development funds, which has clarified their roles, speeded delivery and improved coordination with bilateral agencies in EU countries; and the creation and strengthening of institutions at the regional level, such as sub-regional development banks in Asia, regional infrastructure funds and emissions trading mechanisms. The widespread adoption of continuous learning and evaluation practices, results-oriented administration and evidence-based decision making has begun to create a new management culture in development cooperation organizations. Efforts to improve coordination within donor countries has led to more coherent and mutually reinforcing initiatives from aid agencies, ministries of finance and foreign affairs, and also*

sector ministries (e.g. health, agriculture, environment) that expanded their international programmes.

Many bilateral trust funds in multilateral and international organizations have been merged or closed, and resources transferred to core budgets. Experimentation and risk taking now are an integral, albeit limited, feature of bilateral assistance, with many agencies willing to explore alternatives to the standard policy prescriptions of the international financial institutions. The EU has revamped and expanded its development assistance programmes, which has led to a clearer delineation of roles for on- and off-budget funds, and to a better division of labour and coordination with bilateral agencies. As a result, Europe has more effective voice in the international development scene.

After a decade of gradual rapprochement – prompted by sustained pressure from key shareholders – the World Bank has began to work more frequently in joint initiatives with other multilateral development banks and with international organizations, particularly with the UNDP. An evaluation of the costs and benefits of decentralizing its activities led in the early 2010s to a consolidation of the Bank's field presence in some regions, and to greater reliance and coordination with regional and sub-regional development banks and with the UN in specific countries. The World Bank has made a major leap in consolidating its knowledge base in sector and macroeconomic policies. It now places emphasis on its scientific, technical and engineering expertise in specific project and programme areas (energy, water, sanitation, agriculture, information technology, among others), building on its comparative advantage of global reach and capacity to mobilize knowledge and experience from one part of the world to another.

The Poverty Reduction Strategy process and the ideas associated with the Comprehensive Development Framework have led to more effective development strategies, policies and implementation, and also to greater co-ordination between international cooperation agencies, particularly in the low-income countries. After protracted discussions and negotiations, the issue of IDA grants vs loans was largely resolved, partly with several donor countries providing upfront resources to pay back IDA loans for some countries and partly through the HIPC initiative. This has allowed IDA to renew operations with a more or less clean slate in most low-income countries, with a small component of grants to complement its soft loans on a case-by-case basis, with less rigid and detailed conditionality and with a clearer sense of country ownership.

A broad agreement has been reached between the World Bank and the regional and sub-regional banks regarding division of labour. Two new sub-regional development banks were established in North East Asia and Central Asia in the late 2000s, and – in an unusually effective display of international cooperation – the support from the Asian Development Bank, the European Bank for Reconstruction and Development, the European Investment Bank, the World Bank and the United Nations Development Programme helped to design and launch these two new institutions in record time. The international financial institutions also recognized the need for an independent assessment of the debt burdens of developing countries and the types of relief efforts that each of these countries required. This led to the creation of an advisory panel on debt cancellation and restructuring for developing countries, which has began to make rec-ommendations to multilateral and bilateral agencies, and has also worked closely with UN and regional agencies, as well as with the new G-20 group of developed and developing countries that meets annually at the Heads of State level.

UN reforms have made significant headway, partly as a consequence of a renewed emphasis on international cooperation following the recognition of the shortcomings of unilateral action in security, political and economic affairs. Nearly two decades of reform have led to a streamlined, more efficient, better coordinated and professionally managed UN system, and have also strengthened its intellectual and policy design capabilities. A clearer emphasis on the normative roles of the UN, complemented by highly focused operational interventions to test new approaches, has led to better coordination with bilateral agencies and international financing institutions. All of this has increased the credibility and impact of UN pro-grammes and activities. The new Secretary-General has given additional momentum to reform efforts, which have moved to the more politically challenging arena of international peace and security – including reform of the Security Council, establishment of a standing UN military force, conflict prevention, enforcement of human rights provisions, control of arms proliferation and cooperation against terrorism.

Core funds have steadily increased in several of the key UN agencies that improved their performance significantly during the decade. Institutional mergers have occurred and several agencies of at best marginal value have disappeared. A few agencies and programmes that dragged their feet in reform efforts have lost support and are in a rather precarious situation. A rationalization of trust funds has helped considerably in this process, as bilateral agencies became more willing to channel contributions through the UN system. At the regional level, the moderate success of the NEPAD initiative has inspired similar peer-review arrangements in Central and East Asia, and this has strengthened regional and sub-regional initiatives for resource mobilization.

A combination of new international norms and standards for financial institutions and more effective regulation has reduced the vulnerability of developing countries to external shocks and has limited contagion effects. The creation of the Asian Reserve Fund (modelled on the Latin American Reserve Fund) in the early 2010s has added an additional layer of protection for countries in that region, while the establishment of private regional investment funds, public–private partnerships and guarantee schemes by regional and sub-regional development banks has led to major increases in resources for infrastructure.

Individuals and private foundations have increased their contributions to development financing. The creation of a lottery for global environmental programmes generated a significant increase in financial resources to assist developing countries. This has led to a greater than doubling in the level of resources channelled through Global Environment Facility and to additional financing provided through regional environmental entities. The adoption of guidelines for international partnerships for development has reduced asymmetries in the dealings between foundations, charities and NGOs on the one hand, and developing country public, private and civil society organizations on the other. There is greater participation of developing countries in the governance structures of these partnerships, many of which have succeeded in working together, in pooling administrative and financial support services, and in working closely with bilateral agencies, international organizations and international financial institutions.

These improvements in institutional arrangements have been the result of an unusual combination of forward-looking leaders in several key donor countries, international organizations and developing countries, coupled with innovative and risk-taking heads of private foundations and NGOs. Informal schemes (e.g. the Utstein group) and new institutional structures (e.g. the G20 at Heads of State level) have complemented formal mechanisms (e.g. the DAC at OECD), and have led to greater harmonization and improved coordination in development assistance, and also to better institutional arrangements for tackling global and regional problems. Public opinion has been mobilized in support of development initiatives, which has led to generally moderate, but in some cases significant increases in financial assistance to developing countries. There have been improvements in developing country voice and representation in development financing institutions, and even though they are still far from the egalitarian schemes advocated by development activists, they provide a high degree of autonomy and greater influence for developing countries.

* * *

The institutional arrangements associated with comprehensive reform may be seen as the logical outcome of many incremental but sustained improvements, and of a few radical reforms, that ratcheted up the magnitude and effectiveness of international development finance. They indicate that by 2015 the international community, and in particular a few committed leading donor countries, have succeeded in transforming the development cooperation landscape.

3.2.3 Intermediate outcomes

Short of a total breakdown or a miraculous shift, these two extreme situations regarding institutional arrangements – BASU and CORE – bracket a range of intermediate outcomes and constitute the limits of what can reasonably be expected by 2015. To a very large extent, progress towards *limited* and *major reforms* will be conditioned by the severity of the crises that the international community will face, as well as by the way leaders from the large number and variety of countries, organizations, agencies, firms, and so on, react to these challenges. Reforms may succeed in some fields (for example, in bilateral agencies, international institutions, regional entities, global governance arrangements) and fail to materialize in others, so that a mixed picture is likely to emerge. Yet, these two extremes help us to visualize the kinds of institutional arrangements that would underpin development financing by 2015. Combined with the three other components – financing instruments, types of developing countries and political viability – they give rise to the scenarios described in the next chapter.

3.3 Financing instruments

The second component of the scenarios refers to the financing instruments that link sources of funds with their users in developing countries. There is a large variety of such instruments, which can be differentiated according to their source, potential volume that can be mobilized, institutions to channel funds, activities financed, eligibility criteria, conditions for access, information and administrative requirements, accountability procedures, disbursement mechanisms and volatility of flows, among other features. Of particular concern is the correspondence between the available set of financing instruments and the specific needs of different types of developing countries. A more effective and robust development financing system will have a broader and richer array of instruments, organized to allow all types of developing countries access to a variety of means to finance their development efforts.

Eight categories have been identified to group a large and continuously evolving number of financing instruments. Inevitably, these overlap slightly given that it is difficult to define a clear-cut and unambiguous classification scheme. A couple of these categories have emerged recently, some contain more instruments than others and innovation is present in each of them to varying degrees. The description of instruments also includes those in existence and several proposed but not yet created. These categories focus on the role of external financing and do not consider the measures and instruments to mobilize domestic financing or policies to prevent capital flight. However, as indicated in section 3.1, an effective international development financing system should stimulate and complement domestic savings and investment, and should not in any way substitute for internal resource mobilization efforts in developing countries.

The scenarios to be constructed in the next chapter differ in terms of the richness and adequacy of their sets of instruments to match developing country requirements. Table 3.1 shows the eight categories and the main subcategories of financial instruments, which will be briefly described in this section.[3]

3.3.1 Bilateral instruments

Bilateral instruments involve the direct provision of financing from donor to recipient countries. Resources are channelled primarily through aid agencies as part of ODA, and also via the international programmes of line ministries (Health, Education, Agriculture) and independent agencies (export financing, technical assistance).

However, donor countries also channel a portion of their development assistance through international organizations and international financial institutions to different degrees. The amount of resources channelled through bilateral and multilateral entities is one of the key decisions made by donor countries and, as indicated in chapter 1, the proportion of development assistance flowing through one or another set of channels has varied significantly during the last five decades. International organizations and international financial institutions that receive part of these bilateral funds are considered separately in sections 3.3.2 and 3.3.3.

Bilateral instruments include: (i) *regular loans*, which can take the form of project, programme or sector loans, structural adjustment loans or export credits; (ii) *soft loans* to central and regional governments and to financial intermediaries (private sector and government agencies) usually focused on poverty reduction initiatives; (iii) *grants* to governments and NGOs to finance programmes and projects, humanitarian relief, post-conflict reconstruction, pre-investment studies and portions of national budgets, and also for helping to secure access to multilateral

Table 3.1   Summary list of financing instruments[1]

Source	Type of instrument
1 Bilateral instruments	• Regular loans • Soft (concessional) loans • Grants for public and civil society organizations • Debt relief • Funds to promote private investment in developing countries • Tax incentives (for firms in developed countries)
2 International organizations agencies (UN system, regional and other international organizations)	• Regular grants (from their core budgets and trust funds) • Special purpose grants
3 International financial institutions *a. Multilateral Development Banks (World Bank, regional and sub-regional banks, and their associated institutions)*	• Regular loans • Soft (concessional) loans • Grants (mostly to public institutions) • Risk mitigation and risk management instruments • Equity participation • Debt reduction • Other (e.g. resource mobilization)
b. IMF and regional monetary funds	• Short-term financial assistance • Concessional funds • Debt management and debt relief • Issuing SDRs (IMF) • Other (e.g. trust fund management)
4 Private sources *a. Corporations*	• FDI • Concessions • Grants, donations, social responsibility activities
b. Commercial and investment banks	• Loans • Risk mitigation and risk management • Portfolio flows • Debt relief
c. Private foundations, not-for-profit and non-governmental institutions	• Grants and donations
d. Individuals	• Donations • Foreign worker remittances
e. Global and international lotteries	• Lotteries and games of chance to fund development programmes

Table 3.1   Summary list of financing instruments[1] (*continued*)

Source	Type of instrument
5 International capital markets *a. Bonds and other debt instruments*	• Bonds and related instruments
b. Equity investments	• Equity investments through stock markets
6 International taxes, fees and charges	• Creating international tax arrangements • User fees, charges and assessed contributions
7 Market creation	• For the provision and financing of regional and global public goods
8 Global and regional partnerships	• Special purpose official funds (international, multilateral and bilateral) • Public–private funds and partnerships for specific purposes

Note: See Table 3.5 for a more detailed list of financial instruments.

and private financing or in the form of bilateral funds with special conditions (e.g. the US Millennium Challenge Account); (iv) *debt relief*, which includes debt renegotiation and rescheduling, debt forgiveness, the use of funds to support multilateral debt reduction (e.g. the HIPC initiative) and debt swaps and counterpart funds; (v) *funds to promote private investment in developing countries*, which can take the form of loans, equity positions and joint ventures with private enterprises, and guarantees and insurance to manage political, regulatory and currency risks; and (vi) *tax incentives* to promote charity, corporate giving and individuals' donations, FDI, and the generation of knowledge and provision of goods and services (e.g. medicines for HIV/AIDS, research into developing country diseases), and which imply foregoing tax revenues.

Bilateral development assistance is one of the tools at the disposal of developed country governments as an element of their foreign policies, and is usually aligned with their strategic objectives and interests. The mix of aid motivations varies from one donor country to another and also over time. At the beginning of the twenty-first century, there appear to be three main sets of rationales for development assistance: international solidarity and religious motivations, narrow and enlightened self-interest, and the provision of international public goods (Table 3.2).

Table 3.2   Motivations for development assistance

International solidarity and religious motivations

Altruism, ethical and humanitarian concerns, which highlight the moral obligation of donor countries to assist the poor in developing countries:

- Alleviate human suffering and express solidarity with fellow human beings.
- Help to cope with natural and man-made disasters through humanitarian and emergency relief.
- Build local capacities to undertake initiatives for improving living standards.

Religious proselytism:

- Desire to win converts to a particular faith and to spread the word with a missionary zeal.

Narrow and enlightened self-interest

Strategic and security interests, which respond to the geopolitical and military considerations of donor countries:

- At the national level, which justify aid to developing countries of specific geopolitical importance to the donor country.
- At regional level, which considers the interests of regional alliances or treaties.

Political interests, which focus on obtaining political support for foreign and domestic policies:

- With foreign constituencies (through support to former colonial territories and other areas with special historic and cultural ties to the donor country, aid to obtain international political recognition and support).
- Centred on domestic constituencies (obtaining the support of immigrants and ethnic groups of foreign origin in the donor country).

Economic and commercial interests, which emphasize direct commercial and financial benefits to the donor country:

- Benefits may include export expansion, employment generation, support of domestic producers (e.g. food aid); greater security for investments in developing countries, securing access to resources (oil, strategic minerals); obtaining access to a pool of highly qualified potential migrants (e.g. graduate fellowships), and creating demand for exports (e.g. export credit, technology transfers).

Provision of international public goods

Emergence of regional and global problems, which concern both donor and recipient nations and require the provision of public goods:

- Confronting global and regional environmental threats (global warming, destruction of the ozone layer, loss of biodiversity, tropical deforestation) which affect developed countries directly.
- Addressing global population growth and imbalances and health threats (AIDS, epidemics), that create negative spillovers across borders.
- Supporting international cooperation initiatives to avoid regional and global 'public bads' (e.g. crime, drug traffic, money laundering, terrorism).

Table 3.2   Motivations for development assistance (*continued*)

Provision of international public goods (*continued*)
  Maintaining stability of the international system, which aims at securing a
  stable world order to foster the long-term interests of donor countries:
  • Maintaining political stability by preventing and containing local and
    regional conflicts (e.g. peacemaking and peacekeeping initiatives), and
    by promoting the spread of democracy (monitoring and supervising
    elections, strengthening democratic practices and institutions).
  • Ensuring world economic stability through policy reforms in developing
    countries, and through measures to avoid major disruptions of
    international finance and trade (e.g. provide funds to defuse debt crisis
    and sudden reversals of financial flows, funds to stabilise commodity
    prices).
  • Maintaining social stability in the developing regions to prevent
    international migrations (programmes to reduce population growth,
    combat poverty, promote human rights, improve the situation of
    women).
  • Helping developing countries to improve their participation in the
    economy (e.g. capacity building in knowledge, innovation and
    production), and in international agreements to make them more
    equitable, stable and effective (technical assistance, training negotiators).

Source: Adapted from Sagasti and Alcalde (1999: 145).

The bulk of bilateral financing takes place through soft loans and grants, even though rescue packages in the aftermath of financial crises have absorbed a large volume of funds in some years (for example, the US$48 billion from the US Treasury to Mexico after the 1994 peso crisis). Although the outstanding bilateral debt of the highly indebted poor countries (HIPC) has been reduced from US$72 billion in 1995 to US$49 billion in 2003, it remains quite large and is a major proportion of the US$58 billion of low-income country bilateral debt – even without considering the US$61 billion owed by India, Indonesia and Pakistan (OECD Creditor Reporting System, various years). It follows that instruments to reduce the bilateral debt burden for low-income countries should be placed high on the reform agenda.

Most bilateral loans and grants are provided to developing country governments and public institutions, although private consulting firms and NGOs (primarily from the donor country) have gained importance as conveyors of bilateral aid to recipient countries, and in many cases they work with local NGO counterparts. While there are many claims that non-governmental channels are more efficient than official ones in achieving development results, there is considerable debate about this.

In some donor countries NGOs in the development field depend almost exclusively on contracts and grants from bilateral aid agencies for their survival, and are prone to exaggerate their efficiency and effectiveness.

The impact of bilateral aid and financing on local capabilities has long been the subject of scrutiny and controversy, particularly because of the multiplicity of programmes that demand time and attention from recipient country agencies and functionaries. This applies in particular to technical assistance, which accounts for about a third of total bilateral aid, and which has long been perceived as principally donor-driven. Technical assistance, however, also remains a development imperative in order to provide knowledge and expertise and to build and consolidate capacities in developing countries. Issues surrounding the impact of bilateral aid and financing on local capabilities are also central to the current impetus to improve coordination and streamline procedures in the field (Berg 2002). A further bilateral aid impact issue that is now moving to policy centre stage involves questions of performance-based allocations versus those predicated on need irrespective of performance (see section 2.5 of this report).

3.3.2 UN system, regional and other international organizations

The financing instruments utilized by international organizations and agencies primarily take the form of relatively modest grants for specific activities and projects in the field, and particularly for capacity building and technical cooperation.[4] These institutions provide: (i) *regular grants*, usually from their regular budgets and occasionally from trust funds, to finance directly executed projects and programmes at the country, regional and headquarters levels, to support projects and programmes executed by recipient government agencies, and to finance technical cooperation, institutional development and capacity-building activities; (ii) *special purpose grants* with resources obtained from trust funds and other voluntary contributions, which are usually channelled through specific purpose programmes (research support, environmental sustainability, agricultural development, and so on). Examples include the Transfer of Knowledge through Expatriate Nationals (TOKTEN) fund at the UNDP, the International Foundation for Science (IFS) that receives donations from bilateral agencies and private foundations, and the International Development Research Centre (IDRC) that obtains the bulk of its resources from the Canadian government, among many others. Many proposals are regularly put forward to create 'vertical' funds within international agencies to provide grants to developing countries for specific purposes – for example, the Global Demilitarisation Fund, the Global Hunger Fund, the Global Water Fund – although few have seen the light of day (see section 3.3.8).

The most important set of international organizations and agencies is the UN system, which is composed of three sets of institutions. First, there is the United Nations Secretariat, financed through assessed contributions by member countries. Second, there are the UN offices, programmes and funds, which report to the General Assembly or the Economic and Social Council, and are funded primarily by voluntary contributions, although funds for peacekeeping operations are obtained through assessed contributions. Third, there are the specialized agencies, linked to the UN through cooperative agreements and supported by their own scales of assessed contributions and voluntary donations.[5]

The total expenditures of the UN system in 2002 were approximately US$12 billion, obtained from assessed contributions and donations to voluntary funds. Of these, approximately US$3.6 billion was provided as grants for specific programmes and projects at the country, regional and headquarters levels. At the end of 2003 member countries owed the UN US$1.6 billion in assessed contributions to the regular and peacekeeping budgets, of which the US accounted for US$760 million. A small number of funds and agencies – UNDP, UNHCR, UNICEF, UNFPA, UNRWA and WFP – account for around half of the total grants provided by the UN system.

The UN funds and programmes that provide grants are financed from voluntary contributions by member countries (and occasionally by foundations). These can take the form of either 'core' funds, which are pledged annually, or 'non-core' contributions, some of which are included in annual pledging sessions but many of which are arranged on a strictly bilateral basis. The former are put at the disposal of the agency to use as its governing council decides, while the latter stipulate conditions (often stringent ones) for their use (for example, hiring consultants from the donor country, allocating resources to particular ends, financing narrowly specified activities). The annual cycle of voluntary contributions and the growing share of non-core contributions have led to uncertainty in funding levels and constraints on the operation of these funds and programmes, which have a negative impact on their performance (Bezanson and Sagasti 2002). Between the two extremes of rigid assessed contributions and purely voluntary funds lies the replenishment system of funding, which estimates requirements for a number of years, gathers donors to negotiate multi-year funding commitments and agrees on burden-sharing between donors. Such a system has been in place for the soft loan window of the World Bank (IDA) since the beginning, although without adequate representation from developing countries. Adopting a replenishment system in some UN funds and programmes – with institutional modifications to give greater voice to recipients – could allow a greater degree of predictability in funding levels, curb the excesses associated with the proliferation of trust funds and achieve a better balance between core and non-core contributions, all of which would improve performance.

There are many international and regional agencies working in a wide variety of fields that rely on a mixture of assessed and voluntary contributions, the former usually covering administrative costs and the latter financing projects and programmes at the local, national, regional and international levels. In contrast to bilateral agencies and private sources of finance that can pick and choose which developing countries to work with, international organizations (and for that matter multilateral financing institutions) have to work with all their member countries, including donors, for which they have to provide a varied range of products and services. This places a considerable burden on these institutions.

3.3.3 International financial institutions (IFIs)

The IFIs comprise the MDBs, the IMF and regional financing institutions such as the Latin American Reserve Fund (FLAR). The oldest of these, the Bretton Woods Institutions (World Bank and IMF), have been in existence for 60 years and, as a whole, have at their disposal a large number of financial instruments to mobilize resources for development purposes.

There are about 25 institutions that operate as MDBs, which stand squarely at the intersection of the international development system and the international financial system.[6] They interact closely with a wide range of entities, including governments in developed and developing countries, international and regional organizations, bilateral agencies, corporations, private banks, capital markets, investors and academic institutions, among other actors in the international development and financial scenes. Multilateral development banks mobilize resources from private capital markets and from official sources to provide loans on better than market terms, and also grants, guarantees and equity to developing country public, private and civil society organizations. In addition, they provide technical assistance and advice for economic and social development, as well as a range of complementary services to the international development community.

The financing instruments used by the MDBs include: (i) *regular loans usually on better than market terms*, which include loans for investment projects; structural adjustment and balance of payments support loans; sector adjustment and programme loans (which usually include a technical assistance component); emergency recovery loans in case of disaster or unexpected events; loans to financial intermediaries (development finance corporations or the establishment of apex funds for microfinance); learning and innovation loans (LILs) for pilot projects, capacity building and testing new approaches or practices; and (as yet only a proposal) pre-arranged fast disbursement loans conditional on previous country performance; (ii) *soft or concessional loans*, which provide low-interest long-term financing with an extended grace period to poor countries, and include loans for public sector investment projects and programmes, for sector and structural adjustment, for emergencies and post-conflict reconstruction and for budget support or through a common pool of resources; (iii) *grants*, which are used for assisting public institutions in specific programmes and projects, for technical cooperation, for capacity building and institutional development, and for emergency operations to deal with natural or man-made disasters; (iv) *risk mitigation and risk management* instruments for private investors, including as total, partial and rolling guarantees (for political, contractual, regulatory, credit and foreign exchange risks), financing for currency and interest hedging operations, and other instruments to promote private investment and trade (e.g. export credits, securitisation, leasing, syndication, underwriting, trade insurance); (v) *equity participation*, which involves direct investments in equity and quasi-equity (common shares, preferred stock, C loans), and also profit- and loss-sharing arrangements (e.g. IsDB facility for joint ventures); (vi) *debt reduction*, which includes financing for multilateral debt reduction, debt reduction loans (e.g. for buying-back existing debt, debt service reduction), funds to clear arrears with multilateral development banks and other creditors, and also the proposed credit buy-down mechanism in which the creditor receives the present value of a soft loan from a donor, effectively turning the loan into a grant; and (vii) *additional financing mechanisms*, such as mobilization of resources from bilateral and other multilateral sources through consultative groups (see section 3.3.8), special purpose investment funds (e.g. financing for carbon emission reduction projects at the World Bank) and issuing bonds in developing countries to strengthening local capital markets.

Not all of these financial instruments are available to all member countries in these institutions. For example, World Bank concessional loans provided through the IDA are available only to countries with income per person levels of less than US$865 and countries above those levels of income are supposed to graduate to regular loans. Conditions for access to other financial instruments depend on country policies and public sector practices (e.g. structural adjustment loans), and also on criteria defined for specific purposes (e.g. access to HIPC grants to reduce multilateral debt, access to equity investment in developing country private firms). The rather high levels of concessional debt of poor countries, particularly in Africa, has led the US government to press for transforming IDA concessional loans into grants. Other donor countries have accepted the idea of partially transforming IDA resources into grants, but oppose what in effect could be the disappearance of World Bank concessional lending (section 2.2.1).

The World Bank and the regional development banks provided more than US$34 billion to developing countries in 2002 (down from the peak of US$44 billion in 1998). Of this total, approximately 20 per cent was allocated to private enterprises. If sub-regional banks are included, the total amount of financing provided by multilateral development banks would increase by about 50 per cent and the proportion allocated to the private sector would be slightly reduced (sub-regional development banks work primarily with the public sector). Net flows from the World Bank and the regional development banks totalled about US$177 billion in the period from 1990 to 2002, although they declined from US$15.4 billion in the first of these years to just US$0.7 in the last. Considering only the non-concessional windows of these institutions, net flows went down from US$9.4 billion in 1990 to a negative US$–6.4 billion in 2002, which means that, as a whole, middle-income and emerging countries paid back to these MDBs more than they received from them. This is a natural consequence of the maturity of the portfolios of these institutions. For example, the regular loan windows of the younger regional development banks had a net positive flow of US$51 billion for the period 1990–2002 in comparison with US$31 billion for the World Bank. In the countries of the Andean region (Bolivia, Colombia, Ecuador, Peru and Venezuela), the World Bank had negative net flows of US$430 million for the period 1990–8, while the IADB had US$145 million and the CAF US$340 million in positive net flows.

The IMF and regional funds in Latin America and the Arab world were created to assist member countries in coping with temporary balance-of-payments problems, but have evolved to play larger roles – including poverty reduction, technical assistance and policy dialogue. In addition, there are proposals to create an Asian Monetary Fund and the possibility of creating other regional funds of this type has been raised. The financing instruments at the disposal of these institutions (mostly the IMF) include: (i) *short-term financial assistance* to cope with financial difficulties, such as the IMF Stand-By Arrangements (SBA), the Extended Fund Facility (EFF), the Supplemental Reserve Facility (SRF), the Compensatory Financing Facility (CFF) and IMF's Trade Integration Mechanism for temporary shortfalls of balance of payments after a process of trade liberalization, as well as the short-term financing facilities of the Latin America Reserve Fund (FLAR) and the Arab Monetary Fund; (ii) *concessional loans* for poor countries through the IMF Poverty Reduction and Growth Facility (PRGF); (iii) *debt management and debt relief instruments,* such as grants for multilateral debt reduction under the HIPC initiative, short-term credit lines for clearing arrears, financing for debt and debt service restructuring (a service provided by FLAR), technical advice to introduce Collective Action Clauses (CACs) in sovereign and other developing country bonds, and the (proposed, but not yet approved) establishment of a Sovereign Debt Restructuring Mechanism (SDRM) for orderly debt defaults; (iv) *issuing Special Drawing Rights (SDRs),* to provide additional short-term financing and international liquidity to developing countries; and (v) *other financial instruments,* such as the multilateral administration of trust funds and international reserves (a service provided by FLAR), the signing of letters of intent with developing countries that give clear signals regarding the appropriateness of macroeconomic policies and release funds from other sources (multilateral and commercial banks, bilateral agencies), and the possibility of selling part of its gold reserves to provide additional funds to poor countries.

In addition to these instruments, the IMF plays a key role in defining standards and procedures for preparing financial statistics and for public accounting practices at the national level, which, coupled with its norm-setting functions, can affect domestic and external financing in developing countries in a significant way. For this reason, several developing countries, including Brazil and Peru, have suggested modifications in the IMF national accounting rules. These modifications aim at separating investments from current expenditures for national accounting purposes, considering external financing as part of the budget, and calculating the fiscal deficit in a different way. If adopted, these modifications would release committed but undisbursed funds from multilateral banks that are now held because constraints on fiscal deficits, established by IMF national accounting practices and letters of intent, prevent the allocation of the required counterpart funds.

Resources at the disposal of the IMF are mainly in the form of quotas made available to member countries and amounted to US$292 billion in 2003. As of March 2004 the IMF had US$90 billion in outstanding loans, of which Argentina, Brazil, Indonesia and Turkey accounted for 72 per cent. Because of country quota limits, recent financial rescue packages for these countries have been complemented with bilateral funds. In March 2004, the Poverty Reduction and Growth Facility, an endowment created with the proceeds of sales of IMF gold reserves, had US$9.9 billion in outstanding loans to 60 developing countries, of which Pakistan accounted for 13.6 per cent and nine countries for 52 per cent of the total.

The possibility of issuing additional Special Drawing Rights (SDRs) appears quite limited at this time. The IMF Board of Governors approved a one-time allocation of SDRs in September 1997 through a proposed Fourth Amendment of the Articles of Agreement. This allocation would double the amount of SDRs at the disposal of member countries, which would reach US$42.9 billion. The Fourth Amendment will become effective when three fifths of the IMF membership (110 members) with 85 per cent of the total voting power approve it. As of end-September 2004, 131 members – with 77.3 per cent of total voting power – had accepted the amendment. However, approval by the US, with 17.1 per cent of total votes, is essential to put the amendment into effect, and the issue will not be discussed again at the IMF Board of Governors until 2008.[7]

3.3.4 Private sector

The private sector entities involved in development finance include profit-making organizations such as corporations, commercial banks, investment firms and credit rating agencies, and not-for-profit institutions such as foundations, NGOs, academic institutions and associations, all of this in addition to private individuals.

The financing instruments used by private corporations include: (i) *FDI*, in the form of investment in wholly owned subsidiaries, partial equity and joint venture investments in developing country firms, and participation in the privatization of state-owned corporations; (ii) *concessions*, which involve the participation of private investors in the provision of public services; and (iii) *grants, donations and social responsibility activities*, that take the form of financial or in-kind corporate gifts to public and civil society entities, and donations to local governments, civil society organizations and educational institutions, among other recipients, in the communities where foreign corporations operate.

Total FDI flows in 2002 reached US$651 billion, 25 per cent of which went to developing countries, and declined to US$560 billion in 2003, which is partly explained by a 53 per cent fall in flows to the US (the US$ 30 billion received by this country in 2003 is the lowest level in 12 years). FDI flows to the group of 50 least developed countries were just US$7 billion in 2003, although this marked an increase from the US$5.5 billion penned in 2002. Most of these amounts were invested in a few countries with oil and mineral resources (World Bank 2004a; UNCTAD 2003, 2004).

Facing growing infrastructure demands and capital constraints, developing countries have been offering private investors opportunities to build public infrastructure projects, and also to operate them for certain periods through concessions. Between 1990 and 2001 about 130 low- and middle-income countries adopted policies to attract private investment in the construction and provision of public services (roads, ports and airports, water supply, telecommunications, energy). During this period private investors took charge of the construction, operation or both of these in more than 2,500 infrastructure projects in developing countries, attracting investment commitments of more than US$750 billion. Middle-income countries accounted for about 89 percent of these private investment flows (Izaguirre 2002).

Information about corporate giving is rather fragmented and difficult to obtain, and some times is included in estimates of total private giving including foundations, NGOs and individuals (see below). American, British and Canadian corporations have increased their grants, donations and social responsibility activities during the last decade, reaching US$12.9 billion in 2002. However, most of these resources were spent at home, and only a very small portion may have found their way to developing countries (*Giving USA 2003*).

The financing instruments used by commercial banks and investment firms include: (i) *loans*, for investment projects of the private or public sector, sovereign loans (individual or syndicated), purchases of developing country sovereign debt (bonds and other debt instruments) and trade-related financial instruments (e.g. export credits, supplier's credits, insurance); (ii) *instruments to mitigate and manage risks,* which provide insurance against political, regulatory and currency risks and may take the form of derivatives, options, futures, swaps and other hedging instruments, complemented by technical advice; (iii) *portfolio investment* in developing countries' capital markets, including socially responsible funds, green funds, among others; and (iv) *debt relief of commercial private debt,* such as the Brady bond scheme, debt swaps and debt cancellation.

International bank loans reached US$95 billion in 2003, of which Central Asia and Eastern Europe received US$29 billion, East Asia US$24 billion, Latin America US$9 billion and Africa US$8 billion. During the last few years there has been a surge in bank lending to Central Asia and Eastern European countries, which has changed the negative net flows of these countries with commercial banks (US$–4.1 billion in 2001) to a positive (US$18.5 billion in 2002 and US$22.1 billion in 2003). Private insurers account for 50 to 60 per cent of the market for political risk insurance, and the rest is divided between national export agencies and the Multilateral Investment Guarantee Agency (MIGA) of the World Bank Group, which now has a small (4–6 per cent) but growing share of this market (UNCTAD 2003).

Sovereign commercial bank debt represented a significant source of funds for developing countries in the 1970s and 1980s, but diminished sharply during the 1990s. In addition, the Brady Plan launched in the late 1980s replaced commercial bank debt for bonds traded in capital markets, and allowed banks to dispose of their developing country debt assets but at a discount. As a consequence, at present debt relief by these institutions does not account for a major portion of development financing. For example, the portion of the total cost of the HIPC debt reduction initiative that has been attributed to commercial creditors is US$850 million (in 2003 net present value terms), which represents about 2.4 per cent of the total for the 27 eligible countries. This indicates that commercial banks do not currently have a significant exposure to this group of countries (IMF and IDA 2004).

The financing instruments at the disposal of foundations, NGOs and individuals include: (i) *grants and donations*, that take the form of financial transfers from developed country grant-giving and operating foundations, as well as not-for-profit organizations, to public, civil society and private organizations in developing countries; (ii) *personal gifts and donations,* in the form of direct contributions to funds, agencies, churches, NGOs, special campaigns and operating foundations; and (iii) *workers' remittances,* which can be directly sent by developing country emigrants to individuals and families in their countries of origin, or channelled through organizations that provide counterpart funds and services.

Grants from private foundations and NGOs have begun to play an important role in development financing, perhaps not so much in strictly financial terms, but because of their freedom to experiment and explore new avenues that are later taken and scaled up by bilateral and multilateral agencies. Private foundations can also leverage the resources they obtain from their endowments by linking their grants to the activities of other sources of development finance – in particular, those flowing from international organizations, international financial institutions, bilateral agencies and developing country governments. This can be done in several ways, including the provision of risk capital for global and regional partnerships involving a variety of public and private donors (section 3.3.8), the use of grants to subsidize and reduce interest rates charged by MDBs, and the creation of endowment funds that are matched by public or private funds.

US grant-giving foundations are by far the most important in the development field, primarily because of tax regulations, opportunities to acquire personal wealth and a tradition of private philanthropy. From 1990 to 2000, total giving by US foundations more than tripled from US$8.8 billion to US$27.6 billion, and international donations increased from US$0.8 billion to US$3.1 billion, with a large part going to developing countries. The most important among these is the Bill and Melinda Gates Foundation, whose grants in 2001 surpassed US$1 billion, 75 per cent of which went to developing countries. It focuses primarily on global health issues and works directly with developing country public and not-for-profit organizations, as well as through international institutions like the World Bank and the Global Fund to Fight AIDS, Tuberculosis and Malaria (see section 3.3.8). Other large US foundations (e.g. Ford, Packard, Rockefeller, MacArthur) donated between US$100 million and US$360 million to developing countries in 2001. US-based operating foundations are especially active in the environmental conservation field, with the World Wildlife Foundation, The Nature Conservancy and Conservation International donating about US$1.4 billion to conservation programmes in 2003, of which part is spent in developing countries (OECD DAC 2003).

Data are more difficult to obtain on donations by European foundations, but it has been estimated that about 25 per cent of the US$1.4 billion in total donations went overseas (OECD DAC 2003). It is also difficult to determine the level of funds provided by NGOs for humanitarian and relief purposes from private sources, primarily because these institutions receive additional funds from bilateral agencies (as US and Canadian foundations also do). Nevertheless, it is estimated that these institutions handle around US$12–13 billion annually, of which about a third comes from official sources.

Philanthropic contributions by firms and individuals in the US amounted to US$241 billion in 2002, of which 76 per cent of the total was accounted for by individuals, 11 per cent by foundations, 8 per cent by bequests and 5 per cent by corporations (American Association of Fundraising Council 2003). This underscores the dominant role that private firms and individuals play on the philanthropic scene. Although there are no reliable statistics, it appears that only a rather small proportion of these contributions are given for development purposes.

Remittances by emigrants from developing countries have become a key source of financing for some of these countries. They rose to US$93 billion in 2003 from US$88.1 billion the previous year when they were equivalent to 5 per cent of developing country imports and 8 per cent of domestic investment. Remittances remain the second largest financial flow to developing countries and more than double the size of net official development assistance flows. In 2002 remittances were larger than both official and private flows in 36 developing countries. Latin America accounted for US$30 billion, about a third of these flows, with South Asia and East Asia-Pacific receiving US$18 billion each and sub-Saharan Africa US$4 billion (Ratha 2003).

One possible source of private individual financing for development would involve the launching of global and international lotteries, through a variety of national, regional and international organizations, including the possible participation of private firms. The annual world lottery market exceeds US$126 billion, Internet gambling involves US$32 billion and the total world market for all types of chance games approaches US$1,000 billion. A number of proposals have been floated – lotteries for the environment associated with airline tickets, credit card purchase lotteries, allocating a portion of national lotteries for development purposes, issuing global premium bonds that involve periodic prize draws – and estimates suggest they could generate at least US$5 billion per year for development purposes, and more specifically for attaining the MDGs (Addinson and Chowdhury 2003).

Private sources of development finance now dominate other types of financing instruments, with FDI, focused primarily on emerging economies, and remittances, focused primarily on low and middle-income economies, taking the lead among these instruments. Yet there is much that could be done to increase and stabilize private flows of all types, and also to improve their contribution to development. For example, new instruments could be designed and existing ones modified to increase the availability of and spread more evenly private flows to all types of developing countries.

3.3.5 International capital markets

International capital markets are closely related to the private flows examined above, but have a distinct character in the sense that they provide a set of standardized financial products that can be used by developing country governments and firms, and also because investors can exit with relative ease – at least in comparison with FDI and some of the other instruments examined in the preceding section. Financial instruments in this category include: (i) *bonds and other debt instruments*, such as government-issued bonds (standard, income-linked bonds, senior and subordinates bonds, among others) and bonds issued by developing country firms (fixed rate, floating rate, callable, indexed and convertible bonds, American Depositary Receipts issued in US stock markets); and (ii) *equity investments*, which involves purchasing shares in developing country firms and markets, and can take a variety of forms (e.g. common, preferred, second tier and temporal shares, among others). In some cases, these instruments are bundled by investment funds and offered as a package to investors (e.g. emerging market funds, funds for infrastructure in developing regions). In addition, the grades awarded by private rating firms to developing country public and private debt can be seen as a special type of instrument that facilitates access to international capital markets.

The total size of capital markets (stock market capitalization, debt securities and bank assets) represented 342 per cent of world GDP in 2003 (US$123 trillion), of which 60 developing countries accounted for only 11 per cent (US$13.5 trillion). In these countries, stock market capitalization amounts to US$3.9 trillion, debt securities US$3.1 trillion (the private sector accounts for 41 per cent of this amount), and bank assets are US$6.5 trillion (IMF 2004).

International capital markets flows to developing countries reached US$78 billion in 2002, of which bonds accounted for US$61.6 billion and equities for US$16.4 billion. Asia (US$35.8 billion) and Latin America (US$18.3 billion) took the lion's share in bond issues, while equity financing was largely concentrated in Asia (US$12.4 billion). However, these inflows have been rather volatile. Bond issues were US$79 billion in 1998, US$89 billion in 2002 and US$61.6 in 2002, while equity financing grew from US$9.4 billion in 1998 to US$41.7 in 2000, and fell to US$16.3 billion in 2002.

The potential of international capital markets to mobilize financial flows to developing countries is exemplified by a private equity firm that manages investments in developing countries, and by three investment funds for African countries launched during the last decade. The Emerging Markets Partnership (EMP), established in 1992, is an international private equity firm with headquarters in Washington, DC and subsidiaries and affiliates in Hong Kong, Singapore, London, Johannesburg, Abidjan, Bahrain and Brunei. EMP and its affiliates currently serve as the principal adviser or manager of private equity funds, with US$5.7 billion in committed resources. These include two Asian Infrastructure Funds, the AIG-GE Capital Latin American Infrastructure Fund (US$1.01 billion), the AIG Emerging Europe Infrastructure Fund (US$550 million), the AIG African Infrastructure Fund (US$407 million), the Islamic Development Bank Infrastructure Fund (which comprises US$700 million in equity commitments, US$50 million for a special projects pool and US$200 million for a complementary finance facility). Different partners join forces in these funds, and in the case of the African funds these include the US insurance company AIG, the International Finance Corporation, the African Development Bank and El Paso Energy Corporation, in addition to other investors. These six funds provide equity and equity-related capital to companies in infrastructure-related businesses, primarily in the transportation, power and telecommunications sectors. Professionals working at EMP or its affiliates locate and evaluate potential private equity investments with appropriate risk-reward combinations.

Another example is the South Africa Infrastructure Fund, which was launched in 1996 with US$130 million in commitments. It provides equity investments in infrastructure (water, wastewater, transportation, energy, telecommunications) and is scheduled to remain in operation for 15 years. Its partners include the African Development Bank, the Standard Investment Corporation and South African institutional investors. A recent entry into the list of African funds is the US$227 million Africa Millennium Fund, constituted on the basis of guarantees provided by the US Overseas Private Investment Corporation (OPIC), and which will invest in telecommunications, energy, water and sanitation projects in sub-Saharan Africa. The fund plans to provide seed capital, short-term equity for construction initiatives and, in some cases, long-term equity. In addition, the Emerging Africa Infrastructure Fund, a $305 million fund recently established by a group of public and private sector institutions – including the Department for International Development (DFID) of the UK with US$100 million in equity, the Barclays and the Standard banks with US$120 million in commercial debt, and other corporations with US$85 million in additional contributions – to provide long-term debt to private sector infrastructure ventures in sub-Saharan Africa, which in some cases can be done in local currencies.

Rating agencies play a key role in securing access to capital markets for developing countries. They study the situation in countries and corporations and classify their debt instruments according to the degree of risk to investors. This has a significant influence on portfolio flows and even on FDI. Three US based agencies – Moody's, Standard and Poor and Fitch-IBCA – dominate the world's rating market. Moody's provides sovereign credit rating for 103 countries, 61 of which are developing countries. Being accorded a high rating, and particularly an investment grade rating, improves access to international capital markets and reduces the cost of issuing debt instruments. UNDP and the US State Department have joined forces in an initiative to finance the process of determining rating for 25 African countries, so as to take the initial steps to tap international capital markets.

3.3.6 International taxes and fees

Proposals for new financial instruments based on different types of international taxes and charges for the use of the global commons have been under study and discussion for several decades, but are yet to be put into practice. At the regional and local levels, taxes on trade, sales, income and wealth, among others, have a long tradition, but resistance to their implementation at the international and global levels has been quite determined.

Financial instruments in this category include: (i) the *creation of international tax regimes*; and (ii) *fees, charges or assessed contributions for the use of global or international commons*, such as charges for the use of land, space and the oceans; levies on the extraction of natural resources; and fees or auction revenues on the use of geostationary orbits to place satellites.

Most of the international tax proposals that have been put forward are linked to global public goods in the sense that they seek to obtain resources to finance the provision of a public good or the prevention of a public bad, or that involve taxing the utilization of what is considered as a global resource or infrastructure. They include, among others: (i) *a carbon tax or a tax on the use of energy*, which involves taxing the carbon content of different fuels and energy sources, and could reduce CO_2 emissions, promote the use of cleaner energy and generate resources for environmental protection and for development purposes; (ii) *taxes on the transmission of data and information through the Internet*, which involves a small tax on transactions through the telecommunications networks that support the Internet; (iii) *taxes on foreign exchange transactions*, in particular the 'Tobin tax' on currency transactions, which could both dampen speculation in foreign currency markets and generate resources for strengthening reserves and financing development programmes; and (iv) *taxes on the international weapons trade*, which could both reduce the level of trade in arms and raise money for development programmes, disarmament initiatives and the compensation of victims of violent conflicts.

The potential amounts that these tax schemes could generate are uncertain but could be very large. For example, a tax on fuel consumption of US$0.048 per gallon (which corresponds to about US$21 per metric ton of carbon) could yield about US$130 billion annually, although it would require the US to participate – something highly improbable in the short and medium term – because 20 per cent of the revenues would originate there (Sandmo 2003). In 1996 a bit tax of US$0.01 per megabyte of information transmitted through the Internet would have generated about US$70 billion in revenues (UNDP, 1999); a Tobin tax with a rate of 0.02 per cent of the volume of currency transactions – US$264 trillion in 2000 – would generate US$53 billion (Cooper 2001); and a tax of 5 per cent on the global sales of arms could generate about US$2.5 billion per year (US Department of State 2003).

As in the case of international taxes, it is difficult to estimate the amounts that could be obtained from fees, charges or assessed contributions for the use of global commons. For example, a one per cent levy on the annual volume of passenger tickets and freight transport is estimated to generate US$2.2 billion a year, and one on passenger tickets alone US$0.8 billion. Charges on the use of the global commons – the geostationary orbit, the electromagnetic spectrum, the seabed and the Antarctica – could generate significant revenues. For example, since launches of new satellites grow slowly and erratically, the proposal for charges to satellites already in orbit could yield as high as US$14 billion a year (Mendez 1992). In the case of the electromagnetic spectrum, 90 per cent of the use rights have been assigned to the richest countries: these allocations could be accompanied by small surtaxes for international purposes, as is done in the US (Mendez 2001a). For Antarctica, user fees on exhaustible resources (such as krill and fisheries) could be implemented under the Antarctic Treaty Organization (ATO) and the UN, but there are no estimates of how much they could provide.

Whatever the potential to raise financing for development, opposition to international taxes and levies is quite strong, especially in the US, where some politicians argue that global taxes are a first step towards 'global government', that they would put resources at the disposal of unelected international bureaucracies and that they would undermine national tax revenues. Yet because of their relative effectiveness in raising resources for development purposes and the possibility that they may address global concerns, some sort of international tax scheme for the provision of international public goods and financing development programmes is likely to emerge in the coming decades, perhaps first at the regional level and later with a broader geographic scope.[8]

3.3.7 Creation of international markets

The financial instruments associated with the creation of international markets cannot be strictly considered as development finance, but rather as financing the provision of global and regional public goods. Nevertheless, they may also benefit developing countries to the extent that their functioning would lead to transfers of resources from developed to developing countries, although this would depend on the specific nature of the institutional arrangements. To create markets it is necessary to assign property rights or allocate quotas, put in place mechanisms for information exchange, define procedures to set prices and establish regulatory agencies. It is also possible to create markets by establishing specific funds to purchase a service or product, such as vaccines to prevent diseases and medicines to treat them, and inviting potential providers to submit bids.

One of the main proposals in this category of financing instruments – associated with climate change abatement and the implementation of the Kyoto Protocol – is the creation of an *emissions trading system* for climate change mitigation, in which participants are assigned tradable CO_2 emissions permits that confer the 'right' to pollute or discharge noxious gases into the atmosphere up to the limit set by the permits. This requires determining the total volume of emissions or discharges for a certain period, and then dividing it into a number of discrete units that are allocated to the various countries and their firms in the form of tradable permits. Under the terms of the Kyoto Protocol, firms and countries that exceed their allotted amounts could purchase a tradable permit from another whose emissions are below the limit allowed. Presumably, emissions produced by developing countries and their firms would be below the allotted limits, which would allow them to sell their spare tradable permits to the developed countries. This would lead to a transfer of financial resources from developed to developing countries. Although estimates are fraught with uncertainties, some calculations suggest that the implementation of the Kyoto Protocol could generate about US\$20–40 billion in resources channelled to developing countries up to 2010 (Ellerman, Jacoby and Decaux 1998).

The net present value of the future costs associated with climate change abatement and the Kyoto Protocol has been estimated to be in the order of $1 trillion (Nordhaus 1999). This is approximately 100 times more expensive than the Montreal Protocol. The burden would fall primarily on the companies of the highly industrialized countries. With the ratification by Russia's Parliament the agreement came into effect in early 2005, but without the participation of the US which is the world's largest contributor to climate change.

The absence of sufficiently large and lucrative markets serves as a disincentive to investment by large pharmaceutical firms in the development of drugs to treat and prevent diseases that affect people in the poorest countries. This has led to proposals (for example, WHO 2001) that the required markets should be created with funds from bilateral agencies, international financial institutions and private foundations to purchase, through competitive bidding, drugs for distribution in developing countries. Similar proposals have been made with regard to research for the production of vaccines and new drugs focused on developing country diseases. Effectiveness and cost considerations can be built into these schemes, together with arrangements to provide the drugs at affordable costs to the users in poor countries.

3.3.8 Global and regional partnerships

Global and regional partnerships are financial instruments that combine two or more of the mechanisms and institutions described in the seven preceding categories, and sometimes are referred to as 'innovative mechanisms'. These partnerships are usually created for specific purposes and focus on an issue of particular interest to several members of the international development finance community. These partnerships can take the form of: (i) *special purpose public or official funds*, which involve international multilateral and bilateral agencies in various ways, such as the Global Environment Facility, the proposed Global Issues Network (Rischard 2002) and the Sustainable Energy Finance Initiative (Dlugolecki 2002), in addition to consultative groups for raising and coordinating multi-donor support to developing countries, and particularly to those under stress (e.g. Iraq, Afghanistan, East Timor); and (ii) *public–private funds and partnerships for specific purposes*, which involve international, multilateral and bilateral agencies working together with private foundations, corporations, NGOs and capital markets. These include the Global Alliance for Vaccines and Immunisation (GAVI), the Global Fund to Fight AIDS, Tuberculosis and Malaria, and the proposed Investment Partnership for Polio. The International Finance Facility proposed by the UK government is a particular type of partnership, not only because it involves capital markets and a combination of bilateral and multilateral agencies, but also because it aims at providing large-scale front-loaded funding for budget support to developing countries (Reisen 2004).

The Global Environment Facility, which finances the incremental cost of taking into account the impact of developing country projects and programmes on the global environment, was created by the World Bank, the United Nations Development Programme and the United Nations Environment Program. It provided US$4.5 billion in grants to developing countries during the period 1991–2003 and has worked with the private sector, government agencies and multilateral agencies to mobilize an additional US$14.5 billion in grants, loans and investment for projects and programmes in biodiversity conservation, climate change abatement, protection of international waters, prevention of land degradation, mitigating ozone depletion and controlling persistent organic pollutants.

The Global Fund for AIDS, Tuberculosis and Malaria combines a large number of donors from the public and private sectors under a complex an innovative governance structure that has committed US$2.1 billion in grants to 224 programmes in 121 developing countries. Its Board of Governors is composed of nine donors – seven governments, one foundation and one not-for-profit organization – and nine recipients – seven governments, one developed country NGO and one developing country NGO. The Gates Foundation, the World Bank, Rotary International and the United Nations Foundation have established the Investment Partnership for Polio, which will buy and forgive a developing country outstanding IDA loans upon successful completion of a polio eradication programme. This scheme could unlock US$2.5–3.0 for each grant dollar provided to fight polio.

The International Finance Facility (IFF) is an innovative proposal that has been put forward by the government of the United Kingdom that seeks to convert a stream of 15-year pledges by bilateral donors into large front-loaded grants by securitizing these pledges in capital markets. Annual commitments would start from the US$15–16 billion in additional assistance agreed by bilateral donors at the 2002 Monterrey UN Conference on Development Financing, and would rise 4 per cent in real terms per year. The IFF would issue bonds in its own name backed by the binding pledges from bilateral donors, and would establish strict prudential management practices to match the stream of income to its disbursements and ensure the integrity of its bonds. This initiative could double ODA to US$100 billion per year for the period 2010–15, a large portion of which could be given in the form of grants (Reisen 2004; DFID 2003a).

3.4 Capacity to mobilize financial resources

The third component of the scenarios refers to the capacity to mobilize external and domestic finance. A few developing countries have received relatively large amounts of foreign direct[9] and portfolio investments, but most are bereft of external financing and struggling to attract it. Domestic savings and tax revenues also differ widely, with some developing countries generating significant amounts to invest locally and others being largely dependent on development assistance. This makes it necessary to distinguish between types of developing countries, so as to tailor institutional arrangements and financial instruments to their needs.

Most schemes that classify developing countries for development finance purposes are based primarily on two criteria: income per capita and level of indebtedness. These are often complemented with other economic indicators such as export performance, and with qualitative assessments of the policy and governance environment. Based on these criteria the IFIs, principally the IMF and the World Bank, provide data and establish categories of developing countries – for example, upper middle-income, lower middle-income, low-income, highly-indebted poor countries, low-income countries under stress – which give an indication of the types of financial instruments that may be appropriate to each category, and in some cases determine country eligibility for an instrument (e.g. access to concessional loans and grants). As countries evolve over time, these categories require periodic adjustments.[10]

Implicit in these classification schemes is the general idea that, as countries improve their capacity to mobilize external and domestic resources, the role of development assistance will become less important and private sources of funds will acquire greater weight. In an ideal situation, development assistance – and the institutions and financial instruments associated with it – would play a much more limited role and focus mainly on ensuring the financing and provision of regional and global public goods, and on supporting countries experiencing difficulties.

However, categories based primarily on levels of income and indebtedness do not capture fully the resource mobilization situation of developing countries. Therefore, it would make sense to define categories on the basis of indicators that reflect more directly a country's capacity to attract external finance, such as international asset accumulation, foreign direct investment and official aid flows, and to generate their own domestic resources, such as fiscal sustainability, savings, financial intermediation and investment. Table 3.3 summarizes the information available for these indicators in more than 150 developing

Table 3.3 Indicators of internal and external resource mobilization capacity (2002)[1]

	Indicators								
	Fiscal sustainability (%)		International asset accumulation (US$ million)		Savings, financial intermediation and investment (%)			External financial flows (US$ million)	
Classification according to income[2]	Fiscal deficit/ GDP	Tax revenue/ GDP	Exports of goods and services	International reserves	Internal savings/ GDP	Bank credit/ GDP	Gross fixed capital formation / GDP	FDI inflows	Net official inflows
Average									
Upper middle	−2.65	21.65	22,577	8,334	22.78	63.82	22.22	1,573	−87
Lower middle	−2.70	19.09	23,668	14,058	13.37	46.64	20.63	1,980	−164
Low	−2.70	14.18	5,190	2,517	8.49	27.92	22.03	212	4
Range (maximum, minimum)									
Upper middle	8.57	38.22	187,367	50,671	48.43	196.06	47.54	14,622	583
	−16.15	7.39	139	45	−8.99	−29.58	10.16	14	−1,067
Lower middle	4.04	33.02	375,418	297,739	47.18	166.44	40.24	49,308	933
	−19.60	6.76	46	27	−30.74	−48.67	3.53	−22	−4,102
Low	5.75	34.41	88,216	71,607	49.97	168.73	91.59	3,030	744
	−9.45	2.97	19	3	−47.00	−8.35	6.28	−1,513	−3,656

Table 3.3 Indicators of internal and external resource mobilization capacity (2002)[1] (*continued*)

				Indicators					
	Fiscal sustainability (%)		International asset accumulation (US$ million)		Savings, financial intermediation and investment (%)			External financial flows (US$ million)	
Classification according to income[2]	Fiscal deficit/ GDP	Tax revenue/ GDP	Exports of goods and services	International reserves	Internal savings/ GDP	Bank credit/ GDP	Gross fixed capital formation / GDP	FDI inflows	Net official inflows
Relative standard deviation (in percentages)[3]									
Upper middle	109	33	66	120	70	49	60	35	589
Lower middle	158	37	251	330	121	79	29	381	458
Low	189	56	779	493	131	156	35	1,526	7,512

Source: Global Development Finance 2003, CD-ROM. Sample: 152 developing countries, of which: (i) 34 are upper middle-income countries, 54 are lower middle-income and 64 are lower-income countries

Notes:
[1] For year 2002 or most recent year available.
[2] According to the World Bank classification.
[3] To compare the variability between categories, the relative standard deviation is calculated. This is defined as the sample standard deviation divided by the sample average in absolute value, and this ratio is then multiplied by 100.

countries and compares them with the income level categories used by the World Bank. The figures indicate that, on average, the capacity to mobilize resources is consistent with a country's income level. Upper and lower middle-income countries have higher tax revenues, international reserves and exports, saving and investment rates, and FDI, while low-income countries receive more official flows.

However, there are great variations in the indicators within each income category. The minimum and maximum values for each of the indicators overlap across income categories, and it is possible to find countries with similar resource mobilization capabilities in each of these categories. In addition, the relative standard deviation of each indicator, which is generally higher in low-income countries, suggests that this category is more heterogeneous in comparison with the other two.

Various options were explored to design a classification scheme linked directly to the capacity to mobilize external and domestic resources, which could help to better match financing instruments with types of countries. Two sets of variables were initially identified to calculate an index for the *external resource mobilization capacity* – FDI, ODA inflows, international reserves and exports – and another for the *internal resource mobilization capacity* – domestic savings, tax revenues, fiscal deficit, bank credit and gross fixed capital formation. For each of these sets, a principal components analysis was carried out in order to identify those that were highly correlated. As a result, FDI inflows and exports of goods and services remained as the key indicators of the capacity to mobilize external financing, and domestic savings and tax revenues as a percentage of the GDP remained as indicators of the capacity to mobilize domestic resources. The sample included a total of 132 developing countries for which 1990–2002 data was available, and the simple average of the annual values of each variable was calculated for the two periods under consideration, 1990–1996 and 1997–2002.

A first approach involved the construction of a composite index by rescaling the ranges, normalizing the variables in each set and calculating their averages. In addition to problems related to the availability and quality of the data, the aggregation of different indicators involves loss of information (countries whose indicators would have different values could have the same averages), and presents difficulties in deciding about the weights that should be assigned to each indicator. For these reasons, rather than calculating composite indexes it was decided to rank countries according to the values of each indicator and to use a two-step process for defining categories and the relative standing of countries within each category. In the first step, countries were classified according to their levels of FDI for external resource mobilization and of domestic savings for internal resource mobilization. In the second step, countries were ranked within each of these categories to determine their relative positions using their levels of exports for external resource mobilization and of tax revenues for domestic resource mobilization. This methodology, summarized in Table 3.4, has the advantage of avoiding the loss of information associated with the calculation of averages across indicators and, in contrast with the construction of indexes, the relative position of countries is not affected by absolute values, standard deviations and correlation effects.[11]

Internal savings and tax revenues were defined as a percentage of the GDP of the country, while FDI and exports were defined in US dollars. This is because domestic resource mobilization indicators are expressed in relation to the size of the economy as the frame of reference, while FDI and levels of exports are expressed as absolute values considering the world economy as the frame of reference (alternatively, it would have been possible to use the share of total world FDI or exports).[12]

A matrix to rank countries was constructed by combining the external and domestic resource mobilization categories defined with this two-step process. Figure 3.1 shows the results of the combination of both rankings comprising data for the period 1997–2002. Four countries – China, Brazil, Mexico and Argentina – which have received very large amounts of foreign investment during this period, were considered as 'outliers' and placed in a special category (category 0) along the external resources axis. The remaining countries were divided according to their rank into three groups (labelled 1, 2 and 3 for high, medium and low capacity), each with the same number of countries. A similar process was carried out along the domestic resource axis to divide countries according to their domestic savings rankings, placing them into three groups with an equal number of countries (labelled A, B and C for high, medium and low capacity). This leads to a matrix with 12 cells, even though some of these combinations (for example, high external resource mobilization capacity with low domestic mobilization capacity) lead to apparently incongruous categories with few special-case countries in them.[13]

To test the robustness of the classification scheme, two six-year periods – 1991–1996 and 1997–2002 – were used to examine changes in the relative position of countries between categories. Figure 3.2 shows the results and indicates that 30 per cent of the 132 countries in the sample have changed category, or their standing within a cate-

Table 3.4   A methodology to classify developing countries in terms of their resource mobilization capacities

External mobilization ranking		
CATEGORY 0 (outliers)	FDI HIGH+	X HIGH X MED X LOW
CATEGORY 1	FDI HIGH	X HIGH X MED X LOW
CATEGORY 2	FDI MED	X HIGH X MED X LOW
CATEGORY 3	FDI LOW	X HIGH X MED X LOW

Classification methodology

Variables: FDI net inflows and exports of goods and services (X), both in US\$.
Sources: Both series are from the Global Development Finance 2003.
Period: 1991–1996 and 1997–2002 average.
Criteria and procedure:
- Each variable has been ranked and divided into three equal groups*
  (HIGH, MED, LOW).
- A two-step process was followed for the construction of the four
  categories:
  - First, the countries were sorted according to their FDI ranking and
    placed in a category, which did not change in the next step.
  - Second, the countries were sorted within each category according to
    their X ranking (exports of goods and services).
- The countries were divided into four categories according to the criteria
  in the adjacent table.

Coverage: 132 developing countries were considered. FDI has full coverage, and X has 3 missing cases**. Afghanistan, Cuba, Iraq, Kiribati, Korea Democratic Republic, Libya, Saudi Arabia, Surinam, Liberia, Samoa, Solomon Islands, Somalia, East Timor were excluded because of lack of data.

---

*   Except for the category FDI HIGH+, which comprises four 'outlier' countries with the highest level of FDI inflows (China, Mexico, Argentina and Brazil). The remaining countries are divided into three equal groups.
**   For the ranking, the missing cases have been placed at the end of their category

gory, between the two periods. Most countries in transition, several of which are now part of the EU, have advanced towards higher levels of resource mobilization capacity; most countries that have improved

Table 3.4   A methodology to classify developing countries in terms of their resource mobilization capacities (*continued*)

Internal mobilization ranking		
CATEGORY A	S HIGH	TAX HIGH TAX MED TAX LOW
CATEGORY B	S MED	TAX HIGH TAX MED TAX LOW
CATEGORY C	S LOW	TAX HIGH TAX MED TAX LOW

Classification methodology

Variables: Internal savings/GDP (S) and tax revenues/GDP (TAX).
Sources: The values of S are from the Global Development Finance 2003 and those of TAX are from IMF International Financial Statistics 2003.
Period: 1991–1996 and 1997–2002 average.
Criteria and procedure:
  • Each variable has been ranked and divided into three equal groups (HIGH, MED, LOW).
  • A two-step process was followed for the construction of the three categories:
    • First, the countries were sorted according to their S ranking and placed in a category, which does not change in the next step.
    • Second, the countries were sorted within each S group according to their TAX ranking.
    • The countries were divided into three categories according to the criteria in the adjacent table.
Coverage: 132 countries were considered. S has complete coverage, and TAX has 21 missing cases *.

* For the ranking, the missing cases have been placed at the end of their category.

their performance are located in Asia; and few African countries, with the notable exception of Botswana, have improved their standing between the two periods. By contrast, countries such as Indonesia, Iran, Colombia and several small-island countries in the Pacific and the Caribbean have lost ground and descended a category in terms of their capacity to mobilize internal and external resources.

Comparisons were also made between the categories defined using this methodology and those devised with other criteria such as income levels, debt service, governance, science and technology capacity and

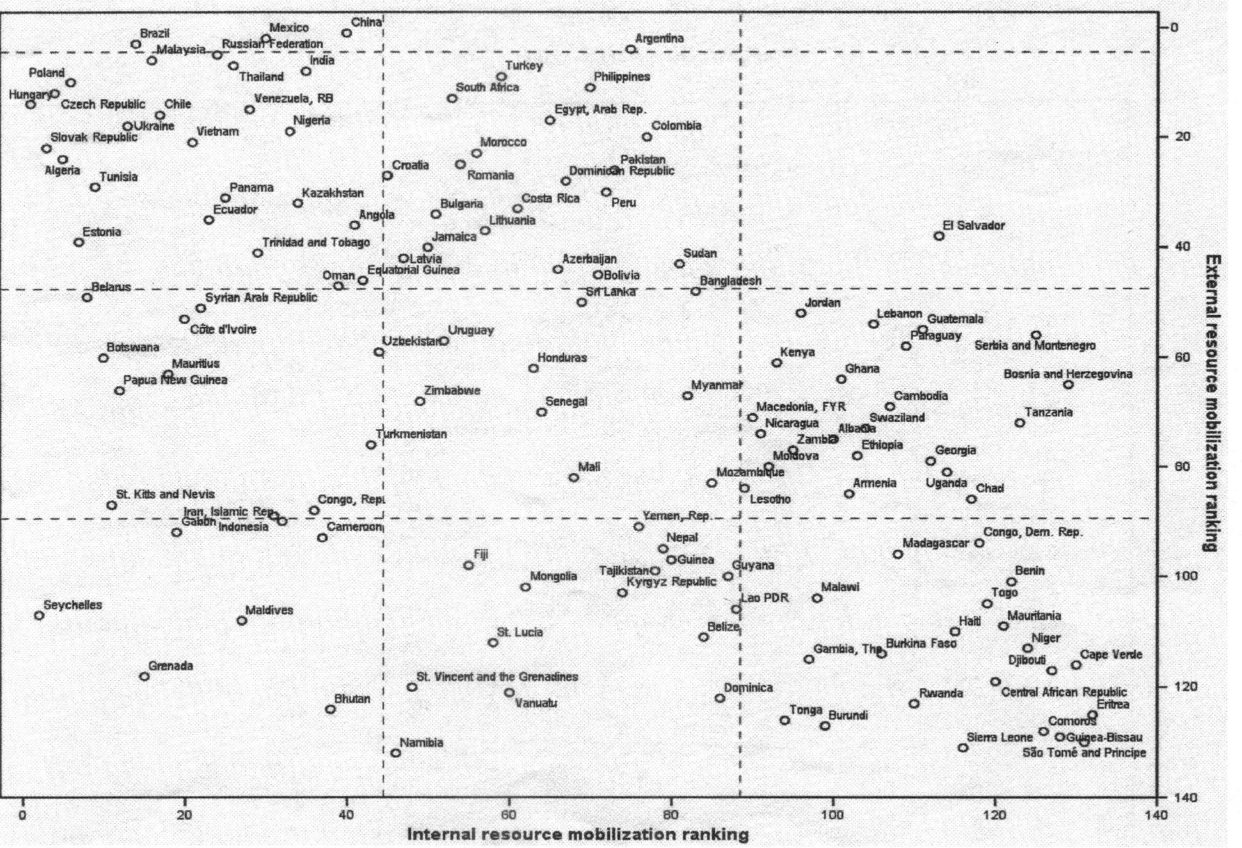

Figure 3.1   Country classification according to internal and external resource mobilization capacity ranking, 1997–2002

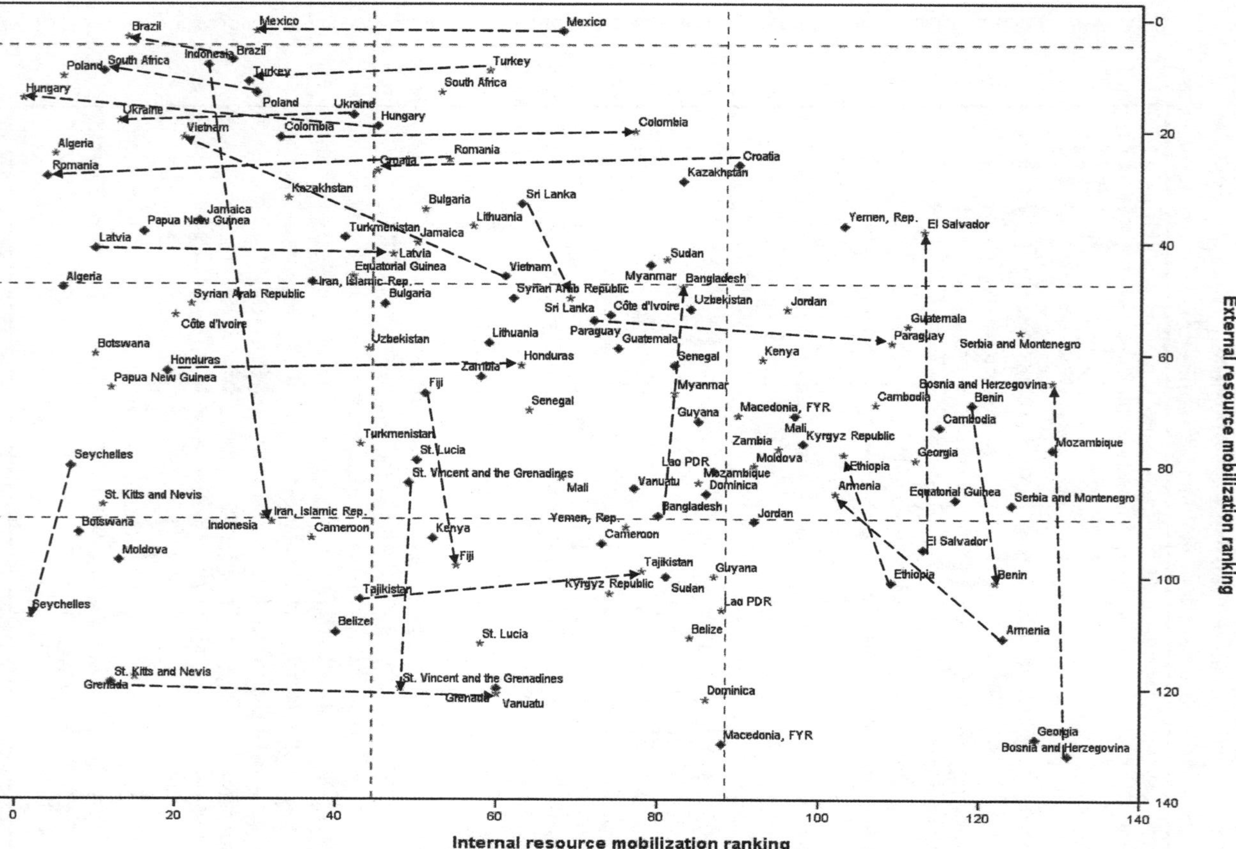

Figure 3.2   Country changes of category and ranking between 1990–1996 (diamond) and 1997–2002 (star)

ODA inflows. The results are presented in Annex B. Some highlights are: most countries categorized as IDA-only, LICUS or Blend (receiving IDA and regular loans) by the World Bank are countries with lower capacity to mobilize internal and external resources (Figure B1); most countries in sub-Saharan Africa are placed in the categories of low capacity to mobilize resources (Figure B2); a higher resource mobilization capacity is associated with higher per capita income (Figure B3); countries with higher debt/GDP ratios have a lower capacity to mobilize resources (Figure B4); and countries with a higher mobilization capacity have higher levels of debt service over exports, which would imply they are able to withstand higher levels of debt service, and that some low-income countries have a smaller debt burden because of the HIPC initiative (Figure B5).

In addition, a comparison with the World Bank's composite governance indicator (Kaufmann and Mastruzzi 2003) suggests that governance levels are not closely associated with the resource mobilization standing of a country (Figure B6), while a comparison of resource mobilization capacities with the Science and Technology Capacity Index (Sagasti 2004) shows a strong positive relationship (Figure B7). Finally, countries with a higher capacity to mobilize internal and external resources receive more ODA inflows (Figure B8), and most countries that have negative ODA inflows have higher resource capacity mobilization, but when ODA per capita figures are used instead of absolute amounts, a higher concentration of ODA is found in countries with relatively lower capacities to mobilize external and domestic resources (Figure B9).

3.5 International political economy and political viability

The fourth component of the scenarios refers to the configuration of international relations that conditions political viability for constructing combinations of institutional arrangements, financing instruments and country categories that in turn define the future for international development finance. Anticipating political will is fraught with uncertainties, but it is possible to advance some reasoned speculations about international power relations and the way they are likely to affect the situation of the development financing system around 2015. The main trends towards unilateral, bilateral, regional, multilateral and private actions in the international development scene will be examined first, before focusing on the role of key political actors and the way in which they could shape outcomes.

3.5.1 Trends in international relations

A first trend that has become highly visible is the drive towards *unilateral action* by the US, which exerts unquestionable dominance in world military, economic, scientific and technological affairs. The rapid transition from the bipolar world of the Cold War to a world order with a single superpower has changed the international development scene. In particular, the future of development assistance will be influenced to a large extent by the behaviour of the US in the next decade. Hegemonic power can be used in enlightened ways, actively engaging the international community, cooperating with others and helping to provide the public goods from which the international community can benefit – as was done by the US after the Second World War by creating the Marshall Plan to aid reconstruction and development in Europe, and by supporting the establishment of the Bretton Woods Institutions. It can also be used in narrowly self-serving ways, by adopting an isolationist, assertive and inward-looking stance – which can do much damage to a multilateral system whose effectiveness is heavily influenced by the financial, political and military clout of one nation, and therefore hostage to the shifting tides of domestic politics in that country. This concern is relevant at present with a US administration that has shown itself willing to withdraw from international social, environmental and trade policy commitments. The refusal to sign the Biological Weapons Convention and the Kyoto Protocol on climate change, together with the continued resort to unilateral policy mechanisms to address international trade disputes, are an indication of a trend towards isolationism. More recently, as shown by the Iraq invasion, the US has been willing to sidestep the UN in pursuing its own security objectives, and of acting unilaterally or through narrow alliances with a couple of middle powers. Whether and to what extent this attitude will carry over to the field of development finance is still an open question.

A second trend is that key donor countries are frequently resorting to *bilateral measures*, both by using country-to-country agreements alongside multilateral processes and by exerting bilateral pressure to enforce multilateral rules. The first, which might be called 'cooperative bilateralism', is exemplified by the continued growth of bilateral trade and investment agreements that often seek to ratchet up the level of multilateral commitment to liberalize trade and investment rules, and also to deal with issues specific to the two countries that are party to the agreement. The second, which may be called 'coercive bilateralism', is exemplified by the increased willingness to use bilateral pressure on issues such as Intellectual Property Rights or the regulation of Genetically Modified Organisms (GMOs) in order to persuade other countries either to upgrade protection or to lower levels of regulation in line with the commercial interests of donor countries and their firms. There is also the use of multilateral institutions to pursue bilateral objectives – the bilateralization of multilateral assistance – which has been the case when international and multilateral agencies are used merely as vehicles to implement bilateral programmes, frequently through trust funds.

A third trend in the international relations scene is the rise of *regionalism*. Regional trading blocs have now evolved in most areas of the world. From the EU to NAFTA in North America, ASEAN and APEC in East and South East Asia, SADC in Southern Africa, and MERCOSUR and FTAA in the American hemisphere, the move towards regional integration looks set to continue. The pace and scope of these integration agreements differs by region, but the propensity towards addressing broader political, social and environmental concerns rather than trade policy alone seems almost inevitable as the spill-overs between these issues increases. The pace of deepening within regional blocs appears to be driven by the market potential of the region and the degree of political trust and cohesion that exists between key members.

The fourth trend refers to the growing interest in *multilateral initiatives*. Despite the presence of unilateralism, bilateralism and regionalism in international relations, the emergence of global concerns has prompted much discussion about the need for new institutional arrangements at the global level. One of the main catalysts for these discussions in the field of international finance was the East Asian crisis of 1997, which prompted reflection about the need for improvements in the international financial architecture, more transparent forms of corporate governance, and stronger regulation of banks and other financial institutions. In particular, the collapse of ENRON and Arthur Andersen, together with scandals in the investment banking and mutual funds industries in the US, have helped to sustain the momentum towards reform in accounting and auditing standards and practices. There have also been discussions between leading academics and politicians about the need for better institutional arrangements to deal with environmental issues at the global level, particularly in light of the poor implementation of commitments agreed at the 1992 UN Conference on Environment and Development in Rio.

Multilateral initiatives have not progressed very far as yet because of resistance to the reform, closure and creation of new institutions, because of doubts about whether they would be in a better position to deal, for example, with financial instability or environmental degradation than existing ones, and also because of opposition from vested interests. There has also been strong resistance to proposals for major new policy instruments within existing institutions, as shown by the failure to create a new Sovereign Debt Restructuring Mechanism in the IMF to allow an orderly debt-restructuring process for countries facing default. However, pressures to include Common Action Clauses (CACs) in the issuing of developing country paper can help to deal with debt problems in cases of financial stress, primarily by restructuring debt without having to obtain universal agreement among bondholders.

Multilateral institutions are increasingly playing a normative role in many areas of development, from health to trade and environment to security. Governments, some more than others, have conceded authority and decision-making power to such bodies and agreed to be bound by the provisions of global treaties. Yet there is also a concern that the more powerful countries use global negotiating processes to try and 'internationalize' or 'export' their own regulatory approaches and preferences (what were referred to as unilateralism and bilateralism above). For example, the debate about guidelines for corporate governance in the wake of the East Asian financial crises focused on the export of US banking standards and systems of corporate governance, though recent scandals raise doubts about their effectiveness. Similarly, in the environmental field conflicts between the regulatory preferences of powerful groups are being fought out through international institutions, but multilateral processes that operate in this way respond poorly to the concerns and needs of developing countries. For example, negotiations on the Cartagena Protocol on Biosafety can be characterized as a struggle between the competing regulation systems of Europe and North America, both of which exclude the viewpoints and preferences of developing countries rich in biodiversity.

In parallel with these trends in the relations between states and between international institutions in the public realm, there has also been a significant growth in *private–public and private regimes* that have important implications for the functioning of the multilateral development system. The emergence of global and regional partnerships between public and private entities, such as the Global Fund for AIDS, Tuberculosis and Malaria (see section 3.3.8) and the Global Compact at the UN, and of private associations that work in the development field, such as the Business Partners for Development initiative and the Business Council for Sustainable Development, have signalled the involvement of non-state actors in a variety of international development initiatives. In addition, public–private bodies are setting elaborate systems of rules and regulations that govern particular areas of international economic relations. For example, the International Standards Organization sets norms that developing country suppliers increasingly have to meet as a condition for entry into developed country markets.

At the same time, private companies and NGOs have established a growing number of certification schemes to meet consumer demands for guarantees about the social conditions (e.g. no child labour) and environmental impact (e.g. no pesticides) associated with the products they buy. While these initiatives aim at dealing with the dilemmas of ethical trade and production, the lack of participation of developing country producers in their design has led, in some cases, to unintended negative consequences. In addition to the standards agreed by bodies such as the ILO and WHO, many developing countries have statutes and regulations that deal with these issues, but lack the capacity to put them into effect. Multilateral and bilateral initiatives for building capacity to meet these standards, and for increasing participation in their design, may be preferable to the efforts some donors have invested in advancing protection of the poor through private regimes that seek to compensate for failings in the system of public regulation.

These trends coexist and interact with each other, and different combinations predominate at particular times. Unilateralism may yield, however reluctantly, to multilateral action when broader support and legitimacy are sought by the dominant power; bilateralism and regionalism may be seen as a threat to multilateralism, but concerted bilateral and regional action can reinforce efforts aimed at improving the functioning of the multilateral system; corporations and NGOs may be seen as competing with public entities in the establishment of policy regimes, but they can also complement and expand official development initiatives. The evolution of the international development financing system will depend to a significant extent on achieving an appropriate balance and a convergence of unilateral, bilateral, regional, multilateral and private actions.

3.5.2 Key actors

As the single superpower, the US now plays the leading role in influencing the shape of international power relations. Yet, since 2002, global opinion surveys reveal a deep and growing disquiet about the way in which the US is playing that role. When American respondents were excluded, an ICM survey in 2003 of 11 countries reported that 60 per cent of the sample had a very unfavourable or fairly unfavourable attitude towards the American President. Despite the flood of sympathy in the immediate aftermath of the events of September 11, 2001, the world has subsequently grown increasingly uneasy with the US. At the time of the presidential election in November 2004, a poll of 34,330 people older than 15 in 35 countries conducted by the polling company Globescan in collaboration with the Programme on International Policy Attitudes of the University of Maryland reported that just one in five people surveyed would support the re-election of President Bush. The same survey provided support to a previous attitude survey by the Pew Research Center, which found very low levels of international support for US foreign policy. According to the Pew's Global Attitudes Report favourable ratings for the international role of the US were dramatically low in a number of Middle Eastern countries, including key allies Turkey (12 per cent) and Pakistan (10 per cent). Egypt recorded the lowest percentage of citizens with a favourable opinion of the US (6 per cent). The US had also lost public support among key Western allies such as Germany (25 per cent), Russia (28 per cent), France (31 per cent) and even Great Britain (from 75 per cent in 2002 to 48 per cent in 2003)

In all these surveys, the main factor presented to explain the sharp decline in international support for the US is Iraq. Events leading up to the Iraq conflict caused a diplomatic debacle that split the UN Security Council, generated deep divisions among political leaders within the EU, and created rifts in the Transatlantic alliance. The central question raised by this is whether the rift and negative attitudes towards the US are temporary phenomena that will dissipate over time or whether they highlight deeper and more enduring fault lines. A recent and controversial study by Robert Kagan (2002a, 2002b, 2003) argues that a permanent shift is occurring. According to his analysis, differences between European and American foreign policy may reflect a deep and enduring cultural rift that has been slowly developing during the last fifty years among the publics on both continents. The main divergence in strategic perspectives, he suggests, concern the appropriate deployment of military might over transnational negotiation, approval of the role of unilateral action over multilateral cooperation, and preferences for the policies of coercion over persuasion. The change, he argues, is not simply due to the Bush administration or a by-product of globalization, and the rise of multilateral institutions such as the EU, NAFTA, and the WTO, and new conventions and regulations of international and multilateral governance on issues ranging from trade to human rights and environmental protection. Rather, in his interpretation, the

Transatlantic differences over foreign and security policy which came to a head in the Security Council debates over resolution 1441, have become ideologically rooted in popular culture in the US and Europe due to their divergent historical experiences and contemporary strengths in the world.

The thesis provided by Kagan lends support to the view that the second Bush administration will be characterized by greater assertiveness, by actions aimed at consolidating American global predominance, by an increasing emphasis on unilateralism and rejection of multilateralism and by an ever-growing recourse to coercion over negotiation. But there are also indications that would suggest movement in exactly the opposite direction. The Bush administration craves the legitimacy that only the UN can confer on its policies in places such as Iraq. The initial public response of President Bush to the tsunami disaster was to announce that America was taking charge, that the tsunami presented an opportunity to promote 'American values' in the world and that the US had 'established a regional core group with India, Japan and Australia to help coordinate relief efforts' (Tisdall 2005). There was no reference to the global coordinating role of the UN. Yet only days following that announcement, recognition of the magnitude of the tsunami disaster led the American president to disband his 'core group' and to acknowledge the UN's overall control. This suggests that multilateral approaches may not be the first or preferred option of the Bush administration, but that the complexity and magnitude of the problems of peace, security and human well-being may make such approaches unavoidable and perhaps even increasingly palatable. The Iraqi quagmire is demonstrating that even superpowers have their limits. Also, the impact of America's unilateral assertive stance on the international development system is likely to prove rather paradoxical. While in some cases it will constrain or become an insurmountable barrier to international collective action, it also appears to be serving as a catalyst for imaginative multilateral arrangements that would not depend on the willingness of the US to participate.

A further, major constraint to American unilateralism is economic. Throughout the 1990s, the aggregate global demand created by United States consumption served as the principal engine of global economic growth. The result, however, was a large imbalance in the global economy. The annual current account deficit of the US rose continuously to over 4 per cent of GDP by the end of that decade, while the gross national debt exploded to almost 70 per cent of GDP. Simultaneously, however, the US moved steadily into a significant fiscal surplus. Yet, since the advent of the first Bush administration in 2000 not only has the current account deficit continued to increase – to about 6 per cent of GDP – but the previous fiscal surplus has been rapidly converted into an annual deficit of historically unmatched proportions.

The result is not merely a severely imbalanced American economy, but also a global financial system that is under great strain. According to the OECD'S latest Economic Outlook, the current account deficit will rise to 6.4 per cent of America's GDP by 2006. This will continue to fuel global liquidity that is already growing faster than ever before in real terms. This has also made inevitable the dollar devaluation of 35 per cent that has already occurred against the Euro. It also makes inevitable the announced intent of the second Bush term to reduce America's fiscal deficit by half over the next four years. This combination of factors means that it will probably become increasingly difficult for the US to address its own international concerns on other than a multilateral basis, notwithstanding a preference to do otherwise.

These trends are further compounded by the fact that other major players in the global economy are not well placed to ease current dangers. The fiscal implications of EU enlargement are uncertain, but the most probable scenario suggests pressures similar to those that accompanied German reunification in the 1990s. Combined with other structural factors, it appears highly unlikely over this decade that the EU can supplant the US as the engine of global economic growth. And while Japan may have begun to emerge from recession and deflation, the constructive steps taken in the manufacturing and services sectors have not been matched by action in its financial sector. These factors, combined with the rapidity and extent of Japan's demographic transition, indicate continuous but slow growth as a likely trend. More recently, the rapid pace of economic growth in China, which has accounted for over 20 per cent of world trade growth for the past three years, has fuelled the expansion of economic activity in many developing countries, particularly those that produce commodities such as oil, cement, soybeans, copper and iron. Yet there are serious concerns. China's high growth rates are being fed by runaway credit expansion and unsustainable levels of investment and these suggest the possibility of a hard landing, which would suddenly reduce demand for such commodities and negatively affect these developing countries.

One consequence of sluggish world economic growth and fiscal constraints will be a reluctance to significantly expand American, European and Japanese development assistance, particularly in view of increasing social demands in these countries.

Three broad possibilities can be sketched for the evolution of American foreign policy over the next 2 to 3 years. In the first, the inherent conflicts between neo-conservatives, aggressive nationalists, the Christian Right, moderate republicans and secular republicans would obviate the more ideological options and would cause policy to return to the 'realist' philosophy embodied under the administration of George Bush Senior. In this possibility, Washington retains overall international hegemony but nonetheless feels constrained (by its own relative economic weakness) to accommodate the interests of other important and emerging powers. Manifestations of this policy would be seen in the assigning of priority to the strengthening of traditional US alliances, especially the North Atlantic Treaty Organization (NATO). The realist approach would also suggest an increasing willingness to act multilaterally, rather than unilaterally.

A second alternative that is being accorded growing emphasis by France and China envisages a geopolitical rebalancing whereby the US becomes less dominant and coalitions emerge to establish a more 'multipolar' world. Here, a greater balance of power is established and collective action – be it against 'rogue states' or for humanitarian intervention – is authorized and coordinated by the (possibly enlarged and more representative) UN Security Council. Given America's overwhelming military superiority, the most effective means to constrain it and achieve increased 'multipolarity' would likely be economic and could include denying critical financial aid to its overseas adventures, or, possibly, selling dollars, despite the risks that this could entail for the international economy.

This may already be happening. Central bankers in Middle Eastern oil-producing countries, along with Russia and China, are shifting a greater percentage of their reserves out of dollars and into Euros. In a new book *Washington Post* correspondent T.R. Reid claims that 'what is now underway is specifically designed to challenge the global hegemony of the dollar' (Reid 2004).

The third possibility, which may not be incompatible with the second, is global chaos in which the major powers simply fail to impose order and stability over vast stretches of the globe, even, in some cases, within their own spheres of influence, as – in the EU's case – during the break-up of Yugoslavia in the early 1990s, or, in Washington's case, the effective abandonment of Haiti in the past 10 months.

The British historian, Niall Ferguson (2003), suggested in an article in *Foreign Affairs* that an end to US domination would create a serious 'power vacuum' in the coming years, leading to an anarchic nightmare of a new Dark Age: an era of waning empires and religious fanaticism, of endemic plunder and pillage in the world's forgotten regions; of economic stagnation and civilization's retreat into a few fortified enclaves.

Ferguson argues that the two most likely rivals to US 'hyperpower,' the EU and China, are much weaker than they appear – Europe because its aging population and dropping fertility rates condemn it 'to decline in international influence and importance'; China because its corruption and governance problems, its heavy dependence on exports and its weak banking system make it ripe for a major breakdown. Ferguson also concedes, with regret, that the US colossus itself has 'clay feet' – the imbalance between its 'hard' and 'soft power'; its dependence on foreign capital; and its lack of experience in and patience for nation-building and empire maintenance, which have begun to assert themselves in public opinion, despite last month's election results.

At the dawn of 2005 and Bush's second term in office, the question is which scenario is most likely to be pushed – either deliberately or negligently – by his administration which, despite its revived multi-lateralist rhetoric, still appears committed to the unipolar world that most analysts believe is now quite beyond its grasp.

Familiarity with the assertiveness of President Bush's administration may lead to an underestimating of the potential for the three possibil-ities sketched above. Even before the events of 9/11, it appears that administration hard-liners had three aims in connection with interna-tional development: to increase US aid outlays somewhat, but on terms that would 'project American power' while weakening USAID which was seen as an unreliably 'liberal' institution; to weaken the World Bank, which they view as insufficiently susceptible to American influence, by requiring it to make more grants and fewer loans – so that its resources would diminish substantially over time; and to appoint a committed conservative as president of the World Bank. Hard-liners in the US administration have not gained the upper hand on every occa-sion, but they have usually prevailed, especially since 9/11 and at least until a year after the Iraq invasion. This has certainly been the case with regard to these three aims. American aid outlays have been increased, but much of this has been channelled through the Millennium Challenge Account (MCA) at the expense of USAID. The US proposal to require IDA to make more grants and fewer loans was adopted as part of IDA 13 and the recent confirmation of Paul Wolfowitz as President of the World Bank will place one of the leading neoconservatives of the Bush administration in that position.

Three major geopolitical concerns have recently prompted *Japan* to rethink its traditional foreign, security and aid policies. The first is the emergence of China as a formidable power with demonstrated determination to achieve a dominant political influence in the Asian region. The second – related to the first – is anxiety about the future of the long-standing post-Second World War security pact with the US. The third (and the most overwhelming current preoccupation) involves Japanese alarm regarding potential conflict with North Korea, exacerbated by the rather aggressive interventions of the US administration in these matters.

The North Korea situation has prompted the Japanese Defence Ministry to request large budget increases, mainly for high-tech weapons systems, although these are not likely to materialize because of fiscal constraints. Japan's overall fiscal deficit had soared by 2002 to over 10 per cent of GDP (and will remain at approximately 7 per cent in 2005) and its gross national debt to 150 per cent of GDP, which is forcing severe spending reductions in the national budget. In addition, Japan has been spending vast sums on defence over the years, and it possesses a far more potent military capacity than is usually realized (Japan's total defence spending in 2003 was second only to that of the US). Yet should some kind of agreement be reached with North Korea and other key countries, primarily the US, China, Russia and South Korea, the abysmally poor condition of North Korea will require a major development and humanitarian assistance effort, which may open the door to new multilateral initiatives in this part of the world (see section 4.2).

Japan has been undertaking a major re-examination of its framework for international development cooperation, prompted in part by major reductions in ODA funding – more than 22 per cent in real terms between 2000 and 2004. It has reached the conclusion that Japan can no longer aspire to 'buy influence with aid' and needs new approaches and alliances in order to increase its influence and developmental impact. In this light, Japanese support for reforms of the international development system may or may not materialize, depending on political circumstances and on whether the traditionally cautious attitude of Japanese policy makers yields to more audacious initiatives. While it appears that Japan may be inclining towards greater support for multi-lateralism – not least because of concerns about the behaviour of the current US administration – it is likely that it would not go so far as to risk alienating the dominant superpower.

There are concerns regarding the role that the *EU* is likely to play in the reform of the international development system in the coming years. First, the enlargement of the EU will distract it from development concerns, and constrain development budgets; second, certain key member states will hesitate to make major changes in economic and trade policy – most notably in the Common Agriculture Policy; third, any member states will be reluctant to cede significant portions of their development budgets to the EU; and, fourth, certain key member states will be reluctant to scale down aid to favourite developing countries – mainly former colonies – partly because of broad foreign policy concerns relating to spheres of influence.

But there are also encouraging signs. There appears to be increasing recognition on the part of several member states that their bilateral aid programmes need to be better integrated with larger collective efforts in order to achieve effectiveness and impact. There is also evidence, inter alia, from the Utstein Group, of a shared view that European bilateral programmes are badly fragmented. This, complemented by a modicum of anti-Americanism since President Bush took power, has generated a strong desire for a distinctive and effective European internationalism. European commitments to increase bilateral aid are likely to materialize in the next few years and the EU development assistance programmes are poised for revamping. Added to the innovative and determined initiatives of several EU countries to renew the international development finance system, this makes it quite probable that European countries and institutions will provide the main impetus for reform during the next few years.

The *UN* and the *World Bank* are not independent players in their own right (i.e. in the sense that they are governed by their nation-state membership), but their behaviour can exert influence and condition the outcome of efforts to reform the international development financing system. The UN is starved of funds, but has substantial legitimacy, partly because all countries have the same weight in the General Assembly and the Security Council allows some of the more powerful ones to exert significant influence. Nevertheless, as has been made unequivocally clear in the recent report by the Secretary-General's High-Level Panel (United Nations 2004), the present structure of many of its bodies needs substantive restructuring to reflect the economic and political circumstances of the early twenty-first century, which are vastly different from those which prevailed in the mid-twentieth century. According to the High-Level Panel, the UN simply cannot serve as an appropriate and credible political actor in the absence of fundamental restructuring. The Panel's release of its report in December 2004 was accompanied by an appeal for urgent action. There are, however, already indications that the call for urgent political reforms to the Security Council has been rejected in powerful quarters, most notably by both the United States and China. Relative to its recommendations for reforms in the political arena, those relating to the development structures and institutions of the United Nations may face less determined opposition, although this remains to be seen. The report draws attention to the fact that UN agencies can perform a number of important tasks that cannot be assumed by either the multilateral banks or bilateral agencies, particularly regarding normative issues, giving voice to developing countries and providing global public goods. In addition, the UN family of organizations can offer an intellectual and policy alternative to a hegemonic World Bank. There may be potential, therefore, for the UN system, and in particular the Secretary-General and his senior associates, to play an important role in facilitating reform of the international development finance system. However, this would require a substantial strengthening of the professional and management capacities of the UN system, and deliberate leadership on the part of the Secretary-General and his senior staff.

There are growing concerns, very much in evidence in developing countries, about the extent to which the World Bank has taken on expanded roles over the past decade ('mission creep' is the terminology used by some observers). In recent years, the Bank has come to occupy and dominate policy and programme areas that were previously the comparative advantage of other agencies, multilateral and bilateral alike. In many countries, the dominance of the Bank in development matters now extends from determining the intellectual and policy agendas at the macro, sector and local levels, to being the main provider of both capital and technical assistance, to the management of operational programmes and projects, and to the evaluation of development performance. There are strong views to the effect that the increasingly hegemonic role of the Bank is not in the best interests either of developing countries or of the Bank itself. Yet, in spite of these concerns, the intellectual and financial clout, together with the convening power, of the World Bank makes it the key multilateral player in the reform of the international development finance system. The direction the Bank will take under a wolfowitz presidency will strongly influence reform outcomes.

The *G7-G8* group of developed economies plus Russia does not appear to be an appropriate arena for the pursuit of reforms of the international development system – and particularly of development finance. When G7 summits were conceived in 1975, their intent was for the heads of state and government of the major industrial countries to get together in intimate, informal circumstances to build rapport and to establish the basis on which important policies could be launched or managed in their interest and, presumably, that of the world at large. Bureaucracy was to be either non-existent or kept to an absolute minimum. They have since become something akin to a media extravaganza run by large bureaucratic staffs. Yet, during the last few years there have been efforts to bring in leaders key developing countries, and particularly Africa, when issues that affect them were discussed. However, little of substance appears to emerge out of these gatherings in which the presence of such leaders is seen by some observers as just a sideshow.[14] The unwillingness – at least to date – of the G7-G8 even to accord serious discussion to the UK's proposal for the International Financing Facility vividly illustrates the problem.

Building on the relatively more successful experience of the G20 meetings of finance ministers from developed and developing countries, which have become a forum to discuss issues such as how to deal with financial instability and better manage sudden capital inflows and outflows in emerging countries, there are proposals to create a G20 forum at heads of state level. The idea is not to replace the G7-G8, but to complement it by bringing in leaders from the emerging countries – Argentina, Brazil, China, India, Indonesia, Korea, Mexico, Saudi Arabia, South Africa and Turkey – to a forum for policy dialogue, discussion and negotiation on global economic issues. In particular, Paul Martin, the Canadian Prime Minister, has pressed for the creation of such a forum and has apparently made some headway.[15] Should the G20 emerge as a viable forum for substantive discussions between the leading developed and emerging economies of the world, it would be a natural place to discuss and negotiate reforms of the international development financing system.

The G77 or other groupings of developing countries are far too heterogeneous entities to offer effective political support for the reform of the international development system and of development finance. Many of the more influential members feel little sense of commonality with smaller, poorer countries; several of the former have developed close ties and intellectual links to western countries; and China tends to go its own way. The fragmentation and the fault lines within the G77 are intensifying, rather than diminishing, and as a collective entity the G77 is unlikely to be strong and flexible enough to facilitate reform. It makes more sense to focus on subsets of developing countries that seek common cause on specific development issues requiring collective international action (e.g. Brazil, South Africa, India, possibly China, and others on the Doha round trade negotiations; regional groups in Africa and Latin America). Nevertheless, it appears that developing countries, acting on their own or through highly heterogeneous groups like the G77, will not be a significant player in the reforms of the development finance system at the global level – although groups like the G20 provide them with a better platform to press for change. There is a different situation at the regional and sub-regional levels, where smaller and more focused groups of countries are likely to have a significant impact on institutional and financial arrangements, as was the case of the Andean countries in the creation of the Andean Finance Corporation (CAF).

Other actors who may exert influence in the reform of the international financing system are *NGOs, private foundations* and, to a much lesser extent, private firms. The campaigns for debt relief of the 1990s, organized by coalitions of grassroots, religious and non-governmental organizations, together with prominent personalities from the fields of art and popular culture, had a significant impact on the creation of programmes to reduce the debt of poor countries. These groups can press for reforms, lobby political leaders in their own countries, organize international protests and even disrupt the work of international and multilateral organizations. Their participation in the MDGs campaigns can help to ensure and consolidate increases in development assistance by major donors, particularly in Europe. Private foundations, especially large ones like the Gates Foundation and the United Nations Foundation, can also exert significant influence, and have been responsible for pushing for the establishment of special funds. Other foundations have helped to explore new avenues for development assistance and have supported specific programmes in innovative ways (e.g. Rockefeller and Ford support for the Green Revolution).

Finally, Table 3.5 presents a list of some key events that present opportunities to press for reform of the international development finance system in the coming years. Three events are particularly worth noticing: the UN Special General Assembly meeting on the MDGs in September 2005, which will review progress towards these targets and their financial implications; the presentation and dissemination of the final report of the Task Force on Global Public Goods, which will propose how to define, identify and finance activities to tackle global concerns; and a series of announcements that will take place between 2006 and 2010 regarding increases in European ODA, which will show

Table 3.5 Future Key international events for development finance initiatives

	Events	Appointments	Horizons/replenishments	Publications/committees
2005	• September: Helsinki Conference WTO Ministerial • September: UN special Assembly on MDGs • 20th Anniversary of Live Aid • UK chairing of G8 • 60th Anniversary of BWIs	• April-June: possible UK elections • May: next term of new World Bank President • July: UK half-year presidency of the EU Council • September: New WTO Director General	• Start of the negotiations on the 10th EDF (transition period to budgetization until 2008–2011) • (Likely conclusion of EU perspectives) • Likely launch of World Bank–Gates Foundation Polio Fund	• January: WEF Global Governance Initiative • July: Publication of Helsinki Process findings • December: International Task Force on Global Public Goods
2006	• Russia chairing of G8	• By June (latest): UK elections	• Implementation of Monterrey pledges: aid increases of US$16 billion a year • Spain's commitment to increase aid to 0.33%	• January: WEF Global Governance Initiative

Table 3.5   Future Key international events for development finance initiatives (*continued*)

	Events	Appointments	Horizons/replenishments	Publications/committees
2007	• Germany chairing of G8 • WTO Ministerial meeting		• EU Agreement on Financial Perspectives post-2006 for 5 or 7 years • Expiry of current EDF (9) • April: UK biennial Spending Round • Ireland's commitment to increase aid to 0.7%	• Fourth Assessment Report of the Intergovernmental Panel on Climate Change (could provide further arguments for Kyoto Protocol)
2008	• Japan chairing of G8	• November: US Presidential elections	• June: IDA 15 Replenishment • Scheduled conclusion of Economic Partnership Agreements (EPAs) under the Cotonou Agreement	
2009	• Italy chairing of G8			

Source: Adapted from Rogerson (2004).

whether these countries abided by their commitments made at the UN Monterrey Summit on Development Financing in 2002. These and other events that could be programmed during the next five to seven years suggest there may be a window of opportunity to reinforce existing initiatives and to embark on new ways to reform the international development finance system.

4
The Shape of Things to Come: Scenarios and Their Policy Implications

4.1 Interactions between the scenario components

The previous chapter examined separately the four components (institutional arrangements, financing instruments, financial mobilization, types of developing countries and political viability) of the scenarios for the future of development finance. This chapter develops the scenarios and examines their policy implications. The result is a framework for strategic choices to help explore alternative paths for the evolution of the international development financing system. To begin this examination, it is useful to outline briefly the interactions between these four components, and in particular how the various financing instruments relate to the categories of countries according to their resource mobilization capabilities.

Institutional arrangements provide the scaffolding within which to place the financing instruments that channel resources to developing countries. Depending on the characteristics of the instruments and the type of countries, a particular kind of institution may be required. In effect, it is often difficult to disentangle institutions from the financing instruments at their disposal because of legal, political and administrative constraints that determine the scope of what institutions can do. For example, bilateral aid agencies are subject to donor country budgetary regulations, political preferences and accountability requirements. Usually they do not have the same flexibility as private banks and foundations in providing loans and grants, and in deciding how and to what to allocate the resources at their disposal. Similarly, international financial institutions are limited by their charters – and by the interests and relative power of their government shareholders – in deciding the financial instruments to use and the countries to which these instruments will be directed. It follows from this that the interactions between institutional arrangements, on the one hand, and the set of financial instruments, types of countries and political viability, on the other, are key in determining the shape of the alternative scenarios.

This is illustrated in Table 4.1, which presents a detailed list of nearly one hundred financing instruments grouped into the eight main types set out in the preceding chapter. The columns under 'country categories' indicate the groups of countries to which these instruments are primarily directed. For example, there are financial instruments appropriate for all or most categories of developing countries, such as FDI, bilateral loans, export credit and IMF short-term financing. In contrast, there are other financial instruments which are only applicable to specific groups of countries, such as bilateral concessional loans, post-conflict grants, direct budget support, contingent credit lines, and bond issues with collective action clauses. In addition, the last column of Table 4.1 shows the degree of utilization of the instrument – ranging from proposed but not yet created to widespread use – and indicates to what extent each instrument has become established within the international development financing system.

The correspondence between financial instruments and country categories is further explored in Table 4.2. As indicated earlier, some combinations of external and domestic resource mobilization appear incongruous – for example, extremely high or high external mobilization capacity with low domestic resource mobilization capacity – and therefore no instruments appear in the respective cells. Although of a preliminary and somewhat tentative nature, this attempt to link financing instruments and country categories suggests that an effective international development financing system should have a large array of financing instruments that fully cater to the specific needs of different types of developing countries.

4.2 Scenarios for the international development financing system

The components described in the preceding chapter can be combined to explore alternative paths for the evolution of the international development financing system up to 2015–20. As shown in Figure 4.1, four scenarios emerge out of a combination of the degree to which

Table 4.1 Illustrative list of financing instruments, country categories and degree of utilization

<table>
<tr>
<td rowspan="3">Types of financing instrument</td>
<td rowspan="3">Sub-types of financial instruments and illustrations</td>
<td colspan="7">Country categories[1]</td>
<td rowspan="3">Degree of utilization[2]</td>
</tr>
<tr>
<td colspan="4">External</td>
<td colspan="3">Internal</td>
</tr>
<tr>
<td>0</td><td>1</td><td>2</td><td>3</td><td>A</td><td>B</td><td>C</td>
</tr>
<tr>
<td colspan="10">Bilateral instruments</td>
</tr>
<tr>
<td>• Regular loans</td>
<td>• Project, programme and sector loans (direct or through official financial intermediaries)</td>
<td>x</td><td>x</td><td>x</td><td>x</td><td>x</td><td>x</td><td>x</td>
<td>++++</td>
</tr>
<tr>
<td></td>
<td>• Large special purpose loans (e.g. funds for financial rescue packages)</td>
<td>x</td><td>x</td><td></td><td></td><td></td><td>x</td><td>x</td>
<td>+++</td>
</tr>
<tr>
<td></td>
<td>• Export credits (usually through specialized credit agencies)</td>
<td>x</td><td>x</td><td>x</td><td>x</td><td></td><td>x</td><td>x</td>
<td>+++</td>
</tr>
<tr>
<td>• Soft (concessional) loans</td>
<td>• Concessional loans to governments and government agencies (national, regional, local)</td>
<td></td><td></td><td></td><td>x</td><td></td><td></td><td>x</td>
<td>+++</td>
</tr>
<tr>
<td></td>
<td>• Soft loans to public, civil society and private financial intermediaries focused on the poor (small and micro enterprises, revolving funds)</td>
<td></td><td></td><td>x</td><td>x</td><td></td><td>x</td><td>x</td>
<td>++</td>
</tr>
<tr>
<td>• Grants for public and civil society organizations</td>
<td>• Direct budget support or through a common pool of resources (also for soft loans)</td>
<td></td><td></td><td>x</td><td>x</td><td></td><td>x</td><td>x</td>
<td>++</td>
</tr>
<tr>
<td></td>
<td>• Grants for specific projects and programmes to help the poor</td>
<td></td><td></td><td>x</td><td>x</td><td></td><td></td><td>x</td>
<td>+++</td>
</tr>
<tr>
<td></td>
<td>• Humanitarian relief and post-conflict grants</td>
<td></td><td></td><td></td><td>x</td><td></td><td></td><td>x</td>
<td>+++</td>
</tr>
<tr>
<td></td>
<td>• Grants for public and private investment (mainly pre-investment)</td>
<td></td><td></td><td>x</td><td>x</td><td></td><td></td><td>x</td>
<td>+++</td>
</tr>
<tr>
<td></td>
<td>• Bilateral funds with special conditions (e.g. Millennium Challenge Account)</td>
<td></td><td></td><td></td><td>x</td><td></td><td>x</td><td>x</td>
<td>*</td>
</tr>
<tr>
<td></td>
<td>• Grants to assist in obtaining access to multilateral and private financing</td>
<td></td><td></td><td></td><td>x</td><td></td><td></td><td>x</td>
<td>*</td>
</tr>
</table>

Table 4.1 Illustrative list of financing instruments, country categories and degree of utilization (*continued*)

| Types of financing instrument | Sub-types of financial instruments and illustrations | Country categories[1] | | | | | | | Degree of utilization[2] |
| | | External | | | | Internal | | | |
		0	1	2	3	A	B	C	
• Debt relief	• Debt reduction and cancellation			x	x		x	x	+++
	• Grants to support multilateral debt reduction (e.g. HIPC initiative)			x	x		x	x	+++
	• Debt swaps and counterpart funds		x	x	x		x	x	+++
• Funds to promote private investment in developing countries	• Loans, equity and joint ventures (e.g. US Overseas Private Investment Corporation, UK Export Credits Guarantee Department)		x	x		x	x		++
	• Guarantees and insurance for political, regulatory and currency risks		x	x		x	x		++
• Tax incentives (for firms in developed countries)	• For FDI in developing countries			x	x		x	x	*
	• To promote charity, corporate giving and individual donations				x			x	+
	• For the generation of knowledge and provision of goods and services (medicines, research on specific developing country problems, technology transfer)			x	x	x	x	x	+

Table 4.1 Illustrative list of financing instruments, country categories and degree of utilization (*continued*)

| | | Country categories[1] | | | | | | | |
| | | External | | | | Internal | | | |
Types of financing instrument	*Sub-types of financial instruments and illustrations*	0	1	2	3	A	B	C	*Degree of utilization[2]*
2 International organizations and agencies (UN system, regional and other international organizations)									
• Grants (from their regular budgets and trust funds)	• Funds for directly executed projects and programmes at the country and regional levels			x	x		x	x	++++
	• Support for government executed projects and programmes			x	x		x	x	+++
	• Technical cooperation grants	x	x	x	x	x	x	x	++++
	• Institutional development and capacity-building grants			x	x		x	x	+++
• Special purpose grants	• Specific funds and programmes (TOKTEN, IFS, IDRC, heritage conservation, agricultural research, access to information technologies)	x	x	x			x	x	++
	• Funds to support the core component of delivery systems for global and regional public goods (conflict prevention, biodiversity, climate change)	x	x	x	x	x	x	x	*
	• Creation of special funds (e.g. commodity stabilization funds, UN Security Insurance Agency, Global Demilitarization Fund, Global Hunger Fund). See also *global and regional partnerships*			x	x		x	x	*

Table 4.1 Illustrative list of financing instruments, country categories and degree of utilization (*continued*)

Types of financing instrument	Sub-types of financial instruments and illustrations	External				Internal			Degree of utilization[2]
		0	1	2	3	A	B	C	
3 International financial institutions									
a. Multilateral Development Banks (World Bank, regional and sub-regional banks, and their associated institutions)									
• Regular loans	• Project, programme and sector loans for the public and private sectors	x	x	x		x	x		++++
	• Structural adjustment loans and balance of payments support (at macroeconomic level)		x	x	x		x	x	+++
	• Emergency recovery loans (in case of disaster or unexpected events)	x	x			x	x	x	+++
	• Sector adjustment and programme loans (for specific sectors)		x	x	x		x	x	+++
	• Loans to financial intermediaries (e.g. development finance corporations)		x	x	x		x	x	+++
	• Learning and innovation loans (for pilot projects and capacity building)			x	x		x	x	++
	• Pre-arranged fast disbursement loans conditional on previous performance	x	x	x		x	x		*
• Soft (concessional) loans	• Project, programme, sector and structural adjustment loans to the public sector				x		x	x	+++
	• Temporary funds for countries with special needs (post-conflict reconstruction, sudden deterioration of external conditions)			x	x			x	+
	• Direct budget support or through a common pool of resources				x			x	*

Note: country categories 0–3 are External and A–C are Internal, grouped under Country categories[1].

Table 4.1   Illustrative list of financing instruments, country categories and degree of utilization (*continued*)

| Types of financing instrument | Sub-types of financial instruments and illustrations | Country categories[1] | | | | | | | Degree of utilization[2] |
| | | External | | | | Internal | | | |
		0	1	2	3	A	B	C	
• Grants (mostly to public institutions)	• For assisting public institutions in specific programmes and projects	x	x	x	x	x	x	x	+++
	• Technical cooperation, capacity-building and institutional development grants			x	x		x	x	+++
	• Emergency operations to deal with natural or man-made disasters			x	x		x	x	+++
• Risk mitigation and risk management (primarily for private investors)	• Total, partial and rolling guarantees (political, contractual, regulatory, credit, foreign exchange risks)	x	x	x		x	x		+++
	• Financing for currency and interest hedging operations	x	x			x			++
	• Other instruments to promote private investment and trade: export credits, securitization, leasing, syndication, underwriting, trade insurance	x	x	x	x	x	x	x	++
• Equity participation	• Direct participation in equity	x	x			x			+++
	• Quasi-equity (common shares, preferred stock, C loans)	x	x			x			++
	• Profit-and loss-sharing arrangements (e.g. IsDB facility for joint ventures)	x	x			x			++

Table 4.1 Illustrative list of financing instruments, country categories and degree of utilization (*continued*)

| | | Country categories[1] External | | | | Internal | | | Degree of utilization[2] |
| | | 0 | 1 | 2 | 3 | A | B | C | |
Types of financing instrument	*Sub-types of financial instruments and illustrations*								
• Debt reduction	• Funds for multilateral debt reduction (HIPC initiative)			x	x		x	x	+++
	• Debt reduction loans (e.g. for buying-back existing debt, debt service reduction)		x	x		x	x		++
	• Funds for clearing arrears with multilateral development banks			x	x		x		++
	• Credit buy-down mechanism			x			x	*	
• Additional financial instruments	• Mobilization of resources from bilateral and other multilateral sources (consultative groups)			x	x		x	x	+++
	• Issuing bonds in developing countries to strengthen local capital markets	x	x			x			++
b. IMF and regional monetary funds									
• Short term financial assistance	• IMF: Stand-by arrangements, Extended Fund Facility (EFF), Supplemental Reserve Facility (SRF), Compensatory Financing Facility (CFF)	x	x	x	x	x	x	x	+++
	• Latin American Reserve Fund (FLAR): liquidity and contingent loans		x	x		x	x		+++
	• For temporal shortfalls of balance of payments (IMF's Trade Integration Mechanism)			x	x		x		++

Table 4.1 Illustrative list of financing instruments, country categories and degree of utilization (*continued*)

Types of financing instrument	Sub-types of financial instruments and illustrations	Country categories[1]							Degree of utilization[2]
		External				Internal			
		0	1	2	3	A	B	C	
• Concessional funds	• Medium-term financing for poor countries: Poverty Reduction and Growth Facility (PRGF)			x	x		x	x	++
• Debt management and debt relief	• Collective Action Clauses for sovereign debt	x	x	x		x			+
	• Financing for multilateral debt reduction HIPC initiative			x	x		x	x	+++
	• Short-term credit lines for clearing arrears, debt service and debt restructuring (e.g. FLAR)			x	x		x	x	++
	• Sovereign Debt Restructuring Mechanisms (SDRM) for orderly debt defaults	x	x			x	x		*
• IMF: issuing SDRs	• Providing additional short-term financing and international liquidity for developing countries	x	x	x	x	x	x	x	*
• Other financial instruments	• Administration of trust funds and international reserves (e.g. FLAR)		x	x		x	x		++
	• Establishment of regional monetary funds (e.g. Asian Monetary Fund)								*

Table 4.1   Illustrative list of financing instruments, country categories and degree of utilization (*continued*)

Types of financing instrument	Sub-types of financial instruments and illustrations	Country categories[1] External				Internal			Degree of utilization[2]
		0	1	2	3	A	B	C	
4. Private sources									
a. Corporations									
• FDI	• FDI: wholly owned subsidiaries, partial equity investment, joint ventures, privatizations	x	x	x	x	x	x	x	+++
• Concessions	• Participation in the private provision of public services	x	x	x		x	x		+++
• Grants, donations, social responsibility activities	• Open corporate grants and donations (financial or in kind) to public and civil society entities	x	x	x	x	x	x	x	+
	• Grants in the locations where the corporation operates (local governments, community associations, civil society organizations). Also in the case of *commercial banks*.	x	x	x		x	x		++
b. Commercial and investment banks									
• Loans	• For investment projects and programmes	x	x			x			++
	• Sovereign loans (individual, syndicated)	x	x	x		x	x		+++
	• Trade-related financial instruments (e.g. export credits, supplier's credits, insurance)	x	x	x	x	x	x	x	+++
	• Purchases of developing country sovereign debt (bonds and other debt instruments)	x	x			x			++
• Risk mitigation and risk management	• Derivates, options, futures, swaps, hedging instruments, technical advice	x	x			x			+++
	• Guarantees and insurance	x	x			x			+++

Table 4.1 Illustrative list of financing instruments, country categories and degree of utilization (*continued*)

Types of financing instrument	Sub-types of financial instruments and illustrations	External 0	1	2	3	Internal A	B	C	Degree of utilization[2]
• Portfolio flows	• Investment in developing country capital markets	x	x			x	x		+++
	• Socially responsible investment (SRI)	x	x			x	x		++
• Debt relief	• Brady bonds, debt swaps and debt cancellation	x	x			x	x		++
c. Private Foundations, not-for-profit and non-governmental institutions									
• Grants and donations	• Funds from developed country operating and grant-giving foundations, and for not-for-profit organizations to public, civil society and private organizations in developing countries	x	x	x	x	x	x	x	++++
d. Individuals									
• Donations	• Direct donations (through churches, NGOs, special campaigns, operating foundations)			x	x		x	x	+++
• Foreign worker remittances	• Sent directly to individuals and families			x	x		x	x	+++
	• Channelled through organizations that provide counterpart funds and services								+
e. Global and international lotteries									
• Lotteries to fund development programmes	• Global and international lotteries for development purposes (operated jointly by national lotteries in developed countries, with the possible participation of private firms: e.g. air ticket lottery, credit card purchases lottery, allocating a portion of national lotteries)	x	x	x	x	x	x	x	*

Country categories[1]

Table 4.1 Illustrative list of financing instruments, country categories and degree of utilization (*continued*)

Types of financing instrument	Sub-types of financial instruments and illustrations	0	1	2	3	A	B	C	Degree of utilization[2]
			External				Internal		
5 International capital markets									
a. Bonds and other debt instruments									
• Bonds and depositary receipts	• Sovereign bonds (standard, performance-linked bonds to exports or GDP growth, convertible bonds, senior and subordinate bonds, bonds with collective action clauses, among others)	x	x			x			+++
	• Private sector bonds and American depositary receipts (ADRs) in US stock markets	x	x			x			++
b. Equity									
• Equity	• Direct equity	x	x			x			+++
	• Quasi-equity (preferred, temporal shares)	x	x			x			
6 International taxes, fees and charges									
• Creating international tax arrangements	• Currency transaction tax (Tobin tax), bit tax, carbon tax, tax on arms exports, international air transport tax	x	x	x	x	x	x	x	*
	• Taxes on the use of the global commons (mining of the seabed, Antarctica, outer space use)	x	x	x	x	x	x	x	*
• User fees, charges and assessed contributions	• Fees for auction revenues for global commons (e.g. geostationary satellites)	x	x	x	x	x	x	x	*
	• Levies and fees on natural resource extraction and the use of land	x	x	x	x	x	x	x	*

Country categories[1]

Table 4.1   Illustrative list of financing instruments, country categories and degree of utilization (*continued*)

Types of financing instrument	Sub-types of financial instruments and illustrations	Country categories[1]							Degree of utilization[2]
		External				Internal			
		0	1	2	3	A	B	C	
7 Market creation									
• For GPGs	• Provision [mitigation] of global public goods [bads] (e.g. emissions trading)	x	x	x	x	x	x	x	+
8 Global and regional partnerships (bilateral and multilateral agencies, international funds and organizations, foundations, private corporations)									
• Special purpose public funds (international, multilateral and bilateral)	• Existing, such as the Global Environment Facility (GEF)	x	x	x		x	x		+++
	• Proposed (e.g. Global Fund, Global Issues Network, Sustainable Energy Finance Facility)	x	x	x	x	x	x	x	*
	• Roundtables for multi-donor support to developing countries under stress (e.g. Iraq, Afghanistan, East Timor)				x			x	+++
	• International Finance Facility		x	x			x	x	*
• Public–private funds and partnerships for specific purposes	• Joint government, private and NGOs mechanisms (e.g. GAVI, Global Fund to Fight AIDS, TB and Malaria (GFATM)		x	x				x	++

Notes:

1. The **country categories** columns are organized as follows:
   - **External** refers to the capacity of a country to mobilize external resources, and ranges from 0 for the few outlier countries that mobilize large amounts of external resources to 3 for those countries that have a very limited capacity;
   - **Internal** refers to the capacity of a developing country to mobilize internal resources, and ranges from A for those countries that mobilize significant amount of domestic resources to C for those that mobilize a very limited amount.
2. The **degree of utilization** column classifies instruments according to categories that use the following symbols:
   - *   Proposed
   - +   Being designed and tested
   - ++   Limited use (in some cases at pilot scale)
   - +++   Moderate use (focus on some countries and sectors)
   - ++++   Extended and widespread use

Table 4.2   An illustrative account of financial instruments and country categories

	CATEGORY A	CATEGORY B	CATEGORY C
CATEGORY 1*	*Emphasis on instruments to avoid sudden withdrawals of external financing and to mitigate risk, to continue attracting foreign private investors.* <u>Illustrative instruments:</u> • Contingent credit lines from international financial institutions. • Collective action clauses for sovereign bonds.	*Emphasis on instruments to complement domestic resources (promoting FDI and portfolio investment flows), and to reduce external financial vulnerability.* <u>Illustrative instruments:</u> • MDB or bilateral guarantees and loans to catalyse external resource mobilization. • MDB local currency bond emissions to strengthen domestic capital markets. • Measures to smooth debt service (refinancing, debt swaps).	
CATEGORY 2	*Emphasis on instruments to improve the country risk profile in order to attract foreign investors.* <u>Illustrative instruments:</u> • MDB guarantees, syndicated loans and equity investments to give comfort and attract private investors. • MDB regular loans (project, programme, sector, policy-based). • Bilateral agency guarantees for foreign direct investors.	*Emphasis on instruments to increase access to capital markets, to mobilize official sources of finance and to improve debt management.* <u>Illustrative instruments:</u> • MDB and bilateral guarantees for foreign direct investors. • Private–public investment funds for special purposes (e.g. infrastructure). • MDB and bilateral regular and blend loans. • Instruments to smooth debt service (refinancing, swaps).	*Emphasis on instruments to promote access to a broader and predictable array of sources of finance.* <u>Illustrative list of instruments:</u> • MDB and bilateral blend and soft loans. • Bilateral–private investment funds (complemented by grants) for special purposes. • Debt reduction instruments. • Grants from bilateral agencies, MDBs and foundations. • Measures to facilitate remittances by emigrants

Table 4.2   An illustrative account of financial instruments and country categories (*continued*)

CATEGORY A	CATEGORY B	CATEGORY C
C A T E G O R Y 3	*Emphasis on instruments to create capacity and a favourable policy environment to mobilize external resources and reduce poverty.* <u>Illustrative list of instruments:</u> • MDB soft and blend loans. • Bilateral and MDB debt reduction and rescheduling. • Grants from bilateral agencies, private foundations and international organizations. • Technical assistance from MDB and international organizations to improve policy environment.	*Emphasis on instruments to reduce poverty, support the provision of basic social services and create capacity.* <u>Illustrative list of instruments:</u> • Bilateral and multilateral budget support grants. • Bilateral and MDB debt cancellation. • Multi-year capacity and institution-building grants from individuals, foundations, and international organizations. • Measures to improve aid coordination in the field.

Note:
* Category 1 includes the few outlier countries placed in category 0, primarily because the distinction between these categories relates to the size of foreign inflows.

institutional reforms are put in place in the agencies and organizations of the international development system, the range of financial instruments available, the categories of developing countries that make use of them, and the political viability of one path or another.

Table 4.3 summarizes the main components and attributes of the four scenarios – *Inertia, Limited Reforms, Major Reforms* and *Transformation* – which should be seen primarily as heuristic devices to assist in the exploration of possible paths for the reform of the international development financing system. Each of these will be briefly described, highlighting some of their main features, indicating how agencies and organizations interact with each other, how financing instruments are used in different types of countries, and assessing the performance of the system as a whole.

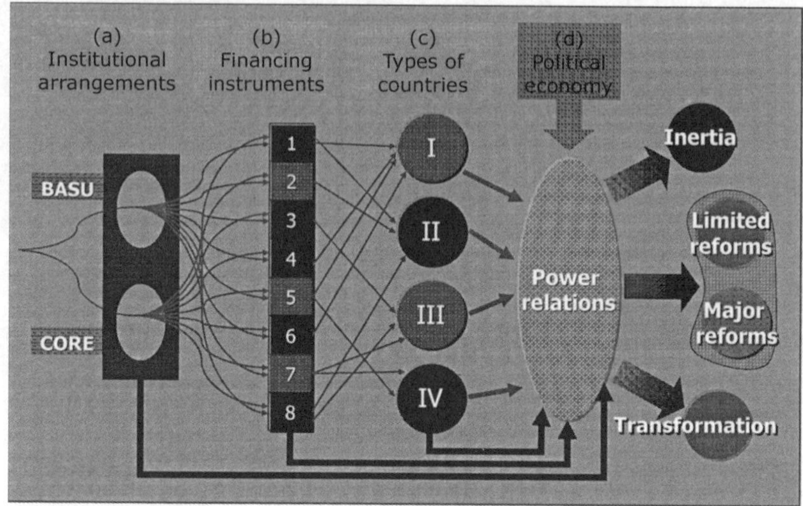

Figure 4.1 Structure of the four scenarios and their components

Rather, the scenarios have been constructed to show how different outcomes should accumulate – from Inertia to Transformation – as a result of (i) the degree to which institutional reforms are implemented; (ii) the emphasis placed on one or another set of financial instruments; (iii) the way in which countries are classified and priority given to one or another category; and (iv) the extent to which political will materializes to support reforms.

4.2.1 Inertia

The first scenario corresponds to a 2015 situation similar to or slightly worse than the one prevailing at the end of the twentieth century. Most of the undesirable features described in section 1.4 of chapter 1 still prevail, resource levels have stagnated again following modest increases in the first several years of the 2000s, and development financing has not become significantly more efficient or effective. The 'Business as Usual' (BASU) set of institutional arrangements presented in section 3.2.1 of chapter 3 broadly portrays the situation obtaining in 2015. There has been little change or innovation in the range of available financing instruments, there is a persistent mismatch between instruments and country needs, and political obstacles to reform have proved impossible to surmount.

Table 4.3 The international development financing system: summary of components and attributes for the scenarios

		Scenarios		
MAIN		*B: Reforms*		
CHARACTERISTICS	*A: Inertia*	*B1: Limited Reforms*	*B2: Major Reforms*	*C: Transformation*
Institutional arrangements, structural features	Business as usual (BASU), no change in existing institutional structures, possible deterioration, GPGs not on the horizon. No significant institutional mergers or exits. Focus on narrow interpretations of security, the 'war on terrorism' and 'global' goods.	Minor and disconnected improvements make headway, priority given to poorest countries. Pilot GPG financing experiment launched. A few important improvements in coordination at the country level and some gains in division of labour, but few if any mergers or exits. Focus remains on narrow interpretations of security but efforts to achieve MDGS are sustained.	Major interrelated institutional reforms improve support for all types of developing countries. Expansion of GPG financing schemes. Several organizations are merged to achieve critical mass. Broader issues and underlying causes of human insecurity dominate development thinking and institutional arrangements.	Comprehensive reforms (CORE) lead to institutional transformations (closures, mergers, reorganizations, clear division of labour, new entities). GPGs provision and financing fully institutionalised. Equitable development and poverty elimination in poor countries becomes major concern of rich and powerful countries.

Components

Table 4.3 The international development financing system: summary of components and attributes for the scenarios (*continued*)

MAIN CHARACTERISTICS		Scenarios			
		A: Inertia	B: Reforms		C: Transformation
			B1: Limited Reforms	B2: Major Reforms	
Components	*Financing instruments*	No major new instruments in place, minor changes in existing instruments.	Significant change in a few instruments, modest increase in flows, experiments launched.	Significant change in several key instruments, a few new instruments are now in place.	Broader and more effective set of financial instruments, some of them automatic, is in place.
	Country types	Mismatch between instruments and country types; some have a 'feast' and others 'famine'.	Better match between financial instruments and country types, but improvements focus only on poorest countries.	Improvements still partial, but much better balance between instruments and country types.	Comprehensive improvements offer full range of instruments to fit all types of countries.
	Political viability	May happen easily in the absence of political will and leadership.	Could well happen with limited political will and leadership.	Requires sustained support from a few determined leaders willing to assume political costs.	Requires broad-based concerted, forward-looking, responsible leadership.

Table 4.3   The international development financing system: summary of components and attributes for the scenarios (*continued*)

MAIN CHARACTERISTICS	A: Inertia	B: Reforms		C: Transformation
		Scenarios		
		B1: Limited Reforms	B2: Major Reforms	
Adequacy	Amounts and structure inadequate, particularly for achieving MDGs, stagnation of aid flows.	Serves reasonably well most emerging and poorest countries, modest increase in flows, and MDGs remain distant.	Significant increases in flows to all types of countries, some MDGs are achieved.	Financial flows to all types of countries increase substantially, several countries achieve many MDGs. Absorption capacity concerns re-emerge.
Predictability	High variability in bilateral and multilateral flows, high instability of private flows.	Bilateral and multilateral flows more stable, continued instability of private flows.	Predictable official flows, financial architecture improvements reduce the instability of private flows.	Predictability improves without leading to complacency.
Responsiveness	Swings between performance and need allocation criteria, lack of balance.	More responsive to needs of the poorest countries, erratic performance allocations.	Better balance between performance and need allocations, improvements in speed of response.	Variety of instruments allows full accommodating of both performance and need criteria.
Diversity and choice	'One-size-fits all' attitude prevails, no alternative to standard and rigid IFI conditionality.	Limited choice, more flexible conditionality by IFIs, bilateral agencies evolve their own policy prescriptions.	Broader set of policy prescriptions available, more ownership and less conditionality.	Ownership and well-tailored policy prescriptions prevail, conditionality takes back seat.

Attributes

135

Table 4.3   The international development financing system: summary of components and attributes for the scenarios (*continued*)

| MAIN CHARACTERISTICS | A: Inertia | B: Reforms | | C: Transformation |
		B1: Limited Reforms	B2: Major Reforms	
		Scenarios		
Domestic resource mobilization	No positive impact on domestic savings, aid dependency, tradeoffs external vs domestic flows.	Trade-offs between external and domestic flows less severe, reduced aid dependency of poorest countries.	External flows begin helping to mobilize domestic resources and to consolidate financial system in all types of developing countries.	Full synergy between external and domestic resource mobilization, external flows help local savings.
Capacity to absorb shocks	No anticipation capacity, slow in responding to shocks.	Better response to shocks in poorest countries under stress, but no significant improvements for other types of countries.	Better monitoring and surveillance, together with more effective instruments improve response to shocks.	Reasonably fast responses to shocks based on crisis anticipation and appropriate instruments.
Voice, representation, accountability	One-way accountability to donors, little voice for developing countries, donors not accountable.	Limited two-way accountability for donors and poorest countries, voice increases for all countries.	Broader two-way accountability for donors and recipients, effective representation increases for all.	New institutional arrangements open the way for more effective voice and representation for all.

Attributes

Table 4.3 The international development financing system: summary of components and attributes for the scenarios (*continued*)

	MAIN CHARACTERISTICS	Scenarios			
		A: Inertia	B: Reforms		C: Transformation
			B1: Limited Reforms	B2: Major Reforms	
Attributes	*Flexibility efficiency, learning*	Rigid, cumbersome, little coordination, overlap and duplication, no learning.	Organizational stiffness prevails but field coordination improves, evaluation initiatives launched.	Flexibility and coordination improves at all levels, better evaluation practices lead to organizational learning	Evaluation and learning are fully internalized, flexibility and effective coordination are the norm.

The way in which the institutions, financing instruments and groups of countries involved in development financing behave and interact with each other can be described in the following terms:

- *Agencies and organizations in the development financing system prefer to act on their own. Turf battles and rivalries are the norm and coordination efforts are ritualistic and limited. Agreements in principle at the level of heads of agencies and organizations seldom filter down to the field. Moreover, resource limitations foster a 'chase the money' attitude and a preference to launch 'flavour of the month' initiatives. As a result, too many agencies and organizations end up doing the same thing, raising transaction costs for both donors and recipients, and leading to pro-gramme fragmentation in the field.*
- *Bilateral agencies still account for over 60 per cent of ODA flows to developing countries. Some of these agencies have experimented with new approaches to the provision of development financing (e.g. direct budget support, pooling of resources, use of civil society organizations), but inconclusive and negative experiences with these attempts have sapped the appetite for innovation. A return to 'tried and true' development finance mechanisms, coupled with intellectual timidity, has caused most bilateral agencies to follow the lead of the World Bank and the IMF, curtailing alternative independent analysis and policy prescriptions and reinforcing their intellectual hegemony.*
- *Agency closures, exits or mergers are extremely rare. As a result, underfinanced institutions with largely irrelevant programmes are (barely) kept alive and are a drain on resources. At the same time there is a proliferation of rather small trust funds for specific purposes, which are under the control of individual donor countries. A gradual but growing shift from concessional loans to grants in IDA and multilateral development banks, coupled with little if any donor compensation for this, has undermined the financial integrity of MDB soft loan windows, loosened the interactions between poor countries and multilateral development banks, and weakened incentives for governments in poor countries to introduce policy reforms.*
- *Policy and decision making in most organizations and institutions are dominated by donors, and especially by the most powerful countries. Priorities are generally defined on the basis of their specific political and economic interests, which lead to conflicts, inconsistencies, overlap, duplication and the blurring of mandates. As interests shift and realign over time, predictability and continuity in programme design and execution are undermined, financial flows become unstable and accountability dissipates.*

- *Development finance organizations have a limited capacity to anticipate, analyse and respond to shocks and rapidly changing situations in the field, and there is little flexibility to adapt programmes to changing circumstances. Bureaucratic inertia reigns and only cosmetic adjustments are made in response to shifting donor priorities and new developments in recipient countries. With the exception of the World Bank, the IMF and some regional development banks, the in-house policy research, design and advice capacities of international organizations are inadequate. Many international organizations are incapable of developing or absorbing new ideas, of learning from mistakes, and of evaluating results and assessing effectiveness.*

- *There is little accountability on the part of international, bilateral and developing country agencies. Monitoring and evaluation focus primarily on budgetary matters and on individual projects. The reporting requirements of different organizations waste the time and scarce resources of agencies and recipients in developing countries. International agencies and organizations compete with each other by recruiting qualified developing country staff to manage their specific programmes, leaving the very poorest countries in particular with little capacity to design and manage programmes on their own and to interact with those of international agencies and organizations. An emphasis on achieving short-term 'results' in the poorest countries, justified partly as a way of building domestic constituencies in donor countries for development assistance, has backfired because of the paucity of highly visible and immediate 'achievements' and has displaced resources away from long-term capacity-building initiatives that could lead to lasting changes.*

- *FDI and portfolio flows remain highly concentrated in a few emerging countries, which are still highly vulnerable to financial crisis, triggered, in most cases, by circumstances beyond their control. Many emerging and middle-income countries have experienced sudden capital withdrawals more than once during the decade, as skittish and volatile capital markets redirected short-term capital flows to what were perceived as less risky options at the time. Few middle-income countries have managed to acquire an investment grade rating for their debt issues, which has restricted their access to international capital markets, and there have been no significant financial innovations that could facilitate such access.*

- *Despite many proposals and some attempts by the international financial institutions (for example, through new guarantee programmes), it has proven exceedingly difficult to mobilize private investment to the poorer countries. Just a handful of investment funds for infrastructure in Africa and Asia remain in operation and these have mobilized only a limited amount of resources. One consequence has been a 'race to the bottom' between middle- and low-income countries that are bending over backwards to offer tax, infrastructure and other incentives to attract foreign investors.*

- *Foundations and charitable donations (especially from religious groups) provide a significant share of private flows to poor countries, and remittances have grown to become the most important sources of external financing for many developing countries.*

- *Experimentation with new development financing schemes has been brought almost to a halt, after a proliferation of partnership arrangements led to increased programme overlap and duplication, wasting effort and resources. Determined opposition to automatic financing mechanisms by powerful donor countries has succeeded in stifling research and studies on this subject.*

After an intensive international campaign to promote the MDGs in the early and mid-2000s, and despite subsequent attempts to downplay the importance of the specific targets and to emphasize progress in their direction, by 2015 the failure to achieve these goals has generated a mood of pessimism and disillusion with development assistance. The emphasis placed on selectivity and performance-based lending by some key bilateral agencies, coupled with the meagre increases in development assistance, has left several poorly performing countries bereft of external financing and with no hope of advancing towards the MDGs. In addition, the provision of external financing to developing countries has not been usually accompanied by efforts to improve domestic resource mobilization, with the result that most low-income and poor countries remain heavily dependent on development assistance. Moreover, the inability of the international community to reach agreement on institutional and financial proposals to improve the provision of global and regional public goods has contributed to the gloomy assessment of the prospects for international development cooperation.

* * *

The messy and dysfunctional character of bilateral agencies, international organizations and private investors in the *Inertia* scenario leaves no doubt that outcomes, results and impacts are well below what could be potentially achieved. High transaction costs, inter-organizational friction and excessive management and reporting burdens on developing countries, all generate irritation. This is exacerbated, on the one hand, by high expectations out of line with real performance, which lead to frustration and, on the other, by low expectations (sometimes bordering on cynicism) that discourage reform efforts.

4.2.2 Limited reforms

The second scenario describes a situation in which a minimum of reforms have been put into effect, there is a modest – but still clearly inadequate – increase in resource flows to developing countries, and in which most reforms are increasingly aimed at the plight of the poorest countries but exclude lower middle-income and middle-income countries. Narrow, short-term security agendas continue to crowd out those related to long-term and sustainable development. There has been change for the better and there might be light at the end of the tunnel, but improvements are too limited and fragile to arouse enthusiasm and maintain commitment.

The way in which the institutions, financing instruments and groups of countries involved in development financing behave and interact with each other can be described in the following terms:

- *A number of partial reforms allow international agencies and organizations to improve coordination in the field, particularly in the poorest countries and those that demand special attention from donors (e.g. post-conflict and natural disasters cases). However, the situation has not changed for other low- and middle-income countries, where lack of coordination and limited resources continue to lead to programme fragmentation, inter-agency rivalries, and pervasive inefficiencies.*
- *Bilateral aid agencies account for about 50 per cent of ODA flows as multilateral and international institutions begin to improve their effectiveness, and as a few donors decide to channel more resources through them. Tying of aid has been slightly reduced and some agencies have begun, albeit in a rather timid way, to experiment with new and more open approaches to the provision of technical assistance.*
- *Resource limitations are still acute and do not foster cooperative behaviour between agencies and organizations. Discussions about curbing the proliferation of trust funds have advanced significantly, and a couple of UN programmes and agencies have seen steady increases in their core budgets. Pressures to shift multilateral bank assistance from concessional loans to grants have been resisted with partial success and, although the size and effectiveness of soft loan windows have been reduced, they have not disappeared or become completely ineffective.*
- *Even though policies, decisions and priorities are still primarily defined on the basis of donor country political and economic concerns, these have become aligned with the problems and aspirations of the poorest countries. Consultation processes between donors and recipients have become more frequent and coordination between international agencies and*

organizations has improved, especially in the field and in some 'flagship' programmes.

- *While in-house policy and research capabilities still require strengthening in most agencies, a few of them have advanced substantially and are exercising leadership and providing credible alternative policy prescriptions to developing countries. This has had an impact on programme design and implementation, and has allowed a breaking of the hold of the 'Business as Usual' attitude in several development assistance institutions.*

- *Accountability has improved to a limited extent, and focuses on a few programmes and countries where agencies have adopted these partial reforms. Emphasis is still placed on the efficiency of resource use, but the evaluation of results and effectiveness has begun to make headway.*

- *Improvements in organizational features still remain piecemeal and patchy, and depend almost exclusively on the support of a few key donors, foundations and agency leaders. They are not backed by institutional reforms that could provide durable support for a transformation of the development financing system. Lack of flexibility and inertia prevail, organizational learning is rare, and rivalries between agencies and programmes lead to inefficiencies.*

- *While private sector flows still remain focused on a few of the larger developing countries, new financial instruments have succeeded in broadening the range of options available to mobilize private resources to poor countries. Guarantee schemes, interest rate subsidies, socially responsible investment regimes, special investment funds and similar mechanisms have induced investors in international capital markets to increase their exposure in low-income countries, while political, currency and regulatory risk mitigation instruments have increased FDI in these countries.*

- *In spite of a major proposal to establish institutional and financial arrangements for the provision of international public goods, determined opposition by a few powerful countries has succeeded in limiting these initiatives to a few regional arrangements, mostly in Europe and Latin America. The possible trade-offs between providing funds for development assistance and providing them for the provision of international public goods have been vastly exaggerated by opponents of the latter, who have managed to enlist many developing country representatives in their cause. In a similar vein, and notwithstanding the efforts of an unusual coalition of developed and developing countries, proposals to establish international tax schemes have been stymied and studies on this subject have barely managed to attract support from a few foundations and forward-looking bilateral agencies.*

- *Foundations and charitable donations still play an important role, especially in the poorest countries, but their relative weight has diminished in relation to public and other private sources of finance. Remittances remain the dominant source of external financing for some countries with large emigrant populations, and the speed and reliability of such transfers has increased significantly, while their cost has been reduced.*

The MDGs campaign has proceeded by fits and starts, under heavy pressure, mostly from developed country NGOs, and hectoring by top UN officials. A handful of developing countries have clearly met these goals and are heralded as examples of what can be done to reduce poverty, but the majority of countries have managed to meet just one or two of the agreed targets. A variety of explanations are being offered to account for what is generally perceived as a failure of the MDGs campaign, but there is widespread agreement that donor countries bear much of the responsibility – primarily for not having provided the amounts of development assistance that were considered necessary to achieve the goals. The few countries that succeeded in meeting the MDGs did so as a result of an unusual combination of massive external financing, improved domestic resource mobilization, good strategies and policies, and vastly improved governance. Despite prodding from many advocacy groups and activists in developed and developing countries, donors and the international community in general are in no mood to launch a new worldwide campaign to improve the lot of poor people in the developing world.

* * *

In the *Limited Reforms* scenario, bilateral agencies, international organizations, financial institutions and private sector investors, considered as a whole, have marginally improved their effectiveness, primarily as a result of piecemeal but visible reforms, and of better co-ordination – especially in the poorest countries. These marginal improvements offer a glimmer of hope for the reform of the international development system. Yet there is a long way to go before these improvements are widely adopted and become the norm. High expectations and frustration, together with low expectations and scepticism, still characterize the prevailing attitudes towards the international development system.

4.2.3 Major reforms

The third scenario describes a situation in which substantive reforms succeed in changing several key features of the international development financing system, there are significant resource increases – which nevertheless remain insufficient, and in which reforms benefit all types of developing countries. The breadth and scope of improvements is noticeable and the international development community has been capable of sustaining commitment to reform.

The way in which public and private institutions, financing instruments and groups of countries involved in development financing behave and interact with each other can be described in the following terms:

- *Reforms of the international development financing system are still partial, but much more balanced, extensive and profound. Under the leadership of key like-minded countries, of several international institutions, of a few international civil society organizations and of a couple of major private foundations, a critical mass of commitment has been mobilized to improve the way in which development finance operates. This has taken place against significant opposition, and reforms advance as far as to the point where they collide with powerful political, strategic, ideological or economic interests.*

- *There is better coordination and a more sensible division of labour between agencies and organizations in many field locations and, to a limited extent, at headquarters. Some significant institutional mergers and exits have occurred and others are receiving serious examination. An orientation towards results and effectiveness provides a more rational basis for cooperation between agencies, which includes the frequent design and execution of joint programmes. However, there are still some holdouts that insist on 'doing their own thing' and refuse, for a variety of reasons (autonomy, finance, personalities, brand name, patronage), to coordinate and work jointly with other institutions in the international development system.*

- *Bilateral agencies account for about 45 per cent of ODA flows, as more effective multilateral and international delivery systems are now in place and a greater proportion of aid is channelled through them. This has also helped to reduce the tying of aid and, in particular, of technical assistance, which has become more focused, transparent and efficient, and in which technical cooperation between developing countries financed by bilateral agencies plays a growing role.*

- *Priorities are defined in a more sensible and balanced way, primarily through joint efforts and meaningful dialogue between international agencies and donors on the one hand, and different groups of developing countries on the other. This has allowed significant efficiency improvements and has reduced overlap and duplication.*

- *International agencies and organizations have become more flexible and adaptive. Evaluation processes have now been generalized and widely accepted, thus enhancing organizational learning capacities. Significant improvements in the functioning of several bilateral agencies and UN programmes show that reform is possible, although persistent turf battles and conflicts still block the path towards comprehensive institutional reforms.*

- *Even though private foundations and corporations, together with international civil society organizations, play a more active and substantive role in international development finance, their interactions with official agencies remain problematic. This is primarily because of differences in accountability procedures, organizational culture and a mismatch in objectives and time horizons. This leads to improvements in the access to financial resources for a broader range of developing countries, but the contribution of the private sector could be much more substantive if some of these difficulties were to be removed.*

- *Private flows to developing countries have increased significantly and become more stable, and are spread more evenly between the different categories of developing countries. Thanks to a number of innovations in financial instruments, including guarantees provided by MDBs, private flows to middle-income and, to a lesser extent, to poor countries have increased. Better and more diverse policy advice, together with greater co-ordination between developing countries, has prevented a 'race to the bottom' to attract foreign investment.*

- *The ranks of emerging and middle-income countries with investment grade ratings have increased significantly, which has allowed their governments and firms to issue bonds and other debt instruments in the international capital markets. A wave of innovation in capital markets, in particular the generalized use of GDP-linked developing country bonds, has allowed a better match between levels of indebtedness and payment capacity, thus smoothing external capital flows and expanding developing country access to private sources of capital.*

- *Remittances continue to play a major role in development finance for many developing countries. Joint efforts between the governments of developed countries that host emigrants and developing countries where they originate have succeeded in improving the flows of remittances, lowering the cost of transfers and also in leveraging these resources to a certain extent through matching grants.*

- *Private corporations, together with international civil society organizations and foundations, play a more active and substantive role in international development finance, and this has led to improvements in access to financial resources for a broader range of developing countries. Nevertheless, the interactions between corporations, NGOs, foundations and official agencies remain problematic, primarily because of differences in accountability procedures, organizational culture and a mismatch in objectives and time horizons. This continues to place limitations on the contribution that private sector entities could otherwise make.*

- *Several foundations – particularly the large ones – have succeeded in leveraging their endowments and resources by partnering with bilateral and multilateral institutions, have helped to renew and innovate the design and implementation of development assistance programmes, and have also succeeded in launching some pilot schemes for the financing and provision of regional and global public goods.*

The MDGs campaign has been considered a modest success. It has been able to mobilize and focus political will on achieving specific targets regarding poverty reduction and improvements in the quality of life; as a result, many developing countries were able to meet a few of these targets. Although increases in development aid were allocated primarily to the poorest countries, several large lower middle-income countries with a large proportion of poor people also received substantial assistance. This has been credited with achieving an overall but modest reduction in the absolute number of poor people in the world. Substantive progress has also been made in advancing towards the 0.7 per cent target for ODA, particularly in the European countries.

* * *

In the *Major Reforms* scenario there is a significant and visible change for the better in the performance of bilateral agencies, international organizations and private investors. The effectiveness of the system has improved noticeably, expectations are broadly in line with results and scepticism about the international development enterprise has somewhat diminished. Yet there are persistent critics, most prominently in the international media and in political circles in some major donor countries, who view development assistance as a misguided and counterproductive enterprise, and whose political influence may reverse the progress achieved in this scenario.

4.2.4 Transformation

The fourth scenario describes a situation in which a critical mass of reform efforts have acquired a momentum of their own, and have succeeded in making the international development financing system much more efficient and effective through fundamental and sustainable changes. The structure of the system comprises a much more coherent set of well-established and innovative institutional arrangements and financing mechanisms, all of which have succeeded in more than doubling financial flows to developing countries. By 2015 these reforms have led to a richer and more structured set of institutional arrangements, broadly along the lines of 'Comprehensive Reform' outlined in section 3.2.2 of chapter 3. They have also managed to create a broader and more nuanced set of financial instruments that now find their specific uses in different types of developing countries. Determined and concerted leadership was required to achieve the critical mass of reforms, many of which faced opposition from some influential and powerful players.

The way in which the institutions involved in development financing behave and interact with each other can be described in the following terms:

- *Broad and comprehensive reforms extend to most international and regional agencies and organizations, leading to an institutional rationalization with major mergers and exits, more effective programmes, better coordination of policies and mandates, and improved accountability. Only a very few and marginal agencies remain recalcitrant and impervious to the reform movement. Temporary programmes with sunset clauses, continuous monitoring and periodic evaluations become the norm and allow for the weeding out of failures without excessive cost or delay. In addition to budget and financial matters, accountability focuses on results and effectiveness. Harmonized reporting procedures allow interagency comparisons and reduce the burden on developing countries.*
- *Clearer mandates and a more adequate division of labour, both at headquarters and field levels, allow for more effective coordination and harmonization of institutions in the international development financing system, reduce transaction costs and improves efficiency, and generate positive synergies in a large number of countries, sectors and problem areas.*
- *Bilateral aid agencies account for less than 40 per cent of ODA flows and the proportion of aid channelled through multilateral organizations has increased, primarily because many of them have improved their effectiveness and earned the trust of donor countries. Tying of aid has been reduced and most bilateral agencies have transformed the way in which they provide technical assistance. Support for technical cooperation among developing countries, reductions in the number of donor country experts involved, and a more balanced process for identifying, designing and carrying out technical assistance programmes have become the norm.*
- *Priorities are defined in a collaborative manner through close interactions between, on the one hand, international agencies, private sector entities and civil society organizations and, on the other, the different types of developing countries. The views and preferences of these*

countries are expressed not only individually, but also through groups that are determined on the basis of their capacities to mobilize domestic and external financial resources. Checks and balances mitigate the disproportionate power of some countries to set the agenda and priorities of the international development system. International and multilateral institutions are more open, transparent and democratic, and are considered the preferred option for the design of development programmes and initiatives.

- *Several international and regional agencies are streamlined and consolidated, which leads to increased core resources and more predictable funding. Collaborative programmes between international organizations and multilateral development banks have become quite frequent, especially at the regional and sub-regional levels. Pilot tests of automatic financing mechanisms have been launched in some regions and for some specific problem areas.*

- *The policy, management and strategic planning capabilities of most agencies and organizations have improved significantly. Increased inter-agency cooperation leads to greater exchange of information and better decision making. Experimentation and innovation are encouraged and promote organizational learning, which now takes place across official, private and civil society organizations.*

- *A richer set of financial instruments, backed by a capital increase in the early 2010s, has allowed the World Bank to renew and expand its role in middle-income countries, while increases in lending have helped to offset the negative net flows of the mid-2000s. The World Bank has largely abandoned its 'one-size-fits-all' policy recommendations and lending instruments, adopting a more nuanced and country-based approach to the use of financial instruments. Rigid graduation criteria have been abandoned in all MDBs. As a result, the World Bank, the RDBs and the SRDBs employ a large variety of financial instruments, ranging from balance of payments support loans to grants, and from guarantees to equity positions, in all types of borrowing countries.*

- *As financial innovation has broadened the range of instruments to channel resources to developing countries, international capital markets and private firms have become fully engaged in development financing and work side by side with official institutions. Private foundations, which can take more risks, continue to explore new avenues for development financing, often in concert with multilateral, international and bilateral organizations. This has been the case for possible automatic financing mechanisms and has led to the creation of public markets closely linked to the provision of regional and global public goods. Charitable donations remain an important source of finance, but these now focus primarily on a few very poor countries experiencing severe crises.*

- *In several developing countries remittances have been fully integrated into their domestic financial systems, and often act as catalysts for the provision of local public goods with resources matched from official sources.*
- *Initiatives to finance the provision of global and regional goods have led to the creation of specific accounts within the few consolidated special purpose (vertical) funds that remain, and innovative financing mechanisms have been put in place to support the provision of these international public goods.*
- *As a result of several academic studies and of the work of an international task force on stable sources of development financing that was created in the early 2010s, the general principle that development assistance should rely more on automatic sources of funds (international taxes and fees, creation of markets) has begun to be accepted in official circles, even though it is still a long way from being implemented.*

There have been major advances towards achieving the MDGs, and – although many developing countries fell short of meeting specific targets – tangible progress has kept optimism alive and has created a positive climate for international development cooperation. These targets have been credited with mobilizing public and private support for international development during the late 2000s and early 2010s, and negotiations are under way to expand the initial set of MDGs. The relative success in increasing official and private financial flows to developing countries has underscored the need for institutional arrangements and financing instruments aimed at improving domestic resource mobilization and absorption capacity, which has become one of the key objectives of development financing.

* * *

In the *Transformation* scenario there are vast and recognizable improvements in the functioning of the international development financing system. Success in improving living standards in several countries and credible advances towards achieving the MDGs mobilize support and restore confidence in the international development enterprise. The gap between expectations and performance is reduced as performance improves and expectations become more realistic. Only a small (but still influential) core of critics and cynics find themselves increasingly at odds with mainstream thinking and public opinion.

Although it is possible to posit an even more desirable and revolutionary scenario, *Transformation* configures a preferred set of outcomes that may also qualify as a realistic and achievable 'vision' for development finance. Whether by 2015 there has been substantive progress towards *Transformation* starting from the current situation will depend – not only on the power relations context and on circumstances, but also on the leadership and ability of those pushing for reform. Clear objectives and strategic directions, careful assessment of interests, identification of winners and losers, persistence combined with flexibility and a capacity to organize support coalitions – together with good timing and luck – are all essential to guide the complex decisions and choices to be made in reforming the international development financing system.

With a sense of perspective, the difference between the situation of the development financing system in the late twentieth century and that depicted in the *Transformation* scenario for 2015, could be viewed as analogous to the difference between the situation of the system of international organizations in the late 1930s and that prevailing in the early 1950s. It is worth noting that, in addition to the impact that the Great Depression and the Second World War had in raising awareness of the need for concerted action, it took audacious, forward-looking and determined intellectual and political leadership to bring about those institutional changes.

4.3 A framework for strategic choices

The main strategic question derived from the description of the four scenarios in the preceding section is how to move from *Inertia* towards *Transformation*. This transition involves intermediate steps through *Limited Reforms* and *Major Reforms* and will be the result of the initiatives and actions of many actors on the international scene. Even though the likely paths for the evolution of the development financing system will traverse through the two intermediate scenarios, exploring the conditions under which the improbable feat of leapfrogging towards *Transformation* is achieved may yield interesting insights.[1]

Chapter 3 set out a rich menu of possible reforms available to policy and decision makers to improve the international development financing system. A key question of how to proceed on this menu entails choosing possible strategic issues and directions based on judgements of viability, efficacy and impact. The choices made should reinforce each other, leverage further reforms, produce visible results and generate sustainable and swift progress towards achieving the situation depicted in the *Transformation* scenario. The ideal of *Transformation*, however, will necessarily prove elusive in the complex context of international development finance. Falling short of the ideal, a pragmatic approach would involve careful selection from a full agenda of strategic issues of a limited number of initiatives that might be realized within a five- to seven-year time horizon. Although such an approach would be piecemeal and gradual, its aim would be to bring about incremental and sustainable changes that would mutually reinforcing and that would aggregate over time to systemic transformation. Preferences and values will, of course, enter swiftly at this stage, for attitudes and commitments to development assistance will bias the choice of strategic issues.[2]

The task now is to derive from this analysis and the heuristic logic of the scenarios a suggested framework of strategic choices and their implications. This follows and the choices have been grouped according to whether they relate primarily to institutional arrangements, financing instruments and country categories. This is a practical way of articulating strategic options, even though it is true that several of the issues are closely interrelated, some overlap, and some could be assigned to different categories.

4.3.1 Institutional arrangements

As indicated earlier, 'institutional arrangements' refers to the organizational architecture of the various entities that are involved in mobilizing and channelling financial resources to developing countries, and may be considered as the scaffolding on which to place financing instruments and link them to different categories of countries. Four strategic choices emerge as priorities among the many options for reforming institutional arrangements:

- *Support and press for reforms in the UN, regional organizations and other international organizations.* This relates, in particular, to the incremental but sustained reform efforts at the UN, the European Commission and other regional organizations. Increased and concrete expressions of support are necessary if the UN Secretariat and UN agency reforms outlined in chapter 2 are to be deepened or even sustained. This would imply consolidating the advances of recent years (e.g. professional recruitment of staff, results-based management, streamlined administrative procedures) and continuing to move forward more broadly (e.g. consolidation of programmes and institutions). It is also important to maintain the pace of reform and to regain the credibility of international and regional institutions, primarily because of their relative weakness in comparison to the international financial institutions. This will include, in particular, steps to improve coordination between agencies and organizations in the field (e.g. through UNDAF, PRSP, CDF) and to conduct studies, research and related activities that will offer rigorous and practical policy advice alternatives to the international financial institutions.

- *Devise and put in place institutions to deal with global and regional public goods.* The recent debates on the relationship between development assistance and the provision of global and regional public goods indicate the prominence that supranational concerns have acquired. The Report of the Task Force on Global Public Goods (see section 2.3) due in 2005 will help to define priorities and make recommendations on institutional and financial arrangements, and will also elucidate the question of how to provide and finance global and regional public goods without negatively affecting development assistance (see section 4.2.2).

- *Promote and champion international capital market institutional innovations* to better accommodate the financing needs of different types of developing countries. These would include the establishment of better procedures of sovereign debt restructuring, creating and expanding private investment funds (e.g. for infrastructure), leveraging aid commitments and endowments through bond issues and financial engineering techniques, and improved monitoring of macroeconomic and financial performance. Some of these would require extensive additional study and painstaking attention to detail before they could be considered for adoption. Financing such a study would incur very little cost and should be accorded urgent and high priority in order to sustain momentum.

- *Establish the G20 at the heads of state level.* The G20 group of finance ministers, which comprises the G7-G8 and the most important emerging economies, has had a short (since 1999) but encouraging track record as a free and open forum for the informal and open exchange of views and ideas on matters affecting global financial stability. The inclusion of large non-western nations, which represent the vast majority of the global population, to expand current arrangements at the G7/G8 level would help to re-focus the rather inward-looking perspective of what is perceived as an exclusive club of rich countries. Care should be taken to ensure that G20 meetings do not pre-empt decision making in other international fora, and that developing country members consult regularly with other developing countries in their regions whilst presenting their views to other G20 members. The G20 should not compete with other institutions or entities, but facilitate deliberation and decision in other fora.[3] Proposals have been made to establish periodic meetings of this group at the heads of state level (Box 4.1). The issue of how Europe would be represented in such a body is one that requires careful consideration.

- *Eschew the proliferation of single-purpose, free-standing special funds or secretariats* as a substitute for the reform of existing institutions. Such proliferation without mergers or market exits generally serves to increase transaction and coordination costs, the bulk of which fall on developing country administrations. Where special problems exist (e.g. the provision of international public goods, certain forms of humanitarian relief, conflict prevention, corruption, weak states) that cannot be addressed effectively through existing organizations, explore innovative institutional arrangements combining public, civil society and private organizations to deal specifically with such problems.

- *Explore innovative but time-constrained institutional arrangements to deal with special problems.* Temporary organizations, established for a particular purpose and a specific period, and with 'sunset clauses' to ensure they do not outlive their usefulness need to be examined carefully and could provide a response to bureaucratic rigidity, organizations outliving their usefulness and the high administrative costs of international organizations. They could be combined with lighter and more agile permanent entities, and can accommodate a variety of financial and administrative procedures adapted to specific needs.

- Address explicitly and *bring into the open some of the more obvious imbalances, conflicts and contradictions between different official channels for development finance,* such as the fact that there are no national constituencies for multilateral agencies. In particular, increasingly vocal and influential NGOs generally oppose openly or covertly the channelling of development finance through multilateral institutions, and their advocacy of grants instead of concessional loans includes strong elements of narrow self-interest.

Another institutional innovation that merits close observation is the deep involvement of the World Bank group and external actors in the Chad–Cameroon oil pipeline project, which involves US$3.7 billion of investment, and should generate US$1.2 billion for Chad and US$540 million for Cameroon over 25 years. This involvement includes capacity-building projects and a revenue management programme,

BOX 4.1. **The G20 at heads of state level**

The G20 is composed of ten industrial countries (the G7 countries plus Russia, Australia and the EU president) and ten emerging market economies (Argentina, Brazil, China, India, Indonesia, Korea, Mexico, Saudi Arabia, South Africa and Turkey), and has caught the attention of world leaders as a useful forum for policy dialogue.

Some of the structural reasons why it makes sense to establish a more representative and diverse group of countries to facilitate deliberation on issues of global concern include: demographic and economic changes, the new challenges posed by globalization, the key role played by emerging economies in economic and financial crises, and the significantly different cultural perspectives that are brought to the table.

It seems axiomatic that the urgent need to find global solutions to global problems will depend on arrangements that embrace diverse and rich perspectives, views and ideas coming from the different civilizations and cultural traditions that make up the world. The nations of the G20 include four Asian countries (China, India, Indonesia and Korea), three Islamic countries (Turkey, Indonesia and Saudi Arabia), three countries from Latin America (Argentina, Brazil and Mexico), and a leading country from Africa (South Africa). The G20 is a body that is more representative of the global population today, and more so yet of the world of the future.

The focus of the new G20 forum would be on global economic governance broadly construed to include trade, finance, health, environment, education, human security, poverty reduction, and conflict resolution and hence would go beyond the realm of ministers of finance. The G20 would provide guidance to the panoply of international organizations working on these issues, creating linkages between issues and institutions, facilitating coordination and a division of labour, creating more vision and strategic direction, and helping to settle conflicts. G20 meetings at ministerial-level could continue to meet twice a year, and ministers with different portfolios could rotate to accord with the pressing issues of the moment. These semi-annual ministerial-level meetings could prepare the agenda for the annual G20 heads of state meeting. This sequence would build on the experience and the success of the G20 since 1999 and provide new energy, a more representative structure, and greater legitimacy to global governance at the highest political level.

In particular, the G20 could allow a more fluid exchange of views on international development financing issues, building up and expanding the work it has done while meeting at the ministers of finance level. At the very least, its exchanges of views would clarify, facilitate and speed up deliberations and negotiations in other institutions that deal with financing issues. Canadian Primer Minister Paul Martin, who in his prior capacity as Finance Minister spearheaded the creation of the ministerial level G20 in 1999, has formally proposed the creation of the G20 at heads of state level in 2004.

Sources: Bradford and Linn (2004); Martin (2004); Centre for Global Studies /Centre for International Governance Innovations (CFGS/CIGI) report on the 'G20 at heads of state level meeting' (2004)

which aim to ensure that oil resources are channelled to health, education, rural development, infrastructure, water and the environment. Should such an intrusive scheme succeed, it may provide guidelines for achieving transparency in the use of external financing in resource-rich countries with weak and inefficient state institutions.

4.3.2 Financing instruments

Several key issues emerge in each of the eight groups of financing instruments that were described in chapter 3. But before examining these in turn, it will be useful to present an overview of the estimated annual revenues that the various financing instruments are generating or could generate. Figures are not strictly comparable and there may be a certain degree of double counting, for example, in contributions from private foundations and individuals, and in bilateral ODA and grants by NGOs. Nevertheless, the figures in Table 4.4 give an idea of the approximate order of magnitude of each financing channel.

FDI and workers' remittances provide the largest volumes of funds to developing countries, although the former appears to be highly concentrated in a few emerging countries and the latter in several mid- and low-income economies in certain regions of the developing world. Bilateral ODA, disbursements from international financial institutions, loans from commercial banks and access to capital markets are next in line, although if net flows instead of disbursements are considered, international financial institutions and commercial banks would drop down several notches. Grants from international institutions, foundations and NGOs, together with funds obtained from partnerships, close the ranks in terms of resources mobilized. Among the financing instruments that have been proposed but not yet put into practice, a carbon tax could generate the largest level of funding, with emissions trading coming second, well ahead of global lotteries and fees on the use of the global commons.

Bilateral instruments

Four principal strategic choices emerge when examining the use of bilateral instruments in development financing:

- *Increase bilateral ODA in a sustainable manner and significantly reduce bilateral debt.* Without action on these two crucial and interrelated issues it will be difficult to make any progress towards a more effective international development financing system. Donor countries should live up to the commitments made at the Monterrey summit

Table 4.4   Estimated annual revenues from development financing sources

Source	Total amount
1 Bilateral instruments	• Bilateral ODA in 2002 was US$40.7 billion, of which 97% or US$39.7 billion was in grants, and 39% of grants or US$15.5 was allocated to technical assistance. • Bilateral ODA in 2003 was US$49.5 billion, of which 99% US$49.1 was in grants, 35.3% of grants or US$17.3 was allocated to technical assistance.
2 International organizations and agencies (UN system, regional and other international organizations)	• Total UN system expenditures: US$12 billion in 2002. • Total in grants (mostly to developing countries): US$3.6 billion in 2002.
3 International financial institutions	
a. Multilateral development banks (World Bank, regional and sub-regional banks, and related institutions)	• World Bank and RDBs disbursed US$34 billion and SRDBs US$16.5 billion in 2002. • Net inflows of US$0.7 billion from WB and RDBs in 2002.
b. International Monetary Fund and regional monetary funds	• IMF net flows were US$14 billion in 2002 and US$8 billion in 2003. Only Latin America maintained large positive flows (US$11.9 billion in 2002 and US$11.4 in 2003). • Total available in IMF quotas: US$267 billion in 2002 and US$292 billion in 2003. Resources available from other monetary funds: US$3–4 billion in 2002.
4 Private sources	
a. Corporations	• FDI net flows: US$147 billion in 2002 and US$135 billion in 2003
b. Commercial and investment banks	• Total disbursements: US$23.4 billion in 2002 • Net inflows: US$–6 billion in 2002
c. Private foundations, not-for-profit and non-governmental institutions	• Grants by NGOs: US$12.3 billion in 2002 (To avoid double counting, this amount could be a good estimation of total private donations to developing countries)
d. Individuals	• Workers' remittances: US$88 billion in 2002 and US$93 billion in 2003.
e. Global and international lotteries	• A Global Lottery could generate US$5 billion per year, estimated in 2003.

Table 4.4   Estimated annual revenues from development financing sources (*continued*)

Source	Total amount
5 **International capital markets**	
a. Bonds and other debt instruments	• US$61.6 billion in gross issuance (US$33.4 billion in net inflows) in 2002
b. Equity investments	• US$16.3 billion in gross investment in 2002 • US$14.3 billion in net flows in 2002
6 **International taxes, fees and charges**	Potential revenues per year: • Carbon tax: US$130 billion; Bit tax: US$70 billion; Tobin tax: US$53 billion; Arms sales tax: US$2.5 billion • Airport ticket fee: US$2.2–0.8 billion; Geostationary orbit fee: US$14 billion
7 **Market creation**	• Emissions trade: US$20–40 billion of potential revenues per year for developing countries
8 **Global and regional partnerships**	• GEF: US$4.5 billion in grants (1991–2003) • Illustrative multi-donor pledges: Afghanistan US$8 billion, Iraq US$32–35 billion • Global Fund for AIDS, Malaria and Tuberculosis: US$2.1 billion disbursed since its creation in 2000. • IFF: up to US$50 billion annually for the period 2010–15, increasing gradually to that level between 2005 and 2010

Sources: See references in chapter 3, section 3.3.

and increase their bilateral financing beyond the specific Monterrey commitments that extend only to 2006. In addition to strong political will in the face of competing domestic demands for the use of limited resources, pressure from civil society and public opinion is essential to strengthen the resolve of political leaders. This should take place in parallel with additional and significant bilateral debt reduction initiatives, especially in the poorest countries. The multilateral portion of this debt has been reduced substantially over the past three years, but the bilateral portion has not followed suit. However, as some donor countries are opposed to additional debt reduction, burden-sharing problems and difficulties will continue to emerge.

• *Clarify the relation between the EU development budget, the European Development Fund, and European bilateral aid.* European nations are perhaps the most important actors in the process of reshaping the international development financing system. This is not only because of the high proportion of bilateral ODA they represent, but also because they can exert influence on the development financing system through direct bilateral interventions and through joint EU initiatives. A restructuring of the relations between European bilateral and regional entities should include harmonization of practices, policy coordination and joint positions in international development financing discussions and negotiations. In a sense, this would involve combining bilateral interventions with actions in a *m*ultilateral forum with small 'm' (Europe) to influence Multilateral institutions with a capital 'M' (UN, World Bank, IMF).

- *Reduce bilateralization of multilateral aid.* This would require a reduction in the number and a rationalization of bilateral trust funds established in international and multilateral institutions. The greater control and visibility they give to donor countries is offset by the higher transaction costs, the weakening of multilateral institutions (especially in the UN system), and by a distortion of developing country priorities. Progress on this issue is closely related to increases in core funding for UN agencies and programmes.
- *Revamp technical assistance.* Too large a proportion of bilateral aid (about a third) is still allocated to conventional technical assistance, which is often tied to the use of donor country consultants. Apart from its donor-driven character, this form of bilateral assistance has a number of undesirable consequences for capacity building in the recipient countries. While ideas have been put forward on how to revamp long-standing technical assistance practices, vested interests and the support provided by donor consulting firms and consultants to aid budgets, make such reforms an uphill proposition (Fukuda-Parr, Lopes and Malik 2002; Berg 1993).

Action on these four strategic choices should be complemented by often-repeated – but seldom heeded – calls for better coordination among donors, increased participation of developing countries in programme design and delivery, and greater independence of bilateral agencies from the dominant ideas and policy prescriptions of the World Bank and the IMF.

UN, regional and other international organizations.

There are two major strategic choice issues that emerge when considering the role that these institutions can play in development financing:

- *Consolidation of mandates, lines of work, programmes and financing mechanisms.* While some institutional reforms have begun to improve the efficiency of international organizations, particularly those in the United Nations system, there is a need to offer an independent assessment of the international development architecture, focusing on the mandates, lines of work, programmes and ways in which they fund activities in developing countries, which would lead to a more effective set of international institutions and agencies. While some bilateral donors have sought to develop their own visions of a more effective international system, an initiative that involved several 'like-minded' donors and leading developing countries could help design a more adequate set of institutional arrangements, mobilize the political will to advance in this direction, and improve the effectiveness of the grants provided by UN, regional and other international organizations to developing countries.

- *Funding patterns of international organizations: core vs non-core, and voluntary vs replenishment system.* The erosion of 'core' or freely disposable contributions to the budget of international institutions, together with the growth of complementary or 'non-core' funds allocated to specific purposes under the direct control of donors, distorts priorities, constraints decision making and undermines technical and professional capacities. The proliferation of non-core trust funds in international organizations increases transaction costs and raises cross-subsidy and free-riding questions, primarily because some donors do not pay the full cost of administering these trust funds (Bezanson and Sagasti 2002). It is necessary to increase and consolidate the core budget of those UN agencies and programmes that are performing reasonably well, while at the same time continuing to expand complementary resources. A first step towards rationalization would be to require full transparency and disclosure on all trust funds and that they include financing for the full core and incremental costs of their management and administration.

  Steps should also be taken to modify the annual cycle of voluntary contributions that provides funds to most international organizations. This implies starting discussions and possible negotiations to establish a multi-year, binding-pledge 'replenishment' model of funding for the core budget of some UN agencies and programmes (particularly the UNDP), along the lines suggested by COWI (2000). To take into account the fact that there will be serious burden-sharing problems to involve all donors in such a system, at least in the early cycles, the possibility of beginning with a 'shadow' exercise limited to a subset of donors (e.g. EU donors) could be explored. In addition, the experience of the IDA replenishment system contains many lessons that should be assimilated, including the major problem of inadequate developing country voice and representation. For this reason, developing country inputs should be sought at the early stages of the replenishment process, including the review of the previous cycle, the determination of the size of the replenishment and the definition of programme priorities.

Initiatives to address this overriding issue that affects the way in which international organizations operate should be complemented with greater efforts to consolidate their lines of work, programmes and projects, and maybe to merge some of these organizations. Programmes aimed at strengthening the policy research, design, implementation and management capacities of developing countries should have high priority, and be undertaken in parallel with initiatives to provide rigorous alternatives to the dominance of the policy prescriptions of the Bretton Woods Institutions.

International financial institutions

International financial institutions have been very active in developing new instruments, changing their product lines and in seizing opportunities to expand their reach. From the many strategic choices relating to the functioning of the MDBs, we have selected five:

- *A systemic perspective of the MDBs.* The MDBs are perhaps the most successful development financing institutional innovation of the mid-twentieth century. They have evolved into a 'family' comprising more than 25 global, regional sub-regional banks and special funds and programmes that mimic some of the features of the MDBs. Coordination and a better division of labour are now becoming more important, especially as the larger and older of these institutions have now moved into negative net transfer situations with their borrowers. The considerable expansion of the range of products and services provided by the World Bank, added to the decentralization of its operations, is leading to overreach and creating a rather loose collection of on-the-field variations on the standard set of instruments available to this institution (loans, grants, guarantees, policy dialogue, capacity building, technical assistance, consultative groups, and so on). In a similar way to the Meltzer Report (2000), but adopting a broader and more balanced perspective, it may be appropriate for an international group of experts to conduct a high-profile review of the functioning of the World Bank, taking into consideration its relations with other

MDBs, the IMF, the UN and other international organizations, bilateral donors and the private sector in general. This review would be commissioned by a leading group of developed and developing countries (perhaps the G20?).

- *Creation of sub-regional development banks.* This is closely related to the preceding issue. The lack of sub-regional development banks in Asia stands in clear contrast to the situation in other regions (which may be explained in part by the relatively high level of domestic savings in many countries of the region). While the Asian Development Bank has been quite active in the region and is generally well regarded, given the size and diversity of the Asian countries it is perhaps time to explore the desirability of establishing sub-regional MDBs in Asia, focusing on specific parts of this vast region. The possibility of creating a Middle East and Central Asia Development Bank has recently been raised in the US Congress,[4] but considering recent security and political developments a more appropriate sub-region to begin exploring this possibility would appear to be that bordering on North Korea and including the Tumen river basin (Box 4.2).

- *The future of concessional loans, multilateral debt reduction and IDA grants.* The debt burdens of poor countries have motivated the HIPC programme, several waves of bilateral debt reduction, and pressures to provide resources from IDA in the form of grants rather than concessional loans. Yet IDA loans contain a very high grant element, for they are long-term, low-interest and have extended grace periods. In addition, borrowing countries often have higher bilateral than multilateral debt burdens. Rather than compromising IDA's future by increasing the proportion of grants (which would reduce future credit reflows and make it even more dependent on donor country largesse), it may be useful to consider the possibility of 'restarting IDA'. This would involve bilateral or other donors buying down outstanding IDA debt, which would amount to a more extended version of credit buy-down schemes proposed for specific purposes such as polio eradication. The question of grants vs soft loans also has to be examined from the perspective of the fiduciary responsibility of donor and recipient countries. Official loan agreements bind multilateral institutions and recipient governments, thereby generating a level of commitment to the appropriate use of funds and policy reforms that is greater than that associated with grants, which could be provided either to government agencies or to NGOs in the recipient country.

BOX 4.2. **A possible Northeast Asian Development Bank (NEADB)**

The possibility that North Korea may end decades of isolation and join the international economic community has emerged in recent years. While tensions persist between North Korea and its neighbours, there have been several visits from senior officials from several governments (South Korea, China, Japan, United States), the United Nations, the European Union and international financial institutions. In addition, during the last few years, government authorities in North Korea have publicly expressed interest in joining the World Bank and the Asian Development Bank. Such membership could help considerably in securing not only financial resources, but also much-needed technical assistance and policy advice for economic policy reforms that could promote peace and security in one of the major problem spots in the world.

However, a number of difficulties may delay the full incorporation of North Korea into the international financial and economic community. Starting with reliable data about the state of its economy and with the disclosure of information, and continuing with an economic system ill suited for integration into the world economy and a lack of government officials with experience in international matters, the obstacles faced may make it difficult to quickly admit North Korea as a full member of the major international financial institutions. These factors are in addition to whatever political and security considerations may remain.

As an intermediate step it may be useful to explore the possibility of establishing a Northeast Asian Development Bank (NEADB) to focus on the subregion around the Tumen river basin, which, in addition to North Korea, includes parts of China, Russia and Mongolia. The NEADB could become a conduit to channel financial and other resources to support the upgrading of the physical infrastructure and the human resources in this region, particularly in North Korea. The NEADB would incorporate countries with substantive interest in the region including South Korea, Japan, the United States and Russia, and could be open to Canada and European countries. The NEADB would work closely with the Asian Development Bank, which has considerable expertise in infrastructure and environment projects in the region, the European Bank for Reconstruction and Development, which has considerable experience in promoting private sector development in transition economies, and with the World Bank, which has experience in policy reforms. The work done by UNDP through the 1990s in the Tumen Region, which included preparing several transport project profiles, could provide a basis for identifying the first set of operations for the NEADB.

The creation of such an institution would allow a step-by-step incorporation of North Korea into the international financial community, while at the same time channelling much-needed resources, technical assistance and policy advice during the initial stages of the transformation of its economy. Considering the experience of other sub-regional development banks, a total authorized capital of the order of US$3–4 billion, of which only a fraction needs to be paid in, should be more than enough to begin operations for the

---

BOX 4.2. **A possible Northeast Asian Development Bank (NEADB)** (*continued*)

Northeast Asian Development Bank. This would allow borrowing resources in the international capital markets for public investment projects, to provide comfort to private investors through guarantees and other services, to ensure co-financing from interested donor countries, and to provide grants for the provision of sub-regional public goods and technical assistance.

Sources: Bezanson and Sagasti (2000); Sagasti (2002b); UNDP Tumen River Area Development Programme website http://www.tradp.org\tsiteind.htm; *The Economist* (13 March 2004, 41–3)

- *Expanding liquidity provision arrangements for developing countries.* This is a task for the IMF, which has at its disposal the means to increase the level of resources that poor countries could draw upon for development purposes. In addition to creating and allocating Special Drawing Rights, there is the possibility of selling part of the IMF gold reserves and allowing developing countries to have access to these resources. Yet, for these possibilities to materialize, it will be necessary to overcome the resistance of key shareholders.

- *Exploring greater voice and representation of developing countries in international financial institutions.* This is a perennial issue in discussions about the operations of the World Bank and the regional development banks. The complex and heavy governance structures of these institutions that are owned by their member states rest ultimately in their relative numbers of shares and voting power. Periodic adjustments have been introduced in the number of shares owned by each member country but, in most cases, the wealthier non-borrowing countries hold the majority of shares. This reflects the initial contributions made by the Bank founders in the form of callable and paid-in capital, which has been adjusted as the Bank's capital increased and new member states joined. But over time, MDBs have also used a major portion of their net income to strengthen their capital and reserves, thereby not requiring additional capital contributions from their members. MDB income is obtained from the interest on outstanding loans to developing countries and from the return on the investments they make in capital markets. The contribution of each source of income has varied with changes in market conditions, but the fact remains that a significant slice of MDB income now comes from the interest paid by the borrowing members, and part of that income is used to shore up the capital base. It could thus be argued that, in addition to their capital contributions, borrowing countries would be entitled to additional shares in proportion to the interest they paid over time to the bank, weighted by the share of net income that has been allocated to capital and reserves. Box 4.3 presents an illustrative calculation of how the voting power of the 20 top shareholders of the World Bank would change if such a contribution were to be considered.

In addition, there are some issues that pertain to the way in which the IMF relates to developing countries and the role it plays in establishing and monitoring compliance with national financial accounting norms and standards. Countries with access to MDB funds have suggested changes in the national accounting rules established by the IMF, which would allow them to mobilize additional investment resources from these institutions. A pilot scheme to test such changes was underway in Brazil in 2004.

Private sources

Private sources comprise a diverse and rapidly changing set of financial instruments that have received a great deal of attention recently. In addition to general measures to promote FDI and attract private donations (improving the investment climate, greater transparency, and so on), three strategic priorities emerge:

- *Enhancing private foreign investment for infrastructure.* Investments in Public infratructure and utilities have been severely neglected in most developng countries and these are areas that could easily absorb significant new investment resources. This is an area where additional interventions could help to create an appropriate risk-reward structure over the lifetime of projects that could attract significant increases in private sources of capital and in the range of countries benefiting from it. In particular, guarantee schemes at the national, regional and international levels could lead to significant increases in private sector flows to this area, which could absorb a large amount of investment resources. These should be complemented by transparency in bidding process, adequate regulation, and guarantee mechanisms (Box 4.4).
- *Remittances and their possible link to the provision of local public goods.* Although these funds have emerged as one of the main sources of external finance for several developing countries, they generally take place in small and dispersed amounts and usually cover con-

BOX 4.3. **Relative voting power of the top 20 shareholders of the International Bank for Reconstruction and Development (IBRD): existing and hypothetical (considering additional developing country contributions to the capital base through loan income)**

Several mechanisms have been proposed to enhance the voice and participation of developing countries in the decision-making processes of the World Bank. Recently the Development Committee (2003) has compiled most of these initiatives and some of them have been discussed. Among these proposals, there is special mention of the governance structure reflected in the voting power of nations (Development Committee 2003).

In the case of the IBRD, one share of stock held corresponds to one vote. From the total of 1,618,661 shares, 46,000 (250 × 184 members), representing 2.8 per cent, are distributed equally among member countries, and the other 97.2 per cent of shares are distributed in proportion to the capital subscribed (composed of actually 'paid-in' and 'callable' capital that would be paid should the need arise). Changes in the composition of shares held imply changes in voting power. For example, at the founding of the IBRD the equally distributed shares represented 10.87 per cent of the total, but subsequent capital increases have altered the proportions of shares held by member countries and the distributed shares today stand at only 2.8 per cent.

IBRD capital and reserves increase not only by additional subscriptions, but also as a result of allocating a portion of net income for this purpose. As IBRD income is obtained from the interest paid by borrowers on IBRD loans and from the returns on the investments made in capital markets, borrowing countries contribute indirectly to increases in the capital base through loan income and the proportion of such income allocated to capital and reserves. The following table indicates what would happen if these indirect developing country contributions were added to their paid-in capital to recalculate voting power. Each member country would have a share of the total vote based on the sum of (i) their paid-in capital, plus (ii) the interest it paid for IBRD loans multiplied by a factor representing the proportion of interest income transferred to capital and reserves (0.28 on average for the last six years). The formula used to calculate this second component for each member country is:

'indirect contribution to the capital base' = [(loan income – borrowing expenses)/net income] × percentage of net income allocated capital and reserves.

sumption and current expenditures, although they are also used for small investments and debt servicing. Transfer costs are high, some flows take place through informal and unreliable channels, and they benefit only the family and relatives that receive them. It may be possible to reduce costs and increase reliability by inducing

---

BOX 4.3. **Relative voting power of the top 20 shareholders of the International Bank for Reconstruction and Development (IBRD): existing and hypothetical (considering additional developing country contributions to the capital base through loan income)** (*continued*)

The hypothetical results that emerge for the 20 top shareholders are:

Country	Actual	Hypothetical	Country	Actual	Hypothetical
Unites States	16.39	14.54	Indonesia	0.94	2.48
Japan	7.86	6.87	Saudi Arabia	2.78	2.44
India	2.78	4.00	Canada	2.78	2.44
Germany	4.49	3.95	Italy	2.78	2.44
United Kingdom	4.30	3.93	Netherlands	2.21	1.93
France	4.30	3.79	Argentina	1.12	1.58
China	2.78	3.34	Belgium	1.81	1.57
Brazil	2.07	2.86	Spain	1.75	1.50
Mexico	1.18	2.77	Switzerland	1.66	1.43
Russian Federation	2.78	2.65	Republic of Korea	0.99	1.33

Note: Only interest paid during the last ten years was considered in this illustrative example
Source: World Bank Annual Reports, various years.

---

senders to use formal channels (banks, savings associations), and it may also be possible to design institutional arrangements at the local level whereby a portion of remittances could be earmarked as a contribution to a local development fund. This would be matched by government authorities as a way of leveraging contributions, and used to provide local public goods (health facilities, sanitation, roads, water, education) under the supervision of the local residents to whom remittances have been sent.

- *Measures to promote FDI in poor countries*. While most foreign investment in production and service facilities in developing countries seeks efficiency, market or resource gains, the poorest countries generally attract only resource-oriented investments. Yet, it is possible

BOX 4.4. **Guarantee mechanisms to balance risk in public infrastructure projects**

Especially for the poorer countries, financing for public infrastructure projects experienced significant declines in the late 1990s and early 2000s. This resulted from the changed priorities of donors, including the World Bank, towards direct investments in poverty reduction. It also resulted from a retreat of private sources of investments as a consequence of financial crises, the unstable investment environment in developing countries, the increased risk aversion of investors and the incapacity of host governments to fulfil their contractual obligations. To rebuild investor confidence it will necessary to address the regulatory and currency risks. This should be done in parallel with measures to develop local financial markets, which would reduce dependency on foreign sources of finance and at the same time help to restore the interest of private investors.

Guarantees are a key instrument for enhancing flows to infrastructure project finance, particularly in developing countries with limited access to external credit. Guarantees from donor countries or international financial institutions can catalyse private finance when other instruments do not suffice, particularly when projects involve significant currency and regulatory risks. These mechanisms relax private constraints and help to obtain the necessary financing for projects that would otherwise not be feasible. Guarantees shold be tailor-made to take into consideration market behaviour and imperfections; otherwise, they might undermine initiatives to enhance private capital flows for twomain reasons. First, they can neutralize incentives to choose only good projects, a clear sign of adverse selection, and also to run them efficiently. If governments bear the risk of failure, private investors would invest in projects that are potentially more profitable but more likely to fail and, having invested in a project, they may have little interest in maximizing its chance of success. Second, guarantees can impose excessive costs on the host and source countries' taxpayers or consumers and expose them to too much risk. Because guarantees rarely show up in the government's accounts or budgets, governments may not know the extent of their exposure.

Financial arrangements for infrastructure projects usually tie the output prices to an estimated dollar exchange rate and the revenues are contractually committed to increase with the host country's inflation rate. This structure imposes a considerable burden on project performance. In the event of a major currency depreciation it is unlikely that the end users in a developing country will be able to absorb the adjustments in local currency – or that the government will be able to provide subsidies – to maintain the price in dollars, euros or yen. Moreover, regulators may deny the tariff increases necessary to offset the devaluation and avoid default on the externally denominated debt.

One of the main challenges in the design of instruments to enhance private flows to developing countries is to deal constructively with the way risk is perceived, and the tendency that investors have not to dissociate the project and country risk. Currency mismatch risk, a usual feature of infrastructure

---

BOX 4.4. **Guarantee mechanisms to balance risk in public infrastructure projects** (*continued*)

projects, limits the credit rating of most projects below the ceiling of sovereign debt rating and in the early 2000s there are fewer investment-grade developing countries than in the mid-1990s. This problem is worsened by the fact that after several crisis episodes, fixed-income investors are increasingly reluctant to incorporate in their portfolio the type of non-investment-grade debt that could be issued by infrastructure projects.

Guarantee mechanisms can address these constraints and help to restore private flows to infrastructure finance. Liquidity facilities are an important step towards mitigating risk, by avoiding temporary cash flow problems. Local currency bonds can help develop capital markets and allow foreign investors to complement the external resources they bring. Sovereign guarantee pools would allow a group of countries to share risk, and may involve the creation of a joint risk assessment and guarantee agency.

Source: Griffiths-Jones and Lima (2004)

---

to design instruments that would make it attractive for foreign investors to move into developing countries (Mistry and Olesen 2003). This would involve, among other initiatives, increasing the level of resources of risk insurance agencies, creating a EU-wide risk cover agency and providing tax credits to private investors.

Some complementary issues in the mobilization of private flows include, first, the importance of harmonizing incentives (i.e. achieving enforceable international agreement on a set of norms and standards) to attract external capital, so as to avoid a 'race to the bottom' between competing developing countries, particularly in natural resource projects where there is the temptation to provide generous tax incentives and to ignore environmental and labour regulations. Second, there is the need to review and adjust the provisions of the Basle II agreement to regulate capital requirements for banks, for it could hinder commercial bank lending to developing countries. Capital requirements for banks that lend to public institutions and private firms in countries with low-rated debt could rise significantly, and the market-sensitive measures associated with the Basle II accord could reinforce the pro-cyclical tendencies associated with commercial bank lending practices. Measures could be designed to fine-tune parameters such as the probability of default and risk weight for lower-rated borrowers, so as to mitigate the negative impact of this accord on the willingness of commercial banks to lend to developing countries.

International capital markets

The issues that emerge in relation to improving access to capital markets refer primarily to the creation of mechanisms to tap investor appetite for relatively more risky financial assets. In spite of the high growth and huge volume of capital markets – and of the great amount of talent and ingenuity that has been focusing on the creation of new financial instruments (Shiller 2003) – their characteristics and regulation are likely to encourage only a fraction of resources to flow to developing countries.

Although radical breakthroughs are unlikely, there are several issues that, if adequately addressed, could facilitate expanded (perhaps significantly) access to capital markets for some developing countries. These include:

- *Creation of special investment funds*, possibly with the participation of bilateral and multilateral development assistance agencies.
- Supporting programmes to *provide country debt ratings to a larger number of developing countries*, following on a recent initiative by the US Treasury Department and the UNDP for several African countries.
- Utilization *of financial engineering techniques* to transform payment flows and spread risk (e.g. securitizing multi-year pledges from donors; currency and interest swaps).
- Use of bilateral, multilateral or private foundation support to *guarantee interest payments on bonds issued by developing countries* or entities that channel funds to them. All of these should be complemented with measures to expand and strengthen developing country capital markets, linking them to their developed country counterparts.

International taxes, fees and charges

As noted earlier, numerous proposals have been made for financial instruments based on international taxes, fees and charges, but none has yet been implemented. The issues they provoke refer primarily to the amounts they are likely to raise, the difficulties in administering them, the technical problems involved and the political viability of the proposals. While these proposals usually do not focus primarily on generating resources for development purposes, but rather on questions such as mitigating climate change, reducing financial speculation and curbing the arms trade, they could also serve as development financing instruments.

- Among the international taxes that have been proposed, a *carbon tax* would appear to be the one with the greatest potential to make some headway during the next five to seven years, even though the obstacles it faces are formidable. Perhaps advantage could be taken of episodes of rising oil prices, when industries and consumers adjust to the new high levels, to introduce a modest tax that would be applied once (or if) prices come down to their historical trend. Moreover, it is likely that any move forward may require concerted action at the regional level, probably in an area where consumers are accustomed to relatively higher oil prices (e.g. the European Union). Whether a portion of the resources such a tax would generate could be earmarked for development purposes is another question.
- *Other taxes and charges*, for example, currency transactions, arms sales and charges for the use of the global commons, appear to be even further away. In any cases, although it remains improbable that global or regional tax schemes will be put in place in the near future, this is an issue that will continue to attract growing attention and will require further research and study.

Market creation

The two issues on the table in this group of financing instruments are, first, the expansion of *emissions trading systems* for greenhouse gases and the *clean development mechanism*, launched as a pilot project a few years ago and still in their incipient stage, and second, the *creation of public markets* for goods and services linked to the provision of international public goods.

- *Emissions trading and the clean development mechanism*. At present, emissions trading continues to function as a quite limited development mechanism, involving a small number of mostly Japanese companies, the government of The Netherlands and the Prototype Carbon Fund established at the World Bank. The recent ratification of the Kyoto Protocol, however, has opened the possibility of creating and emissions trading scheme in Europe in 2005 that will expand the number of developed country participants.

  Estimates of the amount of CO_2 traded indicate that this rose from 13 million tons in 2001, to 29 million tons in 2002 and to 78 million tons in 2003, and that investors purchased 64 million tons of carbon dioxide between January and May 2004[5] at a total cost of about \$260 million. This a modest sum, but as new players join the stage – prompted by the launching of the EU emissions trading scheme in 2005 and by the Russian ratification of the Kyoto Protocol – this figure could increase significantly. Nevertheless, as there are no international commitments to reduce greenhouse gases beyond 2012, and as offset projects in developing countries have long lead times, in the absence of further international agreements a window of opportunity for developing countries to benefit from emissions trading schemes may be closing.

- It is also possible to create *markets for public goods and services*, in particular those related to health. Bilateral agencies, international organizations, multilateral institutions and private foundations could create funds to guarantee the purchase of vaccines or treatments to address developing country illnesses, thus generating an incentive for private sector firms and academic institutions to engage in research and in the production of such goods and services. Initial steps in this direction have already been taken as part of the Global Alliance on Vaccines and Immunisation (GAVI).

Global and regional partnerships

The issues that emerge in this motley group of financial instruments are quite varied and indicative of the search for innovative approaches to development financing at the global, regional and local levels. Most of these instruments focus on particular topics, such as the special purpose global funds that have emerged in the last few years (for example, the Global Fund for the Fight against AIDS, Tuberculosis and Malaria). They involve the joint participation of bilateral agencies, multilateral institutions, private corporations, foundations and capital markets to varying degrees. Many of the proposals can be clearly related to the provision of global and regional public goods, and the pending final report of the *Task Force on Global Public Goods* is likely to make proposals on how to deal with some of the special purpose funds.[6] It is expected that a sharp differentiation will be made between resources allocated to development assistance and those assigned to the provision of global and regional public goods.

- *Special purpose global funds.* As new global and regional issues have emerged and acquired a sense of urgency, the reaction of several leading members in the international development community has been to propose the creation of global or regional funds (to fight diseases, promote clean energy, improve water supply, provide infrastructure, protect the environment, conserve biodiversity, and so on). While these funds have the advantage of focusing attention and raising resources rather quickly, their proliferation may lead to inefficiency (in spite of the aspiration to have lean administrative machineries) and intensify competition for scarce ODA. Moreover, the rationale for these appears to have a great deal to do with a desire to bypass existing institutions in which donors have low confidence or have lost confidence altogether. Perhaps it is not too early to think about a possible rationalization of these initiatives, seeking to group them into three or four 'general funds' (for example, for health, environment, knowledge generation and conflict prevention, among other possible themes). Each of these general funds could have several 'accounts' (for example, the health fund could have several disease-specific accounts) that would share common administrative and technical support services, but which may have slightly different governance procedures depending on their financing structure. While the general funds would be permanent, the individual accounts within each should be temporary entities, with clear sunset clauses. These general funds would be independent international organizations, but would work closely with the UN (and particularly the UNDP), the World Bank, the EU and other relevant UN specialized agencies and international institutions. Limited but significant experience has been gathered with the operation of some of these funds (e.g. Global Alliance for Vaccines and Immunisation, Global Fund for AIDS, Tuberculosis and Malaria), and this experience indicates that problems emerge when the governance cultures of official institutions, international organizations, private corporations and foundations converge in a single organization. A consolidation of specific purpose initiatives into a few general global funds may help in sharing information and spreading governance and management best practices.

- *Local and regional partnerships.* In addition to global fund initiatives, there are many special purpose funds that have been established to deal with local problems, and also proposals to create regional funds focused on specific themes. Among the first, grant giving and operational foundations, together with some NGOs, that support environmental programmes have a long tradition of cooperating with and funding conservation initiatives in biodiversity-rich developing countries.[7] Similarly, there are many partnerships between local governments, NGOs, foundations and private corporations to provide basic health services at the community level in many developing countries. Along a different track, there is a recent proposal to establish a regional trust fund through a partnership between bilateral creditors and government agencies in the Andean region. This trust fund would initially be created with a contribution of 20 per cent of the outstanding bilateral debt of the Andean countries, would receive additional contributions from these countries, and would then issue bonds to tap capital markets. Bilateral creditors would receive full payment of the debt in the form of shares in the trust fund and may redeem these shares at a later stage. Investments in transport facilities at the regional level would be made through a 'regional infrastructure authority' and could involve concessions to private sector builders and operators (Government of Peru 2003).

- *The International Financing Facility and its variants.* In 2003 the UK Treasury and the Department for International Development proposed the creation of a facility to transform a stream of bilateral aid commitments over long periods of time into large contributions at the beginning of the period, which would be done by issuing bonds in capital markets. The general idea is to raise a large amount of funding – up to US$16 billion per year in 2010–15 – to front-load financing of initiatives to achieve the MDGs (Box 4.5). While the proposal appears attractive in principle, it has been the subject of considerable debate and faces several hurdles which are technical in nature (would bond issues count as part of public debt ceilings?), administrative (which entity will issue the bonds?) and political (would this bail out laggard bilateral donors?) in nature. Yet, it may be possible to scale down the size of this proposal, focus on specific development programmes that require considerable up-front investment, ensure the sustainability of subsequent current expenditures, involve a multilateral development bank to issue the bonds, secure bilateral donor commitment to cover the service of the bonds, request a private foundation to provide rolling guarantees for debt service, and engage in financial engineering to determine the most appropriate type of bond to be issued. Such an adaptation of the IFF proposal could work for projects such as water supply and sanitation, construction and operation of health facilities, provision of energy to rural areas, research into the production of vaccines, and similar initiatives. No major institutional changes would be required, resources could be linked to an 'account' of the special purpose 'general' global funds described above and the level of resources generated could be of the order of US$0.5–1 billion. At a later stage it may be possible to replicate and expand these limited facilities to approach the large scale of resource transfers envisaged in the original design of the IFF.

BOX 4.5. The International Finance Facility (IFF)

The IFF aims to bridge the gap between the resources that have already been pledged and what is needed to meet the MDGs by 2015. The Facility would be built on long-term donor commitments, comprising a series of pledges (each of them lasting 15 years) by donors for a flow of annual payments to the IFF. Annual commitments would start from the $15–$16 billion of aggregate Monterrey and post-Monterrey additional sums peldged and would rise by 4 per cent (in real terms) per year. Each pledge would be a binding commitment, in order to provide security against which investors could lend. On the back of these pledges – its assets – the IFF would issue bonds in its own name – its liabilities. For prudential reasons, therefore, the IFF will have to limit the degree to which the donor commitments would be levered; at each disbursement the Facility will allocate a fixed proportion of the donor commitment to that disbursement, taking into account the prevailing cost of long-term debt for the IFF in the donor country's currency and the leverage limit.

The Facility would thus front-load long-term aid flows so that the MDGs could be financed and reached by 2015. The IFF would serve the function of a temporary finance facility; it would be replenished at regular intervals and, at each replenishment, donors would make a fresh series of annual long-term funding pledges (each lasting 15 years) as the basis for further borrowing. After raising and disbursing funds for 15 years, the repayment phase would continued for another 15 years. The Facility would be wound up by 2030. The funds to be raised by donor commitments and by market borrowing could be quickly disbursed through existing mechanisms, in the form of grants rather than loans. It is notable that the IFF would not disburse funds directly to recipient countries, but would instead provide funds for disbursement (subject to conditionally) by existing aid delivery channels which would act as agents on behalf of the IFF.

A key advantage of the IFF proposal is its revenue-raising potential. The facility could double existing ODA from $50 to $100 billion per year during the crucial period 2010–15. Another advantage of the IFF is that it accelerates grant finance rather than loans to the recipient countries participating in the IFF. Another positive potential of the IFF lies in the need for donor coordination, avoiding the need for poor countries to court myriad donors and deal with different regulations.

A weak point of the IFF is that it destabilizes the time profile of aid commitments: The IFF proposes to borrow funds in order to achieve a faster increase in aid in the short term at the cost of reducing future aid when the funds have to be repaid. Growing pension and social security burdens in ageing OECD countries, for example, mean that the opportunity cost of aid will be rising for most donor countries; hence, a continuous commitment to the IFF might be difficult to sustain.

Source: Reisen (2004).

All of these innovative proposals involve, to a greater or lesser extent, the participation of bilateral donors and would require increases beyond their current levels of ODA. This raises the vexing question of 'additionality', especially in light of the commitments made by bilateral donors to increase their levels of aid. In the last analysis, unless donor countries account separately for their contributions to these partnerships – for example, using their health or environment ministries' budgets – the contributions will all have to come from the ODA envelope, and as such will compete with other bilateral assistance priorities. This is particularly the case when large-scale humanitarian assistance and relief operations are undertaken, such as those that took place at the beginning of 2005 following the Indian Ocean tsunami tragedy.

4.3.3 Types of countries

A third group of issues derived from the description of the scenarios relates to the categorization of developing countries, and involves asking whether current institutional arrangements and financing instruments correspond to the particular needs of each group. A move from *Inertia* towards *Transformation* involves devising classification schemes that could help to better match institutions and instruments to country types. As indicated in section 3.4 of chapter 3, categories based on average per capita income levels or debt service burdens may not be most appropriate, especially if a broader range of institutional arrangements and financing instruments evolves. The classification scheme advanced in the preceding chapter focuses on the capacity of developing countries to mobilize external and domestic resources, and leads to nine categories (with three more for outlier countries that receive huge amounts of FDI). These categories appear robust in the sense of being broadly compatible with country rankings derived from other indicators (Annex B). Therefore, a first strategic issue that emerges is *the need to explore alternative classification schemes for developing countries*, taking into consideration primarily their potential to utilize the different financing instruments and institutional arrangements available, which in turn is related to their capacities to mobilize external and domestic finance.

As countries improve their capacity to mobilize external and domestic finance, they migrate from one category to another and change the type of financial instruments that are appropriate to their needs. In general, there will be a progression from the use of bilateral and multilateral grants and concessional loans, complemented by humanitarian

BOX 4.6. **Changes in country capacity to mobilize external and domestic resources**

Few countries have made the full transition from having a very limited capacity to mobilize external and domestic finance, towards full and unrestricted access to external sources of funds and a reliance on domestic savings for a major share of their investment and current expenditure needs. Leaving aside those European countries and Japan that benefited from the Marshall Plan in the late 1940s and early 1950s, several countries in East Asia, and to a lesser extent Latin America and Africa, have made this transition. Other countries have lost ground and receded in the capacity to mobilize resources, either because of the collapese of centrally planned economies, civil wars and violence, external debt crises or economic mismanagement. A stylized account of changes in the use of financial instruments as countries improve their resource mobilization capacity would look as follows:

- Initially a poor country would rely primarily on grants from bilateral agencies and multilateral institutions, which are likely to represent a major share of its public finance. These may be complemented with concessional loans and grants from private foundations and, in special cases that require it, with humanitarian assistance from international institutions and private donors. Export earnings and domestic saving are likely to be very low.
- As economic and social indicators improve and their capacity to mobilize resorces increases, countries would shift towards the use of a mix of bilateral ad multilateral concessional and regular loans (so-called 'blend' countries). They would also qualify for export credits from donor countries, begin to attract FDI (especially in natural resource sectors) and from the rpivate sector windows of MDBs, and would continued to receive donations from private foundations and private individuals. Developing countries with large diasporas would receive significant amounts of external financing through workers' remittances, export earnings begin to grow and become significant source of foreign exchange, and savings and tax revenues increase, helping to develop a domestic financial sector.
- At a subsequent stage countries do not require grants or concessional loans from bilateral agencies and multilateral institutions, but rely to a large extent on regular loans and on direct investments and loans from their private sector windows. Access to official and private export credit grows, and countries begin to make use of international capital markets, issuing sovereign bonds and private debt instruments, and also tapping the secondary markets for public and private debt. FDI continues to grow, and a few local firms venture to invest abroad. Export earnings rise and domestic savings account for a significant portion of investment. Foundations plays a limited role in strategic interventions, and remittances no longer represent a major portion of dexternal financing.

BOX 4.6. **Changes in country capacity to mobilize external and domestic resources** (*continued*)

- When countries gain full access to international capital markets, bilateral agencies and multilateral institutions play a rather limited role, centred on the provision of guarantees, contingency funds and policy dialogue, while loan operations recede to a seondary plane (countries can obtain better terms directly from financial markets). FDI increases and remains at a high level, bonds and other instruments are regularly issued and traded in international capital markets, private sector firms play the dominant role in the mobilization of external and domestic finance, and foundation grants and individual donations are quite limited. Because of their relatively high domestic savings rate and efficient financing system, countries at this stage become a source of finance for other developing countries (through direct investment, export credits, and official and private loans). Finally, instead of being recipients of remittances from their emigrants, they become a source of remittances to poorer countries.

Source: Prepared by the authors.

---

assistance when necessary, to a greater reliance on private sources of finance from international capital markets and foreign direct investors (Box 4.6).[8]

Closely related to classification schemes is the present practice of rigid thresholds for countries to 'graduate' from using one instrument to another. This is most clearly the case with the transition from concessional to regular lending in MDBs, where criteria based on income levels and, to a lesser extent, other variables are explicitly defined in advance. In general, it would appear desirable to fine-tune thresholds that define country categories and determine access to specific financing instruments using several parameters to divide the scale more finely (this may be referred to as 'gradation' instead of 'graduation'). Barriers to access specific financing instruments may also emerge implicitly, as when rating agencies do not provide sovereign credit ratings for developing countries. While simply having a rating, even a good one, does not guarantee access to capital markets, it sends a signal that the country is eventually interested in issuing sovereign bonds, which implies submitting to the macroeconomic policy discipline imposed by those markets. This in turn may stimulate further policy reforms and could even improve prospects of receiving other sources of financing (e.g. investments in public services concessions). Thus a second strategic choice that emerges relates to *the need to be more flexible in defining category thresholds and to remove barriers in order to broaden access to a greater variety of financing instruments*.

A third strategic choice is related to *the relationship between 'perform-ance' and 'need' criteria for the allocation of development assistance funds.* This surfaced in recent years primarily in the wake of World Bank research which claimed to show that aid was far more effective in developing countries with 'good policies'. Yet the trade-offs between need and performance may, in practice, be somewhat exaggerated. No donor country, international organization or international financial institution allocates resources solely on the basis of 'need' or of 'per-formance'; rather, they rely on a mix of these two, and this is apart from a host of political, social and security issues which inconveniently raise their heads when aid allocations are being decided. Therefore – and notwithstanding the recently created US Millennium Challenge Account, which purports to allocate resources primarily on the basis of performance along a range of indicators of good governance, sound-ness of policies and related parameters – it is most likely that aid alloca-tions by bilateral and multilateral agencies will be made on the basis of a mix of need, performance and other criteria. For example, a minimum level ('floor') for allocations may be defined on the basis of 'need' (especially when humanitarian considerations are involved) and additional allocations may be provided according to performance in several different areas. This issue is closely related to the institutional arrangements devised to channel external financing. For example, in the Chad–Cameroon pipeline project mentioned in section 4.2.1, where highly intrusive mechanisms to administer oil revenues were devised (and are still at an early stage), higher allocations of aid may seem justified than otherwise would seem prudent or appropriate. Finally, as pointed out by some developing country officials and NGO representatives, the issues of 'need' versus 'performance' look very differ-ent when viewed from the ground up rather than from the boardroom down.

5
Concluding Remarks: Strategy, Commitment and Prospects

The preceding chapters of this report have reviewed the role that financing plays in the process of development, examined the evolution of international development financing, summarized the main criticisms of development assistance, analysed the main recent initiatives to reform development finance, and explored the possible futures for the mobilization of external financial resources to support development efforts. What emerges clearly from all of this is that at the beginning of the twenty-first century, six decades after international development began to emerge as a field in its own right, the international development financing 'system' is really not much of a *system*. It is rather a collection of disjointed entities that lack coherence, often work at cross-purposes and are not up to the task of mobilizing finance in the amounts and ways required to assist a growing diversity of developing countries in their efforts to reduce poverty and improve living standards.

The institutions that comprise the architecture of the international development system have grown and expanded by accretion, with each layer of agencies, organizations and programmes being deposited on top of previous ones. This expansion has been driven primarily by inertia, special interests and, quite often, fads that have kept alive institutions that should have disappeared, and that preclude the emergence of others that are missing but needed to fill obvious gaps. This has not prevented many existing public and private development organizations from doing good work, but has certainly meant that the overall performance and impact of the international development financing system have been well below what is required to support development efforts – and, in particular, to achieve the MDGs by 2015.

Thus, in spite of the number and diversity of the institutions, instruments and practices that make up the international development finance system, it appears woefully inadequate to respond to the changing demands emerging from the much more complex realities of global interdependence. Moreover, while there have been many attempts to reform its architecture to make it function more effectively as a real system, initiatives have been limited mainly to minor changes in the range of instruments at the disposal of international financial institutions and to joint private–public initiatives of limited reach. Those factors that have a powerful influence on the prospects for development success – such as access to developed country markets and technology, the creation of a supportive security and political context and the establishment of a fair international regulatory environment – are given only modest (and mostly rhetorical) attention. This is largely because international development has simply been absent from the mainstream public policy agendas of large and powerful states.

For a variety of reasons, however, the early years of the twenty-first century have brought about an unprecedented 'window of opportunity' for a conscientious re-examination and re-alignment of the institutions and organizations that configure the international development architecture. As global communications have increased awareness of the plight of the poor in developing countries, as criticisms about the effectiveness of the development financing system have multiplied, and as a general sense has grown that the haphazard approaches to reforms of the past have not been successful, there is a renewed impetus for reform. The specific and time-bounded nature of the MDGs has helped to focus attention on the inadequacies of current international development financing arrangements – even though it is highly improbable that they will be achieved. At a deeper and more fundamental level, the terrorist attacks of September 11 2001 have forced political leaders to acknowledge that a series of international security crises may be looming (and perhaps imminent) unless the widespread poverty, marginalization and growing inequalities that lead to frustration and despair are reduced significantly. Yet there is a risk that these crises and the fear they generate could divert development thinking and practice towards narrow and short-term issues heavily influenced by security concerns – such as the 'war on terrorism'. This could hijack the development enterprise in a similar manner to the impact of the Cold War from the 1950s to the late 1980s.

Nevertheless, recent efforts to define development concerns as a high priority item in the international public policy agenda, together with renewed attempts to reform the international development financing system, appear to be more serious and far-reaching than those of the last three decades. They have managed to engage a wide constituency and have also generated political momentum.

The key issue is whether this momentum can be sustained. The review and analysis of chapters 1 and 2 of this study, the scenarios constructed in chapters 3 and 4, and the framework of strategic choices articulated in chapter 4 suggest that to maintain this political momentum will be a challenging task that will require exceptional political will and leadership. A rich and varied menu of initiatives emerges out of the framework for strategic choices, and these indicate clearly that reforms can be approached sequentially, that each initiative could yield important benefits in and of itself, and that it is possible to combine initiatives that reinforce and support each other. The process of reforming the international development financing system should not conform to an 'all or nothing' or to an 'anything goes' approach. It should rather be informed by a 'radical incrementalism' perspective, in which a long-term vision guides the incremental steps and decisions taken by key actors, so as to advance progressively towards a radically more effective international development financing system.

5.1 Strategic options: taking stock and moving forward

The strategic choices that will determine the evolution of the international development financing system during the next decade and a half will be made by a variety of actors in an increasingly crowded international scene. A set of questions derived from the analyses and explorations in the preceding chapters may be helpful in taking stock of the current situation and of the prospects for international development financing, so as to assist policy and decision makers in framing the various reform issues.

* *How important is finance in the process of development?*
It is essential. The history of development efforts over the past 60 years demonstrates that without adequate and sustained levels of investment (in all its forms) development simply does not occur. However, while the availability of financial resources is a necessary condition it is far from sufficient. The broad area of international development finance lies at the intersection of international development concerns and the field of international finance, and focuses on the mobilization of external resources as a complement to domestic savings and investment in developing countries. Different types of developing countries require and rely on distinct combinations of official and private sources of

external financing to support their own efforts, but none can remain isolated from the international financial system and expect to produce sustainable improvements in the living standards of poor people. Yet, at the beginning of the twenty-first century it has become clear that financial resources on their own are of little help in the absence of strong institutions, good governance, sensible policies and the capacity to generate and utilize knowledge.

- *Are the current structures, channels and mechanisms to provide external development finance appropriate to the needs of developing countries?*

Not really. There is a multiplicity of institutions involved in international development finance but, considered as a whole, they are not up to the task of providing resources to different types of developing countries at the level and in the forms required. Current institutional arrangements are characterized by a lack of overall coherence, by policies that are in conflict and that cancel one another out, by an overall governance deficit and by problems in the delineation of mandates. In addition, there is a lack of accountability, insufficient transparency and inadequate representation of developing countries in decision making. Resource flows are not predictable, some sources of external finance are very unstable, and there is an inadequate match between financing instruments and developing country needs. At the beginning of the twenty-first century, the structure of international development finance is skewed in favour of highly concentrated and mobile (mostly private) flows to emerging economies and against more balanced and steady long-term flows to emerging, middle-income and low-income countries. There is also a need to address and resolve the growing policy contradiction between multilateral agencies as last resort sources of finance and as performance-based sources of capital.

Efforts are under way to redress this situation through the creation of performance-oriented funds, debt cancellation, instruments to catalyse private flows, special purpose partnerships between public and private entities and the provision of direct budget support, among other initiatives, as well as proposals to create new mechanisms (emissions trading, global taxes, provision and financing of international public goods, an International Financing Facility). However, these efforts have not reached, as yet, a required critical mass and some of them are rather controversial and likely to be counterproductive (e.g. replacing multilateral lending on highly concessional terms with outright grants).

- *What would be the main characteristics of a more effective and adequate set of international development financing institutions?*

At least eight. These include: *adequacy* (amounts and forms of financing, match between financial instruments and country needs); *predictability* (stability of funding levels, conditions for access to financial resources); *responsiveness* (balance between developing country needs and performance); *diversity and choice* (variety of financial instruments, institutions and programmes); *capacity to absorb shocks* (response and smoothing capacity to reduce adverse effects of undesirable events); *complementarity of external financing with domestic resource mobilization* (external flows should facilitate and help to catalyse domestic financial resource mobilization and should aim to avoid 'aid dependency'); *voice, representation and accountability* (capacity to accommodate and respond to the interests and views of all stakeholders); and *flexibility, efficiency and learning* (ability to change and adapt, reasonable costs in relation to benefits, continuous evaluation and feedback). These criteria apply to international development financing institutions as a whole and could thus define an ideal system, but can also be used to assess the effectiveness of specific financial institutions. An examination of current arrangements suggests that different components of the international development financing system exhibit these criteria to quite different degrees, and that as a whole it falls short of responding effectively to the needs of developing countries.

- *What are the prospects for international development financing during the next decade and a half?*

Very uncertain. Yet they are arguably much better at the moment than they have been for at least two decades. The MDGs have helped to generate some greater political commitment and to reverse the previous decline in ODA. Further impetus was added by the Monterrey pledges made by many countries to increase ODA further and towards the 0.7 per cent of GDP target. Additional momentum derives from the collective international unease following September 11 which has led, for many, to the association of a deeply disturbing causal linkage been poverty and marginalization on the one hand and interdependent global insecurity on the other. Against these factors that hold promise for development financing prospects, however, is the fact that the international political economy today is characterized by imbalances and distortions of historic proportions and that the development and security agenda has been (and is being) redefined in numerous quarters in terms of a narrow and immediate focus on a 'war against terrorism'. These are factors that risk major negative impacts on the prospects for development assistance. It is also important to note that the next two years may prove especially crucial in terms of these prospects, including those for a post-Monterrey consensus. In 2005 the special session of the UN on the MDGs will take place and the pledges of Monterrey will need to be extended beyond their current framework that extends only to 2006.

Provided reform efforts advance on a number of fronts (several of which are listed below), the set of institutions now active in international development financing could markedly improve their effectiveness. This is envisaged in a *Transformation* scenario where institutional arrangements, financing instruments and different types of developing countries evolve in a positive manner and reinforce each other. Should reforms fail to materialize or to be sustained, however, the outcome would be an *Inertia* scenario that at best would maintain – and would in all probability exacerbate – the difficulties and problems that international development financing faces at present. A broad range of intermediate outcomes is possible, two of which are envisaged in the *Limited Reforms* and in the *Major Reforms* scenarios. For example, reform efforts could focus on improving development financing for the poorest countries, on creating better conditions for emerging countries to access private capital markets, or on establishing and consolidating public-private partnerships to enhance the capacity of middle-income countries to tap multilateral and private sources of finance.

Advancing from the *Inertia* scenario through *Limited* and *Major Reforms* towards the *Transformation* scenario requires a set of initiatives along three closely interrelated dimensions: *institutional arrangements* for development financing, the array of *financing instruments* to channel resources and the *classification of developing countries* to determine the instruments and institutions that are appropriate for different types of countries. For advances to materialize in the next decade or so, a strategic sequence of initiatives along these three dimensions should be in place during the next three to five years.

- *Why is it necessary to explore new ways of classifying developing countries from a development financing perspective?*

Country classification schemes based on income per capita criteria (e.g. high, upper middle, lower-middle, low-income) combined with ad hoc categories (e.g. low-income countries under stress), do not adequately reflect the main features of developing countries. This should focus rather on their capacity to mobilize external and domestic resources. Two strategic issues, which require further analytical and policy-oriented studies, stand out in this regard.

First, *explore alternative classification schemes* that could reflect the external and domestic resource mobilization capacity of developing countries, so as to identify the kinds of financial instruments, which are appropriate to the needs of different types of developing countries. This is closely related to the need for flexibility in defining country category thresholds and for removing barriers that may limit access to some financing instruments. As developing countries evolve in their capacity to mobilize financial resources, the set of financial instruments they employ changes in a natural way in the direction of greater reliance on private sources of capital.

Secondly, *move beyond the perceived trade-offs between country performance and country needs in allocating development assistance*, which have characterized aid debates in recent years. Placing countries in categories based just on indicators of performance or of need is not an effective way of determining the levels and kinds of assistance they should receive, especially when humanitarian and poverty reduction perspectives are adopted to balance aid effectiveness considerations.

- *How can change in the international development financing system be brought about?*

The full menu of strategic issues and options regarding institutional arrangements, financial instruments and developing country classifications can be considered as a 'framework for strategic choices' to advance towards a more effective international development financing system during the next three to five years. While these may appear rather modest in relation to the challenge of moving from the *Inertia* to the *Transformation* scenarios, they indicate a number of viable initiatives that could be taken to guarantee steady progress in this direction.

Past experience has clearly shown that major advances in the structure of international arrangements take place at times of crisis. But taking advantage of such situations requires preparation and a clear vision of where to go – and how to get there – when the crisis arises. Absent a major crisis that would force a fundamental rethinking of development financing – perhaps of the same magnitude of the Great Depression and Second World War that ushered in the Bretton Woods agreements, gradual improvements are the way to proceed. Yet gradualism needs to be combined with vision in articulating an approach to strategic change, in which a clear conception of the desired ideal future informs and guides the steady steps to be taken. Along the way, it is necessary to remain alert to emerging opportunities to speed the pace of change, such as changes in leadership. This also requires an adequate appreciation of the interests, aspirations and limitations of key stakeholders, and continuous monitoring of events.

- *Who are the main actors in the process of moving towards a more effective international development financing system?*

The international development finance scene is quite crowded and changes all the time. Its complexity precludes the possibility that a single actor, no matter how powerful and influential, will decide the direction that the evolution of development financing will take. Such an evolution will be the result of collective if disjointed leadership, with some actors playing leading and others supporting roles, and all of them affecting at different times and in different ways the critical choices that will shape the system. In a sense, given the hardened institutional structures and the natural resistance to change of most entities involved in development financing, and again without a crisis that would motivate radical reforms, change is most likely to take place through leadership 'seeping through' the cracks of institutional arrangements. From this perspective, the role of the key actors may be visualized as facilitating the process of change and spawning initiatives that may gradually begin to steer the evolution of international development financing from *Inertia* through *Limited* and *Major Reforms*, towards *Transformation*.

A multiplicity of actors play leading, secondary and bit parts with scripts that are continuously modified and defy attempts to keep track of a variety of intertwined subplots. The cast of characters will change according to the different initiatives under consideration but it will be drawn from the set of:

- Presidents and prime ministers, heads and senior officers of development assistance agencies or ministries, ministries of finance and foreign affairs, and congressional leaders in donor countries, together with the corresponding authorities in the EU, ad hoc ministerial groups (e.g. the Utstein group) and, to a much lesser extent, the OECD Development Assistance Committee.
- Heads and senior staff of the World Bank, the IMF, the UN and, to a lesser extent, the UNDP, the regional development banks and the specialized UN agencies.
- Presidents, ministers of finance and foreign affairs in developing countries.
- Presidents and senior officers of the leading private foundations and large grant-making NGOs.
- Key executives and senior staff of commercial and investment banks, pension and investment funds, and debt rating agencies.
- Leaders of international civil society organizations, in particular large international NGOs and business associations.

- Leaders of special commissions and task forces (e.g. the GPG Task Force, the International Panel on Climate Change, the Bretton Woods Committee).
- Opinion and academic leaders concerned with development issues, including journalists, well-known artists and mass media personalities.

Not all of these are likely to exercise leadership in a positive way to advance towards the *Transformation* scenario in international developing financing. Some may be expected to prevent change from taking place at all or even to steer change in the wrong direction.

But in the last analysis, determined leadership by key stakeholders and actors (who need not be the leading or most visible ones) is essential to keep a steady reform course. Some of these could form temporary alliances to press for specific reforms or work together with more ambitious and long-term aims. In particular, decisive action by a few developed 'like-minded' countries that champion the development cause, combined with a greater and more effective participation of developing countries, is likely to lead to substantive incremental changes along the path from the *Inertia* through the *Limited* and *Major Reforms* and towards the *Transformation* scenario. Should a major global crisis create the opportunity, such an alliance would also increase the probability of leapfrogging towards a more effective international development financing system.

- *What are the main issues in the reform of institutional arrangements?*
Many of the issues in this group are rather pedestrian (e.g. continuation of basic reforms to the UN system) but remain essential to improve current institutional arrangements in the international development financing system and have been mentioned in chapter 4, section 4.2.1. Among these it is possible to identify five initiatives: (i) continue to *press for and support the current reform efforts of international organizations*; (ii) devise and *put in place institutions to provide international public goods*; (iii) *champion international capital market innovations* to better accommodate the financing needs of different types of developing countries; (iv) *eschew the proliferation of single-purpose, free-standing special funds or secretariats* as a substitute for the reform of existing institutions; (v) recognize and *make explicit the contradictions between issues of voice and of conditionality* associated with the fact that there is no 'level playing field' between donor and developing countries. These asymmetries can be addressed by increasing developing country representation in relevant instances and by creating new fora with a more balanced representation of developed and developing countries.

In addition, it is necessary to prepare the ground for those longer-term fundamental changes in the structure of development financing that will be essential to the criteria of predictability, adequacy and stability. This would necessarily entail recognition that while private flows (including remittances in a globalized order) will play an increasingly important role, there is no substitute for public funding of development assistance. This would further entail recognition that, ultimately, some sort of automatic mechanisms – such as international fees and taxes levied in small amounts – will be the most efficient way of providing development assistance.

- *Which are the main issues and initiatives regarding the array of financial instruments to channel resources towards developing countries?*

The vast array of existing and proposed financial instruments suggests a broad and heavy agenda to focus on during the next few years to improve the prospects for international development financing. These are discussed in detail in chapter 4, section 4.2.2 and will not be repeated here. In general these initiatives involve: (i) modifying, expanding and creating bilateral instruments; (ii) improving financing arrangements in the UN, regional and other organizations; (iii) broadening and deepening the range of financial instruments at the disposal of the international financial institutions; (iv) improving the reach and effectiveness of private sources of development finance and, in particular, FDI and remittances; (v) facilitating developing country access to international capital markets; (vi) exploring the use of international taxes, fees and charges, and seeking to garner political support for such initiatives; (vii) creating international markets that would help transfer resources to developing countries (e.g. emissions trading) and finance public goods; and (viii) supporting the consolidation of global and regional partnerships involving joint public and private initiatives in development financing.

5.2 The way forward: radical incrementalism

This report has argued that a well-functioning, efficient and effective international development financing system is essential for global poverty reduction, for improving living standards in developing countries, for reducing worldwide inequalities, and for achieving the MDGs. Current institutional arrangements and instruments to mobilize external financing for development are woefully inadequate and require major restructuring. As elucidated through the scenaries presented in the preceding chapters, the international development financing system could evolve along quite different paths during the next ten to 15 years. Whether the *Inertia* or the *Transformation* scenario prevails will depend on how the international community and its leadership face the new realities of global interdependence and respond to the demands of development finance.

As mentioned before, in the past a series of crises strengthened the resolve of political leaders to act boldly and to introduce structural reforms in the conduct of international affairs. The tragedies of the First World War, the Great Depression, and the Second World War, among many others that characterized the twentieth century, spurred in the 1940s a series of major institutional innovations. They led to the creation of the United Nations, the Bretton Woods Institutions and the launching of what may be called the 'international development experiment'. Sixty years later, when global interdependence has increased to previously unthinkable levels – and when poverty, destitution, exclusion and violence are continuously but fleetingly brought to our attention under the harsh light and the magnifying glass of the global mass media – the whole array of international institutions designed to preserve peace and promote development is under severe stress. This requires a fundamental shift in the way international economic, social and political relations are managed and, in particular, it poses the challenge of creating a new and more effective international development financing system.

Radical incrementalism – an oxymoron that fits appropriately the paradoxical character of the emerging fractured global order – may well be the best approach for advancing towards the *Transformation* scenario for development financing in the mid-2010s. It implies the simultaneous articulation of a shared vision of the desired future and the design of pragmatic, down to earth, means to approach it. Both vision and pragmatism are required to launch and sustain the reform process along a broad front of initiatives. Political will and courage, together with determined leadership and the ability to mobilize support coalitions, will be essential for steady, incremental progress in transforming the vast and complex international development finance system into a truly effective instrument for development. A sense of utmost urgency must drive and spur reform efforts. Otherwise, tragedies and catastrophes will occur sooner or later, as they did in the twentieth century. These would probably then steel political resolve and catalyse action, but not before incurring a heavy toll in human suffering and widespread misery.

Notes and References

1   The Inheritance: Evolution of the International Development System and of Development Financing

1 This was the fourth point of US President Harry S. Truman's Point IV Program (Truman 1949).

2 The contribution to the rates of growth of output of these other factors has been called the 'residual' and more recently 'total factor productivity'.

3 It averaged almost 90 per cent from 1950 to 1960.

4 At the same time, the 'disciplinary functions' of these institutions increased as a function of the growing importance of 'conditionality' and 'cross-conditionality' in development financing. For developing countries, an agreement with the IMF became a condition not only on loans and concessional assistance from multilateral institutions but also on co-financing from bilateral donors and loans from commercial banks. Having a 'Policy Framework Paper', drawn up primarily by the IMF and the World Bank (in consultation with government authorities), became a prerequisite for mobilizing large amounts of bilateral funds from donor countries.

5 High levels of year-to-year volatility have also been a characteristic of private debt in recent years. For example, net short-term debt (less than one year maturity) moved strongly into negative territory for four years in a row after the Asian Crisis (-US\$30 billion on average during the period 1998–2001) and then jumped to a positive US\$32 billion in 2003.

6 Of 115 emerging-market deals in the international equity market in 2002, 14 deals (about 15 per cent) in six countries (Brazil, China, Indonesia, Malaysia, Russia and South Africa) accounted for 75 per cent (US\$8.7 billion) of the total raised through international placements (World Bank 2003a).

7 Because of a large account deficit and a slowdown in FDI inflows last year, the US Congress is now considering a temporary break on repatriation taxes (the Homeland Investment Act). According to a J.P. Morgan survey (2003), the Homeland Investment Act could bring back earnings, in the form of dividends, ranging from \$265 billion to \$375 billion.

8 The EU, for example, has announced plans for the union as a whole to reach an average of 0.39 per cent of Gross National Income (GNI) by 2006. Also, the US administration has announced proposals for annual increases by 2006 of US\$5 billion to its Millennium Challenge Account and almost US\$2 billion for an AIDS initiative.

9 The fiscal deficit in the United States is estimated at about 5 per cent of GDP in 2004, a level without historical precedent. In addition, France, Germany, Italy and Spain are all projecting deficits of over 4 per cent while Japan's fiscal deficit remains at over 9 per cent.

10 For example, in order to enhance the development impact of remittances, the Inter-American Development Bank's Multilateral Investment Fund (MIF)

teamed up with Brazil's small business agency and the private Banco America do Sul to establish a US$10 million investment fund that will aim to assist enterprises started by migrants who return to their homeland. The fund will seek to capitalize on both the experience gained by the returning migrants and the networks built by these overseas communities. Another MIF initiative, this time jointly with the International Fund for Agricultural Development (IFAD), has led to the creation of a US$ 7.6 million grant facility to support and improve the flow of remittances to poor rural areas in Latin America.

11 In 2000, for example, four countries (the three Nordic countries and the Netherlands) provided 42 per cent of the core financing of the UNDP, UNICEF and UNFPA. In addition to the general political problem of a major asymmetry in burden sharing, this imbalance raises basic issues of subsidy and free-riding.

12 Net income in the MDBs is applied in general to three main functions: (i) to increase reserves and strengthen their financial position and risk-bearing capacity; (ii) to meet administrative expenses to support more complex operations; and (iii) as transfers to soft loan windows for concessional lending, and grants for a variety of purposes (e.g. disaster relief, post-conflict reconstruction).

2 Attempted Change: Recent Attempts to Transform the International Development Financing Architecture

1 For a more complete discussion, see Bezanson, and Sagasti (2000: 10–12).

2 Although these views have been popular for some time in conservative political circles, they acquired much greater prominence in March 2000 with the publication of the report prepared by the International Financial Institution Advisory Committee of the US Congress (the Meltzer Report).

3 The Secretary-General grouped thirty UN departments, funds and programmes under four sector areas: peace and security, humanitarian affairs, development and economic and social affairs. An Executive Committee to coordinate the work of the sector areas was set up and a Senior Management Group (SMG) was established to serve as the Secretary-General's cabinet and the central policy planning body of the United Nations. Additionally, a Strategic Planning Unit was installed to identify emerging global issues and trends and devise policy recommendations for the Secretary-General and the Senior Management Group. The Triennial Comprehensive Policy Review (TCPR) was also introduced to assess the implementation of policy directives. Coordination within the system is now overseen and guided by the Administrative Committee on Co-ordination (ACC), which has recently undertaken a number of measures to enhance policy co-ordination.

In order to achieve the second objective, the United Nations Development Group (UNDG) was created to advance greater coherence and cooperation in United Nations development operations at the country level. To save money, improve operational synergy, and project a unified image of the United Nations in a country, various 'UN Houses' group various UN agencies working in a country. As part of this effort, the role of Resident

Coordinator as leader of the UN country team was strengthened. Two new tools were established to facilitate coordination, and to bring UN assistance more closely in line with the strategies and priorities of the host countries: a Common Country Assessment (CCA), which clarifies national needs, and the UN Development Assistance Framework (UNDAF), which sets out the division of labour among UN entities in assisting governments to promote development and to implement goals from the UN global conferences.

4 Funds made available for HA have more than doubled from US$2 billion in 1990 to US$5.5 billion in 2000. From 1999 to 2001, total humanitarian assistance averaged US$5.5 billion a year and represented about 10 per cent of ODA (Kent, Dalton, von Hippel and Maurer 2003).

5 The new openness of the UN to interacting with civil society and the private sector may also be producing gains in a number of other areas such as the Global Fund on AIDS, the recently formed UN Information and Communication Technologies Task Force to bridge the world's digital divide, and the establishment of the UN Fund for International Partnerships (UNFIP). Most recently, 120 CEOs, senior industry leaders and more than 3,500 NGOs at the Johannesburg World Summit on Sustainable Development committed themselves to over 90 partnership initiatives in the areas of energy, water, health, agriculture, tourism, forestry, fisheries and biodiversity.

6 The report states that: 'International institutions and States have not organised themselves to address the problems of development in a coherent, integrated way, and instead continue to treat poverty, infectious disease and environmental degradation as stand-alone threats... Existing global economic and social governance structures are woefully inadequate for the challenges ahead... At the moment, there is no high-level forum which provides leaders from large industrial and developing economies a regular opportunity for frank dialogue, deliberation and problem solving' (United Nations 2004b: 26).

7 For example the 'Fifty Years is Enough' campaign that accompanied the fiftieth anniversary of the founding of the World Bank and IMF and with regard to the African Development Bank, *The Quest for Quality, Report of the Task Force on Project Quality for the African Development Bank*, 1994 (also known as the Knox Report).

8 Four key elements were identified in the Strategic Compact: refuelling current business activities, primarily by easing budget pressures to protect the level and quality of client services; refocusing the development agenda on issues of social and environmental sustainability, as well as on the roles of the private and public sectors; strengthening the World Bank's role of brokering knowledge, disseminating best-practices; and revamping institutional capabilities by realigning the institution's information systems, reformulating financial management, investing more in staff training and relocating functions, authority and staff to the field.

9 To the end of 2003, IDA will have forgiven £10,97 billion owed to it by HIPC countries and it is estimated that IDA will ultimately bear just over 20 per cent of the total cost that creditors will sustain through the HIPC debt cancellation programme (see World Bank, 'Allocating IDA funds based on performance', March 2003).

10 The IMF Board Poverty Reduction and Growth Facility (PRGF) guidelines in September 2002 – the first revision since 1979 (IMF 2002).

11 In response to the 1997 Asian financial crisis, the IMF surveillance and crisis prevention capacities were strengthened. In 1999, the IMF and the World Bank created a joint Financial Sector Assessment Programme (FSAP) designed to assess the strengths and weaknesses of countries' financial sectors; and the following year under IMF leadership a large number of countries subscribed to the Special Data Dissemination Standard (SDDS), the Code of Good Practices in Fiscal Transparency and the IMF's Code of Good Practices on Transparency in Monetary and Financial Policies. As of March 2004, 71 of the IMF's 184 member countries had completed one or more Reports on Standard and Codes modules (ROSCs).

12 The Internal Evaluation Office has analysed two central issues on IMF activities: country ownership and IMF policies (IMF 2001) and IMF participation in three recent financial crises in South Asia, Mexico and Russia (IMF 2003b).

13 This process included: (i) a 1997 staff review of the ESAF ten years after the facility's inauguration in 1987; (ii) an external review of the ESAF in 1998; (iii) a summary paper on the internal and external reviews – Distilling the Lessons of the ESAF Reviews – discussed by the Executive Board in July 1998 and leading to a first round of changes to the ESAF architecture and staff guidance; and (iv) discussions in the Executive Board and the Interim Committee of the Board of Governors in September 1999 leading to the decision to transform the ESAF into the PRGF and link the PRGF closely to Poverty Reduction Strategy Papers (PRSP).

14 Total social sector lending accounted for almost 50 per cent of total committed loans in 2003.

15 These are, in order, the Corporación Andina de Fomento, Banco de Desarrollo de America del Norte, Caribbean Development Bank, Banco Centroamericano de Integración Económica and Fondo Financiero para el Desarrollo de la Cuenca del Plata.

16 Currently, only 20 per cent of investment in these countries is generated from internal private savings, compared with over 100 per cent in Western Europe.

17 The UK's record of untying aid from domestic procurement is unprecedented. In 2000, 92 per cent of British bilateral ODA was untied contrasted to a low 29 per cent in 1991. Decisions have now also been made on how the principles of untying will be carried through to DFID's non-commercial activities.

18 The distinguished membership of the task force includes K.Y. Amoako, Gun-Britt Andersson, Fred Bergsten, Kemal Dervis, Mohamed T. El-Ashry, Gareth Evans, Enrique Iglesias, Inge Kaul, Lydia Makhubu, Trevor Manuel, Hisashi Owada, Nafis Sadik, Brigita Schmögnerová, Yves-Thibault de Silguy and M.S. Swaminathan. The task force is co-chaired by Tidjane Thiam and Ernesto Zedillo.

19 The EU is a union of 25 independent European states. It was formerly (until 1 November 1993) known as the European Community (EC) or as the European Economic Community (EEC). Its political representation and

decision-making body is the European Parliament (EP) and its executive body is the European Commission (EC).

20 The distribution of the subsidies, however, is on a highly uneven basis. OXFAM calculated that over half of the CAP's 2000 budget of US$41 billion was spent on the biggest 17 farm enterprises in Europe, belying the widespread European myth that the CAP is about employment for small farmers (OXFAM 2002).

21 Section 3.3 of chapter 3 further describes a broad range of financing initiatives. For recent and detailed evaluations of innovative financing mechanisms see Rogerson (2004) and Reisen (2004).

22 The MDGs are clearly serving as a principal catalyst to this quest. Estimates vary widely, but a generally accepted view is that a minimum requirement for the prospects of achieving the MDGs by 2015 would be an additional US$50 billion per year in ODA. This signifies roughly a doubling from present levels.

23 For example, the current Canadian Prime Minister, Paul Martin, proposed to both the Commonwealth Ministers of Finance and the G8 when he was Minister of Finance that serious consideration be given to the Tobin tax. The Presidents of France, Brazil, Spain and Chile have also raised the possibility of creating global taxes for development in their opening statements at the UN General Assembly in September 2004. More recently (26 January 2005), French President Jacques Chirac proposed at the World Economic Forum at Davos the creation of an international tax on financial transactions to help fight AIDS, saying such a measure could raise $10 billion each year. He also proposed that international taxes could apply to fuel used in air and sea travel or on airline tickets.

3   Building Scenarios for International Development Finance

1 Several developing countries noted at the Monterrey Summit that in the 1980s many donor countries chose to co-finance World Bank structural adjustment programmes and, in doing so, adopted the same 'one-size-fits-all' policy framework. This rigid posture reduced the possibility of adapting policy sets to local conditions. In this regard, issues such as overlap and duplication in the provision of external finance may be seen in a different light, for rather than leading to inefficiency they may increase choice.

2 See Annex B for an account of the approach and methodology to define the classification scheme.

3 Table 3.4 in section 3.6 contains a more detailed list of financial instruments with additional information on their degree of use and adequacy to different types of developing countries.

    See table 3.5 for a more detailed list of financial instruments.

4 Some UN agencies provide small soft loans, including UNESCO (to protect cultural heritage), the United Nations Capital Development Fund (apex funds for small and medium-sized enterprises in low-income countries), and IFAD, which operates in part like a multilateral development bank. In addition, there is the United Nations Foundation, a temporary entity created through private donations, which provides grants to UN programmes.

5   The three set of institutions which make up the UN system can be defined more fully as: (i) The UN proper, which comprises six organs (the General Assembly, the Security Council, the Economic and Social Council, the Trusteeship Council, the Secretariat and the International Court of Justice), funded by assessed contributions of member countries; (ii) the UN offices, programmes and funds, such as the Office of the UN High Commissioner for Refugees (UNHCR), the UN Development Programme (UNDP), the UN Children's Fund (UNICEF), the UN Capital Development Fund (UNCDF), the UN Centre for Human Settlements (UNCHS), the UN Conference on Trade and Development (UNCTAD), the UN Environment Programme (UNEP), the UN Population Fund (UNFPA), the UN Industrial Development Organisation (UNIDO), the UN Institute for Training and Research (UNITAR), the UN Relief & Works Agency for Palestinian Refugees in the Near East (UNRWA), the United Nations University (UNU), and the World Food Programme (WFP), which report to the General Assembly or the Economic and Social Council and are funded entirely by voluntary contributions; and (iii) the specialized agencies, linked to the UN through cooperative agreements, such as the World Health Organisation (WHO), the International Civil Aviation Organisation (ICAO), the International Labour Organisation (ILO), the Universal Postal Union (UPU), the United Nations Industrial Development Organisation (UNIDO), the Food and Agricultural Organisation (FAO), the International Maritime Organisation (IMO), the United Nations Educational, Scientific and Cultural Organisation (UNESCO), International Telecommunication Union (ITU), the World Intellectual Property Organisation (WIPO), the International Atomic Energy Agency (IAEA) and the World Meteorological Organization (WMO), which are autonomous bodies created by intergovernmental agreements and are supported by assessed and voluntary contributions.

6   There are four types of MDBs. First, there is the World Bank Group, the only global MDB, which comprises five member institutions – the International Bank for Reconstruction and Development (IBRD) that provides regular loans, the International Development Association (IDA), that provides soft loans, the International Finance Corporation (IFC), that works with the private sector, the Multilateral Investment Guarantee Agency (MIGA) and the International Centre for the Settlement of Investment Disputes (ICSID). Second, there are the regional development banks (RDBs), including the African Development Bank (AfDB) and its soft loan window the African Development Fund (AfDF); the Inter-American Development Bank (IADB), which also has a soft loan window – the IADB Fund for Special Operations (FSO) – and a private sector promotion agency – the Inter-American Investment Corporation (IIC); the Asian Development Bank (AsDB) and its soft loan window Asian Development Fund (AsDF); and the European Bank for Reconstruction and Development (EBRD). Third, there are the sub-regional development banks (SRDBs), which include the Caribbean Development Bank (CDB), the Central American Bank for Economic Integration (CABEI), the European Investment Bank (EIB), the Andean Finance Corporation (CAF), the Nordic Investment Bank (NIB), the Islamic Development Bank (IDB), the East African Development Bank (EADB), the West African Development Bank (BOAD), the Arab Bank for Economic Development In Africa (BADEA) and the North American Development

Bank (NADB). Fourth, there are other funds that operate like MDBs, such as the el Rio de la Plata Fund (FONPLATA), the Nordic Development Fund (NDF), the International Fund for Agricultural and Rural Development (IFAD), the Arab Fund for Economic and Social Development (AFESD) and the Organisation of Petroleum Exporting Countries Fund (OPEC).

7 See the IMF webpage http://www.imf.org/external/np/exr/facts/

8 On 14 September 2004, a group of experts, civil servants, NGO and private sector leaders under the chairmanship of Jean Pierre Landau, the French Inspector of Finances, released a report on global tax schemes titled 'New International Financial Contributions'. The group was appointed by the President of France, Jacques Chirac, and examined taxes on air and maritime transport, financial transactions, multinational companies, profits and arms sales as possible ways of mobilizing resources to achieve the MDGs.

9 In 2003, China replaced the US as the world's largest recipient of FDI.

10 For example, in 1996 the Asian Development Bank (AsDB) changed its criteria for graduation from concessional to regular lending. The AsDB now uses income, indebtedness and other economic, social and financial indicators in a two-step process (see chapter 2). Similarly, a new category – low-income countries under stress (LICUS) – was created by the World Bank in 2003 to describe countries facing severe internal problems (civil wars, state collapse) and requiring special treatment from development institutions.

11 Aggregating the indicator values to elaborate an index may lead to wrong assessments if the values for each country have high levels of standard deviation, which is the case when using several indicators. For example, if a country has a value of 0.5 for each of the indicators of external resource mobilization (FDI and exports), a simple average index will be 0.5. Another country that has a value of 0.9 for the first indicator and of 0.1 for the second will also have an average index of 0.5 and it would not be possible to distinguish between them. With the proposed methodology the second of these countries will be better placed than the first because it attracts more FDI, but could be well below countries with similar FDI inflows because of its low level of exports.

12 For example, China, Brazil and Mexico receive the largest share of world FDI and have the highest levels of exports, but these flows represent less than 3 per cent of their GDP. In contrast, for small countries that export natural resources, or that have a large tourism sector, FDI and exports may represent more than 10 per cent of their GDP. Yet it is clear that these three large countries have a higher capacity to mobilize external financing.

13 Countries in category A-3 (high internal mobilization capacity and low external mobilization capacity) such as Seychelles, Grenada and Maldives, have high values of internal savings in relation to the size of their economy, which boosts their relative position in the ranking process. Along with Bhutan, Gabon and Cameroon, these countries would probably be better placed in category B-3. In contrast, countries in category C-1 (low internal mobilization capacity and high external mobilization capacity), such as El Salvador, are similar to countries in category C-2 because they are dependent on external savings.

14 Jeffrey Garten, Dean of the Yale School of Management, describes today's G7 summits as follows: 'Except for sleep-inducing communiqués, G7 members

barely deal with critical economic reforms within their own countries – the very policies that matter most to the global economy. Instead, they offer plenty of advice on what non-member countries should do. The group (deflects) attention from its inability to make the tough economic choices at home by loading the agenda with the political issues of the day. The G7 has done pitifully little to adjust to [the real issues of international well-being]. It is time to close it down' (*The Financial Times*, 27 May 2003).
15 See Bradford and Linn (2004) and Martin (2004).

4   The Shape of Things to Come: Scenarios and Their Policy Implications

1 For example, a catastrophic climate change scenario beginning in 2010, such as the one explored by Schwartz and Randall (2003), may lead to a serious breakdown of international cooperation or, on the contrary, may prompt increased concerted action of the type described in the *Transformation* scenario.
2 Few countries have stated their views on development cooperation as clearly and comprehensively as Sweden has done in its Government Bill 2002/03:122 *Shared Responsibility: Sweden's Policy for Global Development*, which emphasizes the critical importance of development finance and of aligning domestic with aid policies. A number of reports prepared by the Expert Group on Development Issues of Sweden's Ministry for Foreign Affairs, and particularly those in the Development Financing 2000 initiative that led to the present study, articulate a set of concerns that inform the approach adopted in this section. For example, even though the specific questions of domestic resource mobilization and preventing capital flight are most important for developing countries, they have not been explicitly addressed in this study that focuses on international development finance.
3 There have been and are other groups of countries created at different times and for specific purposes. For example, the informal 'like-minded' group of countries gathered together progressive developed countries (in particular the Nordics) with leading developing countries in many international nego-tiations during the 1970s and 1980s. More recently, the 'Cairns group' put together more than 20 developed and developing countries interested in reducing American, European and Japanese agricultural protectionism. However, they are unlikely to affect general development financing matters as the G20 could do.
4 Congressmen C. Hagel and J. Lieberman introduced bill S.2304 in the second session of the 108th US Congress on 8 April 2004 with the title 'Greater Middle East and Central Asia Development Act of 2004'. This bill would authorize the US government to contribute to the creation of a multilateral development bank, a development foundation and a trust for democracy in that region. On 3 October 2004 the finance minister of Russia, Alexei Kudrin, met with World Bank President James Wolfensohn to discuss the possibility that the World Bank may assist Russia and Kazakhstan to establish a devel-opment bank for the Commonwealth of Independent States (*World Bank Development News*, 4 October 2004).

5   *World Bank Development News*, 10 June 2004.
6   The Task Force on Global Public goods selected six issues to focus its work on: international trade, knowledge, peace and security, financial stability, global commons and control of communicable diseases. Some of these issues overlap with global funds that have been created or have been proposed.
7   For example, the Moore Foundation, The Nature Conservancy and the National Parks Service in Costa Rica have established a trust fund to finance part of the current expenditures involved in running conservation areas.
8   Please note that in the proposed classification scheme, which places developing countries in three bands according to their domestic and external resource mobilization indicators to define nine categories (plus three additional categories for outlier countries in external finance mobilization), advancing from one category to another requires that another country moves back. This is because categories are defined by dividing the range of values in such a way that a third of the countries lies in each of the three bands.

Bibliography

Abramovitz, Moses (1956) 'Resource and Output Trends in the United States since 1870', *American Economic Review Papers and Proceedings*, 46 (May), 5–23.

Acharya, Arnab, Ana Fuzzo de Lima and Mick Moore (2003) 'The Proliferators: Transactions Costs and the Value of Aid', Brighton, Sussex: Institute of Development Studies.

Addison, Tony and Abdur R. Chowdhury (2003) *A Global Lottery and a Global Premium Bond*, Helsinki: World Institute for Development Economics Research (WIDER) of the United Nations University.

African Development Bank (2003) Press release, 25 July, Tunis, Tunisia.

African Development Bank (2004a) 'Stepping Up to the Future: An Independent Evaluation of AfDF VII, VIII and IX', July, Tunis, Tunisia.

African Development Bank (2004b) 'A Proposal for the Strategic Orientation of AfDF Activities under AfDF-X', Tunis, Tunisia: African Development Bank.

American Association of Fundraising Council (2003) *Giving USA 2003: The Annual Report on Philanthropy for the Year 2002*, Indianapolis: AAFRC Trust for Philanthropy.

Asian Development Bank (ADB) (1999) 'Strengthening the International Financial Architecture', *Briefing Notes* No. 12, Manila: Economics and Development Resource Centre, ADB.

Baier, Scott Leonard, Gerald P. Dwyer and Robert Tamura (2002) 'How Important are Capital and Total Factor Productivity for Economic Growth?', Working Paper 2002–2a, Federal Reserve Bank of Atlanta.

Bank of International Settlements (BIS) (2001) *Triennial Central Bank Survey of Foreign Exchange and Derivatives Market Activity in April 2001*, Basle: BIS Monetary and Economic Department.

Bank of International Settlements (BIS) (2004) *Triennial Central Bank Survey of Foreign Exchange and Derivatives Market Activity in April 2004*, Basle: BIS Monetary and Economic Department.

Basu, Moni (2004) 'Poorer Nations may get Investors', *Cox News Service*, 9 June.

Baumert, K.A., James Perkaus and Nancy Kete (2003) 'Greater Expectations: Can Emissions Trading Deliver an Equitable Climate Regime?', *Climate Policy*, 3, 137–48.

Becker, Torbjorn, Anthony Richards and Yungong Thaicharoen (2001) 'Bond Restructuring and Moral Hazard: Are Collective Action Clauses Costly?', IMF Working Paper. Available Online at http://www.org/external/pubs/ft/wp/2001/wp0192.pdf

Berg, Elliot (1993) *Rethinking Technical Cooperation: Reforms for Capacity-Building in Africa*, New York: United Nations Development Program.

Berg, Elliot (2002) 'Increasing the Effectiveness of Aid: A Critique of Some Current Views', paper prepared for the Expert Group Meeting, Department of Economic and Social Affairs, United Nations, New York, 24–5 January.

Bertrand, Doris (2002) *The Results Approach in the United Nations: Implementing the United Nations Millennium Declaration*, Geneva: Joint Inspection Unit Report (JIU/REP/2002/2).

Bezanson, Keith and Francisco Sagasti, *et al.* (2000) *A Foresight and Policy Study of the Multilateral Development Banks*, Study 2000, Stockholm: IDS on behalf of the Ministry of Foreign Affairs, Sweden.

Bezanson, Keith and Francisco Sagasti (2002) *Perceptions and Perspectives on Overlap and Duplication in the United Nations Development System Specialised Agencies*, paper submitted to the Department for International Development, Institute of Development Studies, Brighton, UK.

Bezanson, Keith, Ursula Casabonne, Richard Jolly, Robert Picciotto, Fernando Prada and Francisco Sagasti (2003) *Evaluating Development Effectiveness in Six United Nations Agencies*, paper commissioned by the Department of International Development (UK), Institute of Development Studies, Brighton, UK.

Birdsall, Nancy (2000) 'The World Bank of the Future: Victim, Villain, Global Credit Union?', Policy Outlook, Washington, DC: Carnegie Endowment.

Bleijenberg, A.N. and R.C.N. Wit (1998) *A European Environmental Aviation Charge – Feasibility Study*, Delft: Centre for Energy Conservation and Environmental Technology (CE).

Borensztein, Eduardo and Paolo Mauro (2004) 'The Case for GDP-Indexed Bonds', *Economic Policy* Vol. 19 (38) (April), 165.

Bradford, Colin and Johannes Linn (2004) 'Global Economic Governance at a Crossroad: the Obsolescence of the G7 and the rise of the G20', *Brookings Institution Policy Brief*, Washington DC, April.

Brainard, Lael and Allison Driscoll (2003) *Making the Millennium Challenge Account work for Africa, Global Economics*, The Brooking Institution. Available http://www.brookings.edu/views/papers/brainard/20030710.pdf.

Brown, Gordon (2001) Speech given by Gordon Brown, Chancellor of the Exchequer, at the International Conference Against Child Poverty, London, 26 February. Available at www.hm-treasury.gov.uk/newsroom_ and_speeches/ press/2001/press_18_01.cfm .

Brown, Karen (1996) 'Transforming the Unilateralist into the Internationalist: New Tax Treaty Policy towards Developing Countries', in Karen B. Brown and Mary Louise Fellows (eds), *Taxing America*, New York: New York University Press.

Brzoska, Michael, Bonn International Centre for Conversion (2001) 'Taxation of the Arms Trade: An Overview of the Issues, paper prepared for the United Nations ad hoc Expert Group Meeting on Innovations in Mobilizing Global Resources for Development, June.

Buira, Ariel (2002) 'Reforming the Governance of the Bretton Woods Institutions in Financing for Development', Proceedings of a workshop of the G-24, published by The OPEC Fund for International Development,Washington, DC.

Centre for Global Studies/Centre for International Governance Innovations (CFGS/CIGI) (2004) 'The G-20 at Leaders', Level?' 29 February IDRC, Ottawa.

Childers, Erskine and Brian Urquhart (1994) *Renewing the United Nations System*, Uppsala, Sweden: Dag Hammarskjold Foundation.

Cleveland, Harlan, Hazel Henderson and Inge Kaul (eds) (1995) *Special Issue of Futures: The United Nations: Policy and Financing Alternatives*, The Global Commission to Fund the United Nations, Washington, DC.

Commission on Global Governance (1995) *Our Global Neighbourhood*, New York: Oxford University Press.

Commission on International Development (1969) *Partners in Development* (the Pearson Report), New York: Praeger Publishers.

Cooper, R. (2001) 'Financing International Public Goods: a Historical Overview and New Challenges', in C.D. Gerrard and M. Ferroni and A. Mody (eds), Obstect Public Policies and Problems: Implications for Financing and Evaluation, Proceedings from a World Bank workshop, Washington, DC, 11–12 July 2000.

Cordell, Arthur J. (1996) 'New Taxes for a New Economy', *Government Information in Canada*, 2(42), online at http://www.usask.ca/library/gic/v2n4/cordell.cordell.htm;

Council of Economic Advisers (1998) 'The Kyoto Protocol and the President's Policies to Address Climate Change: Administration Economic Analysis'. Washington, DC.

COWI (2001) 'Joint Nordic Assessment of the CCA/UNDAP Process: haying the Keystone of UN Development Reform: The CCA/UNDAP Experience, Copenhagen. *CCA/UNDAF Experience*, Synthesis Report, October, (mimeo)

COWI and Oxford International Associates (2000) *Mobilising Support and Resources for the United Nations Funds and Programmes*. Stockholm: Swedish Ministry of Foreign Affairs.

Cox, A., S. Folke, L. Schulpen and N. Webster (2001) 'Do the Poor Matter? A Comparative Study of European Aid for Poverty Reduction in India', *ODI Working Paper* No. 124, March.

Culpeper, Roy (1997) *Multilateral Development Banks: Titans and Behemoth?*, vol. 5, Ottawa: The North South Institute.

D'Orville, Hans and Dragoljub Najman (1995) *Towards a New Multilateralism: Funding Global Priorities: Innovative Financing Mechanisms for Internationally Agreed Programmes*, Paris/New York: Independent Commission on Population and Quality of Life.

Darcy, J. (2003) *Measuring Humanitarian Need: A Critical Review of Needs Assessment Practice and itsIinfluence on Resource Allocation*, London: Overseas Development Institute, Humanitarian Policy Group, February.

Denison, E.F. (1964) *Measuring the Contribution of Education (and the 'Residual') to Economic Growth*, Paris: OECD.

Denison, E.F. (1985) *Trends in American Economic Growth 1929–1982*, Washington, DC: Brookings Institute.

Department for International Development (DFID) (2003a) *International Finance Facility*, London, January.

Department for International Development (DFID) (2003b) *International Finance Facility*–A Technical Note, London, February.

Devarajan, Shantayanan, Margaret J. Miller and Eric V. Swanson (2002) 'Goals for Development: History, Prospects and Costs', World Bank Policy Research Working Paper 2819, Washington, DC: World Bank.

Development Committee (2003) 'Enhancing Voice and Participation of Developing and Transition Countries', Progress Report by the Boards of the World Bank and the IMF, DC2003–0012, 12 September.

Dollar, David, and Victoria Levin (2004) 'The Increasing Selectivity of Aid, 1984–2002', World Bank Policy Research Working Paper 3299, May http://econ.worldbank.org/files/35475_wps3299.pdf.

European Commission (2000) *The European Community's Development Policy*, Brussels. European Commission, November.

European Commission (2002) *US Farm Bill*, Brussels: European Commission, 15 May.

Economic Commission for Latin America and the Caribbean (2002) *Growth with stability: Financing for Development in the new International Context*, Santiago, Chile: ECLAC.

Eichengreen Barry (1996) 'The Tobin Tax: What Have We Learned?', in ul Haq *et al.* (eds), *The Tobin Tax: Coping With Financial Volatility*, New York: Oxford University Press

Eichengreen, Barry, and Ashoka Mody (2000a) 'Would Collective Action Clauses Raise Borrowing Costs?', *NBER Working Paper* 7458, January.

Eichengreen, Barry, and Ashoka Mody (2000b) 'Would Collective Action Clauses Raise Borrowing Costs? An Update and Extension', *World Bank Research Paper* 2363, June.

Eichengreen, Barry, Kenneth Kletzer, and Ashoka Mody (2003) 'Crisis Resolution: Next Steps', Brookings Trade Forum, Washington, DC: Brookings Institution.

Ellerman, A., Henry D. Jacoby and Annelène Decaux (1998) 'The Effects on Developing Countries of the Kyoto Protocol and CO_2 Emissions Trading', *World Bank Policy Research Working Papers* No. 2019.

Estrella Faria, Jose Angelo (2002) 'The UNCITRAL Legislative Guide on Privately Financed Infrastructure Projects', *The Journal of World Investment*, 3:2:211–229, Geneva

Feldstein, Martin (2003) 'An Overview of Prevention and Management', in Martin Feldstein (ed.), *Economic and Financial Crises in Emerging Market Economies*, Chicago and London: The University of Chicago Press.

Ferguson, Niall (2003) 'Hegemony or Empire', *Foreign Affairs*, September–October, 154–61.

Flint, Michael (2002) 'Easier Said Than Done: A Review of Results–Based Management In Multilateral Development Institutions', November, DFID, London.

Friedman, Milton (1962), *Capitalism and Freedom*, Chicago: University of Chicago Press.

Fukuda-Parr, Sakiko, Carlos Lopes and Khalid Malik (eds) (2002) *Capacity for Development: New Solutions to Old Problems*, London: Earthscan-UNDP.

Galloway, Jennifer (2004) 'What CACs Lacks', *Latin Finance Number* 153, January 2004.

Gillinson, Sarah (2003) *UN Reform: 1997–2003*, London: Overseas Development Institute

Goldin, Ian, Halsey Rogers and Nicholas Stern (2002) *The Role and Effectiveness of Development Assistance: Lessons from World Bank Experience*, Washington, DC: World Bank.

Gonzalez-Eiras, Martin (2002) 'The Effect of Contingent Credit Lines on Banks' Liquidity Demand' (unpublished, Buenos Aires: Universidad de San Andres). Cited in IMF (2004) *Global Financial Stability Report*, Washington, DC: IMF.

Gottschalk, Ricardo (2003) *Why It Can Be Economically and Morally Rewarding to Invest in Developing Countries*, Sussex: Institute of Development Studies.

Government of Peru (2003) Mecanismas Innovadores para el Financiamiento de Infraestructura Regional, documents presentado a la Cumbre Presidencial del Grupo de Rio, Brasilia.

Graduate Institute of International Studies Geneva (2003) *Small Arms Survey 2003: Development Denied*, Oxford: Oxford University Press.

Griffith-Jones, Stephany and Jose Antonio Ocampo (2004) 'Is there Progress Towards a Development-oriented International Financial System?', *IDS Bulletin*, 35(1), January.

Griffith-Jones, Stephany and Ana Teresa Fuzzo de Lima. (2004) *Alternative Loan Guarantee Mechanisms and Project Finance for Infrastructure in Developing Countries*, Brighton: Institute of Development Studies.

Gugiatti, Mark, and Anthony Richards (2003) 'Do Collective Action Clauses Influence Bond Yields? New Evidence from Emerging Markets'. Reserve Bank of Australia, *Research Discussion Paper* 2003–02 (March).

Hancock Graham, (1992) *Lords of Poverty*: the Power, Prestige and Corruption of the International Aid Business, New York: The Atlantic Monthly Press.

Hansard (2003) House of Commons, the United Kingdom Parliament, Column 305W, Wednesday 22 January.

Hufbauer, Gary Clyde (1999) *Tax Policy in a Global Economy: Issues facing Europe and the United States*, Washington, DC: Institute for International Economics.

Hüfner, Klaus (2004) *Total UN System Expenditures: 1986–2004*, available at http://www.globalpolicy.org/finance/tables/tabsyst.htm.

International Civil Aviation Organization (ICAO) (2001) 'Aircraft Engine Emissions –ICAO's Existing Policies', background information paper for the Colloquium on Environmental Aspects of Aviation, Montreal, 1–11 April.

International Civil Aviation Organization (ICAO) (2002) *Annual Report of the Council*. Available at http://www.icao.int/index.cfm. Montreal: ICAO.

International Development Association (IDA) (2002) *Additions to IDA Resources: Thirteenth Replenishment*, IDNSecM2002–0488, report from the Executive Directors of IDA to the Board of Governors.

International Finance Corporation (2003) *Towards Sustainable and Responsible Investment in Emerging Markets*, Washington DC: IFC.

International Monetary Fund (2001) 'Strengthening Country Ownership of Fund: Supported Programs,' Washington, DC. http://www.imf.org/external/np/pdr/cond/2001/eng/strength/120501.htm.

International Monetary Fund (2002) *Guidelines on Conditionality* prepared by the Legal and Policy Development and Review Departments, 25 September.

International Monetary Fund (2003a) *Special Drawing Rights (SDRs): A Factsheet*, September, at www.IMF.org.

International Monetary Fund (2003b) 'Evaluation of the Role of the Fund in Recent Capital Account Crises–Report by the Independent Evaluation Office'. SM/03/171. Washington, DC, May.

International Monetary Fund (2003c) 'Role of the Fund in Low-Income Member Countries over the Medium Term: Issues Paper for Discussion', 21 July.

International Monetary Fund (2004) 'Global Financial Stability Report: Market Developments and Issues', Washington, DC, World Economic and Financial Surveys, April.

International Monetary Fund Committee (IMFC) (2002) Communiqué *Collective Action Clauses (CACs)* at www.IMF.org September.

International Monetary Fund Committee (IMFC) (2003) Communiqué *Proposals for a Sovereign Debt Restructuring Mechanism (SDRM)* at www.IMF.org 12 April.

International Monetary Fund and International Development Association (2004) 'Heavily Indebted Poor Countries (HIPC) Initiative: Statistical Update', prepared by the Staffs of the IMF and the World Bank, 31 March.

International Monetary Fund-World Bank (2002) *Review of the Poverty Reduction Strategy Paper (PRSP) Approach: Early Experience with Interim PRSPs and Full PRSPs*, 26 March, Washington, DC.

International Monetary Fund-World Bank (2003) Foreign Direct Investment in Emerging Market Countries, Washington, DC: IMF-World Bank.

International Monetary Fund-World Bank (2004a) *Global Monitoring Report 2004*, Washington, DC: World Bank/IMF.

International Monetary Fund-World Bank (2004b) 'Strengthening IMF-World Bank Collaboration on Country Programs and Conditionality. Progress Report', SecM2004–0072/1. Washington, DC, 26 March.

International Monetary Fund-World Bank (2004c) 'Heavily Indebted Poor Countries (HIPC) Initiative: Statistical Update'. IDA/SecM2004–0184. Washington, DC, April.

Izaguirre, Ada (2002) 'Private Infrastructure: A Review of Projects with Private Participation, 1990–2001 Note Number 250, World Bank Private sector and infrastructure network.

J.P. Morgan Securities (2003) 'Introducing the Homeland Investment Act', Economic and Policy Research, New York.

Jha, Raghbendra (2002) 'Innovative Sources of Development Finance – Global Cooperation in the 21st' Australian National University, Canberra.

Kagan, Robert (2002) 'Power and Weakness', Policy Review, No. 113, available at www.policyreview.org/JUN02/kagan.html.

Kagan, Robert (2003) *Of Paradise and Power*, New York: Knopf.

Kanbur, Ravi, Todd Sandler and Kevin Morrison (1999) 'The Future of Development Assistance: Common Pools and International Public Goods', *Overseas Development Council Policy Essay*, No. 25, Baltimore Johns Hopkins University Press.

Kapur, D. (1999) 'Processes of Change in International Organisations', prepared for UN Wider research project 'The New Role and Functions for the UN and the Bretton Woods Institutions'.

Kapur, D., J. Lewis, and R. Webb (eds) (1997) *The World Bank: its First Half Century*, Washington DC: Brookings Institution Press.

Kaufmann, D., A. Kraay, and M. Mastruzzi (2003) 'Governance Matters III: Governance Indicators for 1996–2002', *World Bank Policy Research Working Paper* 3106.

Kaul, Inge, Pedro Conceicao, Katell le Goulven and Ronald Mendoza (eds) (2003) *Providing Global Public Goods: Managing Globalization*, New York: UNDP, Oxford University Press.

Kaul, Inge, Isabelle Grunberg and Marc A. Stern (eds) (1999) *Global Public Goods: International Cooperation in the 21st Century*, New York: UNDP, Oxford University Press.

Kent, Randolph, Mark Dalton, Karin von Hippel, and Ralf Maurer (2003) *Changes in Humanitarian Financing: Implications for the United Nations*, London: DFID and the Inter-Agency Standing Committee (IASC).

Kohler, Horst (2003) 'On the Work Program of the Executive Board', 5 November, IMF Press Release No. 03/199.

Kremer, Michael (2002) 'Pharmaceuticals and the Developing World', *Journal of Economic Perspectives*, 16(4) (Fall), 67–90.

Kristol, William and Robert Kagan (eds) (2002) *Present Dangers: Crisis and Opportunity in American Foreign and Defense Policy*, New York: Encounter Books.

Lall, S. (1997) 'Attracting Foreign Investment', *Economic Paper* No. 31, London: Commonwealth Secretariat.

Lewis, W. Arthur (1955) *The Theory of Economic Growth*, Holmwood, Il: Richard D. Irwin.

Lucas, R.E. Jr. (1993) 'Making a Miracle', *Econometrica*, 61, 251–72.

Lucas, R.E. Jr. (1988) 'On the Mechanics of Economic Development', *Journal of Monetary Economics*, 22, 3–42.

Mackie, J. J. Frederiksen and C. Rossini (2004) 'Improving ACP-EU Cooperation; Is 'Budgetising' the EDF the Answer?', *ECDPM Discussion Paper* 51, Maastricht: ECDPM.

Malloch Brown, Mark (2003) 'Strengthening the Security–Development Nexus: Conflict, Peace and Development in the 21st Century', address to the International Peace Academy Conference, New York, 5 December.

Martin, Paul (2004) 'Address on the Occasion of a Luncheon Hosted by the Conseil des Relations Internationals de Montréal (CORIM)', Montreal, Quebec, 10 May.

Maxwell, Simon and Engel, Paul (2003) 'European Development Cooperation to 2010', ODI Working Paper 219, May.

Mavrotas, George (2003) *The U.K. HM Treasury – DFID Proposal to Increase External Finance to Developing Countries: The International Finance Facility*, Helsinki: World Institute for Development Economics Research (WIDER)

McMahon, Fred (2001) *A Global Tax: Unworkable, Unnecessary and Dangerous*, Vancouver, Canada: The Fraser Institute.

McNamara, Robert S. (1970) 'The True Dimension of the Task', *International Development Review*, vol.1, 5–6.

Meltzer, Allan H. (Chairman), International Financial Institution Advisory Commission (2000) Washington DC, referred to as the 'Meltzer Report' and the 'Meltzer Commission', March.

Mendez, Ruben P (1992) *International Public Finance: A New Perspective on Global Relations*, New York: Oxford University Press.

Mendez, Ruben (2001a) The Case for Global Taxes: An Overview', paper presented to the United Nations ad hoc Expert Group Meeting on Innovations in Mobilising Global Resources for Development, UN Headquarters, New York.

Mendez, Ruben (2001b) 'Financing the UN and the International Public Sector', in Paul Diehl (ed.), *The Politics of Global Governance: International Organizations in an Interdependent World*, second edition, London and Boulder: Lynne Rienner.

Mendez, Ruben (2002) 'Global Taxation: the Rise, Decline and Future of an Idea at the United Nations', Working Paper, Paris: Institut du développement durable et des relations internationales.

Migliorisi, Stefano (2003) *The Consequences of Enlargement for Development Policy*, Volume I, Development Strategies, IDC. Available online at: http://www.europa.eu.int/comm/europecised/projects/org-cd/fichiers/rapp-consequences-enlargement_26_08_03_en.pdf

Minear, Larry and Ian Smillie (2003) *The Quality of Money: Donor Behaviour in Humanitarian Financing*, Humanitarianism and War Project, Feinstein International Famine Center, Tufts University, April.

Mintzberg, Henry (1994) *The Rise and Fall of Strategic Planning: Reconceiving the Roles for Planning, Plans and Planners*, New York: Prentice-Hall.

Mistry, P. and N. Olesen (2003) *Mitigating Risks for Foreign Investments in Least Developed Countries*. Stockholm, Sweden: Ministry for Foreign Affairs.

Nayyar, Deepak and Julius Court (2002) 'Governing Globalization: Issues and Institutions', manuscript prepared by the UNU World Institute for Development Economics Research (UNU/WIDER), Helsinki.

Nissanke, Machiko (2003) 'Revenue Potential of the Tobin Tax for Development Finance: A Critical Appraisal', *WIDER Discussion Paper* 2003/81.

Nordhaus, William D. (1999) 'Global Public Goods and the Problem of Global Warming,' Annual Lecture, The Institut d'Economie Industrielle (IDEI), Toulouse, France.

Nordic Council (1991) *The United Nations: Issues and Options: Five Studies on the Role of the UN in the Economic and Social Fields.* Commissioned by the Nordic UN Project, Stockholm, Sweden: Nordic UN Project.

Nurske, R. (1953) *Problems of Capital Formation in Underdeveloped Countries*, New York: Oxford University Press.

O'Brien, Maria (2004) 'Public Interest, Private Financing', in *Latin Finance*, number 155, March.

OECD (1997) Annex I Expert Group on the United Nations Framework Convertion on Climate Change Working Paper No.4, *Economic Fiscal Instruments: Taxation (I.E Carbon/Energy)*, OCDE/GD (97)188, p. 6

OECD (2003b) 'Philanthropic Foundations and Development Co-operation', *DAC Journal*, vol. 4.3, Paris: OECD.

OECD (2003c) *Glossary of Statistical Terms. International Trade*, http://cs3-hq.oecd.org/scripts/stats/glossary/detail.asp?ID=1029.

OECD (2004a) *Development Co-operation Report 2003*, Paris: OECD.

OECD (2004b) *Indicators of Progress in Harmonization and Alignment Methodology and Questionnaire*, elaborated by the Task Team on harmonization and alignment, DAC Working Party on aid effectiveness and donor practices (Fourth Meeting), Room Document No. 2.

OECD DAC (1992) *DAC Principles for Effective Aid: Development Assistance Manual*, Paris: OECD.

OECD DAC (1996) *Shaping the 21st Century: The Contribution of Development Co-operation*, Paris: OECD.

OECD DAC (2004a) *Improving the Aid Effectiveness of Europe's Largest Donor Country*, Paris: OECD, 27 May.

OECD DAC (2004b) *Modest Increase in Development Aid in 2003*, Press note 16 April.

Overseas Development Institute (ODI) (1997) International Taxes: New Sources of Finance for Development, Development and Cooperation, No. 3 May–June, 1997

Overseas Private Investment Corporation (OPIC) (2002) *Annual Report 2002*, Washington, DC: OPIC.

OXFAM (2002) 'Europe's Double Standards: How the EU Should Reform its Trade Policies with Developing Countries', *OXFAM Policy Briefing*, No. 22.

Patomaki, Heikki and Network Institute for Global Democratisation (2003) *The Tobin Tax: How to Make it Real Towards a Socially Responsible and Democratic System of Global Governance*

Pearce, Brian, Patrick Roche and Nick Chater (2002) *Sustainability Pays*, London: Co-operative Insurance Society (CIS).

Pieschacón, Anamaría and José Alejandro Soto (2001) 'Sistema de Préstamos al FLAR de los Bancos Centrales Miembros', FLAR Documento de Trabajo 01/01, Bogota.

Progressive Health Partners (2000) *Current US Legislative and Administration Proposals Supporting an AIDS Vaccine*,1 March, prepared for the International AIDS Vaccine Initiative (IAVI). Available online at: http://www.globalhumanitarianassistance.org/gha2003cont.htm

Radelet, Steve (2003) 'Will the Millennium Challenge Account Be Different?', *The Washington Quarterly*, 26(2), 171–187.

Rajan, Ramkishen (2000) Examining the Case for an Asian Monetary Fund', *Visiting Researchers Series* no. 3, Singapore: Institute of Southeast Asian Studies.

Rajan, Ramkishen (2001) *Revisiting the Case for a Tobin Tax Post Asian Crisis: A Financial Safeguard of Financial Bonanza*, School of Economics (University of Adelaide), Australia, and Institute of Southeast Asian Studies, Singapore.

Randel, Judith (2003) *Global Humanitarian Assistance Flows 2003*, Development Initiatives. http://www.globalhumanitarianassistance.org/gha2003cont.htm

Ratha, Dilip, (2003a) 'Workers' Remittances: An Important and Stable Source of External Development Finance', in World Bank, *Global Development Finance 2003*, Washington DC.

Ratha, Dilip, (2003b) 'Workers' Remittances: An Important and Stable Source of Development Finance, at http://www1.worldbank.org/prem/prmpo/poverty-day/docs/2003/ratha.pdf

Raymond, Peter (2004) *Comparative Review of IFI Risk Mitigation Instruments*, presentation at the World Bank Water Week Diving for Implementation, 25 February.

Reid, T.R (2004) *The United States of Europe: The New Superpower and the End of American Supremacy*, New York: Penguin Press.

Reisen, Helmut (2002) 'The Tobin Tax: Can It Work?', *OECD Observer*, May.

Reisen, Helmut (2004) *Innovative Approaches to Funding the Millennium Development Goals*, Paris: OECD Development Centre – Policy Brief No. 24.

Rischard, J.F. (2002) High Noon: Twenty Global Issues, Twenty Years to Solve Them, New York: Basic Books.

Rogerson, Andrew (2004) *The International Aid System 2005–2010: Forces for and Against Change*, London: Overseas Development Institute, ODI working paper, Draft 3: 7 January 2004, cited with permission.

Rogoff, Kenneth (2004) 'The IMF's China Card', *Foreign Policy*, May/June, 142, 64.

Rome Declaration (2003) 'Rome Declaration on Harmonization', 25 February, Rome, Italy.

Romer, P.M. (1986) 'Increasing Returns and Long-Run Growth', *Journal of Political Economy*, 94, 1002–10.

Rostow, Walter W. (1960) *The Stages of Economic Growth: A Non-Communist Manifesto*, Cambridge: Cambridge University Press.

Rwegasira, Delphin G. and Henock Kifle (1994) 'Regional Development Banks and the Objectives of the Bretton Woods Institutions' reprinted in United Nations Conference on Trade and Development (1998) *International Monetary and Financial Issues for the 1990s*, Geneva UNCTAD, Vol. 4, pp. 106–116.

Salamon, Lester (1994) 'The Rise of the Non-Profit Sector', *Foreign Affairs*, 73(4), 109–22.

Sanford, Jonathan E. (2004) 'IDA Grants and HIPC Cancellation: Their Effectiveness and Impact on IDA Resources', *World Development*, 329(9), 1579–1607.

Sagasti, Francisco (2002a) 'La Banca Multilateral de Desarrollo en América Latina', *Serie CEPAL/BID Financiamiento del desarrollo*, No. 119, Santiago de Chile: CEPAL.

Sagasti, Francisco (2002b) 'Notes on the Possible Creation of a Northeast Asian Development Bank', unpublished note, 6 May, San José, Costa Rica, University for Peace Program on Development, Security and Peace.

Sagasti, Francisco and Gonzalo Alcalde (1999) *Development Cooperation in a Fractured Global Order: An Arduous Transition*, Ottawa: International Development Research Centre.

Sagasti, Francisco and Keith Bezanson (2001) *Financing and Providing Global Public Goods Expectations and Prospects*, Development Financing 2000, Institute of Development Studies on behalf of the Ministry of Foreign Affairs Sweden

Sandmo, Agnar (2003) 'Environmental Taxation and Revenue for Development', *WIDER Discussion Paper* 2003/86, Helsinki: WIDER.

Sandor, R. (2002) 'Emissions Trading: Financing Environmental Public Goods at Least Cost'. in I. Kaul, K. Le Goulven and M. Schnupf (eds), *Global Public Goods Financing: New Tools for New Challenges*, New York: United Nations Development Programme, Office of Development Studies.

Schaefer, Brett D. and Paolo Pasicolan (2003) 'How to Improve the Bush Administration's Millennium Challenge Account', *Backgrounder*, no. 1629, Washington, The Heritage Foundation.

Schlesinger, Stephen (1997) 'Can the United Nations Reform?', *World Policy Journal*, 14(3)47–53.(Fall), 1997.

Schwartz, Peter and Doug Randall (2003) *An Abrupt Climate Change Scenario and Its Implications for United States National Security*, Global Business Network, October 2003 (found at www.gbn.org).

Seers, Dudley (1969) 'The Meaning of Development', *International Development Review*, 11, 2–6.

Schiller, Robert J. (2003) *The New Financial Order: Risk in the 21ˢᵗ Century*, Princeton, NJ: Princeton University Press.

Singer, Hans W. (1995) 'Revitalizing the United Nations: Five Proposals', *IDS Bulletin*, 26 (4), 39.

SIPRI (2000) *SIPRI Yearbook 2000*, Oxford: Oxford University Press.

Social Investment Forum (2003) *Report on Socially Responsible Investing Trends in the United States*, Washington, DC: SIF Industry Research Program.

Solow, Robert M. (1957) 'Technical Change and the Aggregate Production Function'. *Review of Economics and Statistics*, 39 (August), 312–20.

Soros, George (2002) *George Soros On Globalization*, New York: Public Affairs (Perseus Books Group).

Sparkes, Russell (2002) *SRI: A Global Revolution*, Chichester: John Wiley & Sons.

Stalgren, P. (2000) *Regional Public Goods and the Future of International Co-operation – Review of the Literature on Regional Public Good*, EODI Working Papers, Stockholm: Swedish Ministry for Foreign Affairs.

Statement of Heads of Multilateral Development Banks (2002) *Better Measuring, Monitoring, and Managing for Development Results*, News Release No. 2002/243/S, Monterrey, 19 March.

Statement of Heads of Multilateral Development Banks (2004) *Joint Marrakech Memorandum*, Statement at the Second International Roundtable 'Managing for Development Results' of the heads of the African Development Bank, Asian Development Bank, Inter-American Development Bank, European Bank for Reconstruction and Development, and World Bank, and the chairman of the Development Assistance Committee of the Organisation for Economic Co-operation and Development, 5 February.

Stiglitz, Joseph (2002) '*A Fair Deal for the World: Review*', *The New York Review of Books*, 23 May.

Stiglitz, Joseph (2004) 'Stiglitz Favours Regional Monetary Funds to Contain IMF', *The Hindu*, 19 January.

te Velde, Dirk (2001) 'Policies Towards Foreign Direct Investment in Developing Countries', *Emerging Best-Practices and Outstanding Issues*, vol. 12, London: Overseas Development Institute, pp. 51–2.

The Courier ACP-EU (2002) no. 194, September–October, p. 34

The Economist (2001) Charlemagne, '*Christopher Patten*', 16 August.

The Economist (2001) 'The European Union's aid programme to Albania is a shambles', 25 October.

The Economist (2003) 'Europe's population implosion', 17 July.

The Foundation Center (2004) *Foundation Giving Trends*, New York: The Foundation Center.

The Guardian (2003) 'Arms and the Taxman', Tuesday 1 July.

Tisdall, Simon (2005) 'A Tragedy That Could Make – or Break – the Troubled UN', *The Guardian*, 8 January p. 11.

Truman, Harry S. (1949) 'Inaugural Address', 20 January, in *Documents on American Foreign Relations*, Connecticut: Princeton University Press, 1967.

Ul Haq, I. Kaul, and I. Grunberg (eds) (1996) *The Tobin Tax: Coping with Financial Volatility*, New York: Oxford University Press.

UNCTAD (2003) *World Investment Report 2003: FDI Policies for Development: National and International Perspectives*, Geneva: UNCTAD.

UNCTAD (2004) *World Investment Report 2004: The Shiftt Towards Services.* Geneva: UNCTAD.

UNDP (1969) *A Study of the Capacity of the UN Development System*, (Jackson Report), Geneva: United Nations Inter-Agency Consultative Board, UNDP.

UNDP (1999) *Human Development Report*, New York: UNDP.

United Nations (1994) *An Agenda for Development*, Report of the Secretary-General, General Assembly, Doc. A/49/665.

United Nations (1997) *Renewing the United Nations: A Programme for Reform*, Doc. A/51/950, New York: United Nations.

United Nations (2000a) United Nations Millennium Declaration, Doc. 55/2, New York: United Nations.

United Nations (2000b) *Resource Requirements for Implementation of the Report of the Panel on United Nations Peace Operations*, Report of the Secretary-General, A/55/507.

United Nations (2001a) *Road Map towards the implementation of the United Nations Millennium Declaration*, Doc. A/56/326, New York: United Nations.

United Nations (2001b) *Report of the High-level Panel on Financing for Development* (Zedillo Report), New York: United Nations.

United Nations (2001c) *Towards Global Partnerships*, Doc. A/56/323, 9 October.

United Nations (2001d) 'Financing for Development', Report of the Secretary-General, Session 3 of the Preparatory Committee for the International Conference, Document A/AC.257.

United Nations (2001e) 'Note by the Secretary General: Technical Notes on Existing Proposals for Financing for Development'. General Assembly, Doc. A/AC.257/xx. [http://www.un.org/esa/ffd/aac257_27a1.pdf].

United Nations (2001f) *Medium Term Plan for the Period 2002–2005*, Doc. A/RES/55/6 Rev. 1, New York: United Nations.

United Nations (2002a) Outcome of the International Conference on Financing for Development, Report of the Secretary-General, Doc. A/57/344, New York: United Nations.

United Nations (2002b) *Report of the International Conference on Financing for Development*, Monterrey, Mexico, 18–22 March, New York: United Nations.

United Nations (2003a) *Implementation of the United Nations Millennium Declaration: Report of the Secretary General*, Doc. A/58/323, 2 September.

United Nations (2003b) *Scale of Assessments for the Apportionment of the Expenses of the United Nations*, Doc. A/58/360.

United Nations (2004) *A More Secure World: Our Shared Responsibility*, Report of the High-Level Panel on Threats, Challenges and Change.

United Nations Millennium Project (2004) *Millennium Development Goals Needs Assessment*, New York: United Nations.

United Nations Millennium Project (2005) *Investing in Development: A Practical Plan to Achieve the Millennium Development Goals*, New York: United Nations.

United Nations, General Assembly and Security Council (2000) *Report of the Panel on United Nations Peace Operations* A/55/305-S/2000/809, 21 August.

United States Department of State (2003) *World Military Expenditures and Arms Transfers (WMEAT) 1999–2000*, 28th edition, February.

Van Reisen, M. (2002) *Tackling Poverty: a Proposal for European Union Aid Reform*, London: British Overseas NGOs for Development (BOND).

Vasquez, Ian and John Welborn (2003) 'Reauthorize or Retire the Overseas Private Investment Corporation?', *Foreign Policy Briefing* No. 78, 15 September, Washington, DC: Cato Institute.

Wade, R., and F. Veneroso, (1998) 'The Resources Lie Within', *The Economist*, 7 November, 19–21.

WBGU-German Advisory Council on Global Change (2002) *Charging for the Use of Global Commons*, Berlin.

World Bank (1989) *Strategic Agenda: Strategic Planning Division*, Washington, DC: World Bank.

World Bank (1998a) *Assessing Aid: What Works, What Doesn't and Why?*, Policy Research Unit, Washington, DC.

World Bank (1998b) *Partnership for Development: Proposed Actions for the World Bank, Partnerships Group*, Washington, DC: World Bank.

World Bank (2003a) *Global Development Finance 2002*, Washington, DC: World Bank.

World Bank (2003b) 'The Global Poll: Multinational Survey of Opinion Leaders 2002', prepared for the World Bank.

World Bank 2003c) 'Supporting Sound Policies with Adequate and Appropriate Financing', paper presented to the Development Committee in September 2003. DC2003-0016. Washington, DC.

World Bank (2004a) *Global Development Finance 2003*, Washington, DC: World Bank.

World Bank (2004b) *Global Economic Prospects 2004: Realizing the Development Promise of the Doha Agenda*, Washington, DC: World Bank.

World Health Organization (2001) *Macroeconomics and Health: Report of the Commission on Macroeconomics and Health*, Genera: WHO.

Annex A: Development Financing 2000 Reports

Mitigating risk for foreign investments in developing countries

The study takes as a point of departure the commitments made in Monterrey and Johannesburg for new public–private partnerships. Focus here is on public–private interaction that increases FDI in the least developed countries through risk mitigation. The study aims to increase understanding in official and intergovernmental circles on the specific risk issues faced by private investors in least developed countries (LDCs).

Although many investment regimes in LDCs are now more liberal than those in OECD countries, the response from foreign investors has, for the most part, not been commensurate with the reform efforts LDCs have made. The risks they pose for foreign investors are considerably higher than the risks of investing in alternative locations in the developing world. This study focuses on ways of mitigating these risks and bringing them down to more acceptable levels through a variety of public–private interactions.

The fundamental principle is that risks should be allocated to parties that are in the best position to bear them. To the greatest extent possible, project sponsors must absorb financial and operating (i.e. commercial) risks. It would be unreasonable to expect foreign investors to bear non-commercial risks without full or partial cover.

To fill the gap, political risk cover is available from official and private sources, but it suffers from practical limitations. It does not cover risks that cannot be conceptualized and anticipated in advance. Normal insurance cover is available to protect against natural events (Acts-of-God). But no cover is available for events triggered by cumulative policy failures, global acts of terrorism that have implications for investments generally, or for events triggered by civil society. Thus there are lacunae in the risk cover that foreign investors in LDCs can draw on. These gaps deter increased FDI flows but are not amenable to being filled quickly without more innovative 'product development' on the part of both official and private insurers.

Experience through the 1990s suggests that multilateral institutions have serious 'attitude problems' in galvanizing FDI flows to LDCs. Their *modus operandi*, their vulnerability to the volatility of their frequently changing leaderships and the perverse incentives under which their staff operate do not make them best suited to performing this task. The way in which they function is inimical to productive exchanges with the private sector.

That leaves the onus on bilateral agencies to support FDI to LDCs in ways that do not create permanent dependencies for subsidies or result in the wrong sort of (subsidy-chasing) FDI. There are a number of things that bilateral donors can do, which may be divided into medium-term and long-term initiatives to mitigate risks and unblock FDI flows to LDCs. *Medium-term initiatives include*: (i) working with multilateral partners and the private sector to develop financial systems and capital markets of LDCs; (ii) providing open access to their domestic consumer markets to all products of LDCs; (iii) engaging in 'regulatory-partnership' arrangements between their financial system regulators with regulatory agencies in LDCs to ensure that sound laws, rules and regulations are developed and that they are applied and enforced; (iv) providing seed funding to encourage their non-banking institutions to establish a presence in LDC financial systems that would be shunned by the private sector; (v) encouraging their domestic firms through favourable tax treatment or through grant support for partial cost coverage to develop supply sources so that LDCs can take advantage of the preferential access they have but are not availing of and encouraging developing country investors to invest in LDCs to take advantage of privileged access to donor markets. *Long-term options* for bilateral donors to consider include: (i) providing sustained long-term institutional and human capacity-building assistance to LDC accounting, legal and judicial systems to improve their performance and capacities when it comes to dealing with foreign investors swiftly; (ii) providing support for political and broader governance reforms to improve transparency, accountability and democratic governance; and (iii) supporting the future evolution and development of political and non-commercial risk insurance capacity in their own domestic markets and in the wider regional European market through more productive public–private partnerships between official bilateral insurers and private risk insurers.

Financing and providing global public goods (GPGs)

The study makes a critical analysis of the growing international debate on global public goods (GPGs) and discusses ways in which they could be financed most efficiently. The central concern is of a practical nature, and relates to whether the concept of GPGs can advance thought and action on common concerns that affect a large portion of humanity. The study includes a system perspective for providing and financing for global public goods, analyses of innovative financing instruments, a discussion of the division of responsibilities between the multilateral institutions, and case studies on climate change, biological diversity, financial stability, peace and security, and HIV/Aids.

Globalization is normally seen as the reason for the increasing focus on GPGs in international policy debates. The paradox of globalization lies in its effect of increasing contact between people, but simultaneously maintaining deep fissures between groups of countries and groups of people within countries. This paradox is described as the fractured global order.

The structure of the fractured global order can be conceptualized in terms of three closely interconnected and partially overlapping domains, each of which has its own specific features and ways of interacting with the other two: the domain of the global, that of the networks, and that of the local. The domain of the global comprises the impacts of actions by individual agents on the majority of the world's population. The domain of the networks consists of the multiple channels and nodes that interconnect social groups all over the world and that establish a tangled web of overlapping and intertwined networks. The domain of the local is constituted by human activities anchored in time and space, and which comprise the actual production, exchange and consumption of tangible goods and services by organizations and social groups of all kinds.

Many concerns, issues and activities that were previously national or local in nature have now acquired a wider scope and have moved beyond the control of the nation-state. The emphasis on the 'global' nature of certain public goods must not lose sight of the fact that their actual provision is rooted in the domain of the local.

The last decade has witnessed many efforts at reversing ODA trends. GPGs have become a major part of these efforts. Many established development organizations interpret GPGs as providing a new rationale for development assistance and as a possible basis for mobilising additional funding. The basic proposition is that by focusing significant increases in financing on GPGs, richer countries would be acting in their own direct interest. This appeal to enlightened self-interest is distinct from rationales based on appeals to charity or ethical responsibility.

As a methodological device, the notion of an 'idealized public goods delivery system' is introduced and identifies the elements that must be in place for a global public good to be defined, produced and consumed, and invites, therefore, assessment of what is missing in the case of a particular global public good and how far down in the international public goods delivery system it will be necessary to go in order to arrange for its provision. The idealized public goods delivery system is made up of all of the following components:

- Knowledge, public awareness and political decision as to what GPGs are, their characteristics, effects, and benefits.
- GPG regimes, such as conventions, treaties, protocols, and other legal instruments.
- International organizations and partnerships to interpret, administer, monitor and evaluate the provisions specified in the agreements that give rise to the GPG regime.
- Financing mechanisms.
- Operational policies and procedures – requirements for the consistent and effective application of the principles and norms of GPG regimes.
- Agreements and contracts specifying terms of reference, obligations and rights of the national and local entities involved in the actual production and consumption of the GPG.
- Capabilities and arrangements for the inclusion of national and local entities in the provision and consumption of GPGs.

The conceptual framework underscores the point that there is no way of escaping values, interests and power relations in defining what is a global public good; that the knowledge of epistemic communities is critical to underpin a decision and to establish global public goods regimes; that institutions and partnerships, financing mechanisms, and operational policies and procedures are required at the international level to facilitate the production of the global public good; and that all of the preceding arrangements would be useless without the identification and involvement of national and local entities that will be in charge of actually producing and consuming the global public good.

The study also identified four broad categories of possible *financing mechanisms*:

- Internalizing externalities, to the consumers of the good or the creators of the deleterious effect. This could be done through the creation of a market, or the charging of taxes, fees or levies.
- Private sources, for example through companies imposing internal charges, or contributions from individuals.
- National and international financial institution (IFI) sources, through transfers of various kinds.
- Partnerships, involving a range of different levels and actors, including public–private alliances.

There is no single optimal approach to the financing of GPGs. Although some general principles and questions are useful in the examination of financial issues and alternatives (e.g. to what extent can externalities be externalized? Could a market be created?), a singular set of appropriate financial arrangements will apply for each specific international public good. This implies adopting a systematic case-by-case approach to the identification and choice of financing mechanisms. The report presents a *'financing decision tree'* (a framework to help guide choices and policy decisions), based on integrating consideration of the criteria defining a GPG and the various options for the financing of delivery. The framework involved reference to the following criteria: applicability; sustainability and continuity; fairness; flexibility, and lack of constraining administrative complexity; and political feasibility. The convenience and feasibility of using one or another of these mechanisms will depend on a variety of circumstances and on the specific characteristics of the public good in question.

Five case studies are included in the study: financing biodiversity conservation; climate change abatement as a GPG; funding public goods: the case of AIDS research; peace and security as a GPG: focus on operational conflict prevention; and financial stability as a GPG: towards a new global financial architecture (the first three were reported at the seminar). The common features evident in the case studies are:

- The vital need for clear and precise definitions, to provide rigour of analysis (without this, anything can be called a GPG and the term itself becomes meaningless).
- The recognition and delivery of GPGs must be firmly embedded in political considerations and political processes.

- Even where private sources of financing and the creation of markets are possible, there is an essential and irreplaceable role for the public sector.
- There is no standard pattern and one size does not fit all. Specific approaches to funding are required for each good.

Mobilizing support and resources for UN funds and programmes

Much of the seminal thinking about development since 1980 had emanated from the United Nations Development Funds and Programmes (UNDFPs),[1] especially on issues such as 'social and human development' (UNDP), and putting a human face on structural adjustment (UNICEF). This report argues that it is hence important that donors strive to maintain and strengthen the soft intervention capacity that the UNDFPs have, instead of compromising it further.

The fundamental issue that needs to be addressed concerns the right balance between (i) retaining the soft-intervention type of development capacity that already exists, and (ii) building up competing similar soft-intervention capacity in the IFIs and MBDs. It is not necessarily clear, however, that the IFIs/MBDs are able to do as cost-effective a job in as user-friendly a manner.

The study's assessment is that the present pattern of burden sharing is neither healthy nor sustainable for the system. Current burden-sharing distortions are so significant that it will take some time to correct them. For burden sharing to be accepted as a basic component of replenishment negotiations for funding the UNDFPs, a political initiative should be taken in order to build consensus through the OECD-DAC working group mechanisms.

If a replenishment model were to be applied to the UNDFPs, the optimal replenishment period should cover four years. Replenishments are not cost-free exercises and it would be easiest to negotiate a single replenishment for all the UNDFPs under the auspices of the UNDG. It is, however, doubtful whether the internal coordination mechanisms within the UN system are strong enough for such a pooled approach to be taken.

A foresight and policy study of the multilateral development banks

This study attempts to provide a broad strategic framework for examination of the issues affecting the future of the MDBs. We are in a time of unprecedented pressures on these organizations, as they are bombarded with demands and attacks from a multitude of actors. The MDBs are uniquely placed, however, for more than all other organizations, they interact with all entities that straddle the worlds of development and of international finance. In spite of many problems and shortcomings, independent analyses have consistently confirmed a reasonably positive track record and the fact that there are no other institutions that provide a comparable range of products and services to member countries.

Most donors seek improved coordination among the MDBs and between them and other members of the international development system. In order for this to succeed, they will need to move their policy and practice focus away from its dominant pattern of dealing with single organizations and discrete channels of delivery and move to more systemic approaches that visualize the totality of the systems of international development and international finance.

Currently and for the foreseeable future, MDBs will be pressed to perform a triple role:

- Financial resource mobilization.
- Capacity building, institutional development and knowledge brokering.
- Provision of global and regional public goods.

MDBs need to maintain the delicate balance of these three functions. With regard to *financial resource mobilization*, this will require the MDBs to:

- Develop a broader range of products suited to different client needs and priced accordingly (all the way from large, emergency, fast-disbursing loans for middle- and high-income developing countries, to small, capacity-building, slow-disbursing loans for poor countries).
- Eschew formal graduation policies, and instead differentiate products aimed at specific segments of borrowers, pricing them according to their characteristics.
- Focus on enhancing other financial flows, both official (co-financing, donor coordination) and private (comfort, guarantees), and on helping to increase domestic resource mobilization (financial sector reforms, public expenditure reviews).
- Explore new forms of mobilizing financial resources for poor countries (trust funds to cover recurrent expenditures, export promotion, debt reduction on an exceptional basis).

With regard to *capacity building, institutional development and knowledge brokering* MDB institutions will need to:

- Ensure the availability of the technical and management capacity to engage in more costly and lengthy operations (social sectors, governance, safety nets, and continuous policy dialogue). Some of the MDBs currently simply do not have these capabilities or do not have them in sufficient quantity and quality.
- Build and renew their intellectual capacity to engage in policy dialogue with stakeholders, embracing intellectual diversity and a greater willingness to learn from others.
- Focus on spreading best practices and on building policy-making capacities in borrowing countries.
- Give greater and special emphasis to technological innovation and scientific research capabilities (bridge the knowledge divide).
- Explore the possibility of charging for non-lending (i.e. technical assistance, information, policy dialogue) services to middle- and high-income developing countries.

With regard to the *provision of regional and global public goods* the MDB family of institutions will need to:

- Engage with other regional, international and global organizations in strategic partnerships. The evidence from current practice is that MDBs cannot and should not continue to attempt to provide public goods on their own.
- Ensure they can count on sufficient grant-making resources to cover the cost of contributing to the sustainable provision of public goods.
- Develop jointly with strategic partners rapid-response capacities to help member countries cope with shocks. In addition to the sudden and unforeseen requirements resulting from natural disasters and health epidemics, the benefits of increased economic openness and integration into the global economy also entail increased exposure to volatility.
- Explore new forms of resource mobilization for this purpose (predictable and assured funding, international taxes, international fiscal transfers).

The differences between the MDBs should not prevent visualizing them in an integral manner, as a set of organizations that share common characteristics, play similar roles and conform broadly to the same institutional model. The challenge is to transform a more or less disparate family of institutions into a more efficient network and eventually into an effective MDB system.

In addition to paying attention to the World Bank and the regional development banks, it is necessary to pay greater attention to the smaller sub-regional banks. They often play an important role when viewed from the perspective of the borrowing countries, and should intensify and improve their interactions with other members of the MDB family.

Transboundary water management as a global public good[2]

This study looks at transboundary water management through the lens of international public goods and analyses financial flows and institutional mechanisms in the provision of regional water management. It discussed the possibility of a more coordinated approach to managing and financing transboundary waters, and the importance of politically feasible environments. In addition, it addresses the question of a more proactive role for regional economic groupings such as the European Union (EU), Southern Africa Development Community (SADC) and the Association of South East Asian Nations (ASEAN), and new financing mechanisms and a strengthened institutional framework.

International financial support to transboundary water management is rather piecemeal and scattered. There appear to be significant barriers to the entry of the private sector in provisioning of regional public goods, not least due to the frequent lack of clear regional legal and regulatory frameworks.

The study recommends the establishment of an International Shared Waters Facility (ISWF), under a partnership model and drawing on the established roles of multilateral organizations presently engaged in the sector, including the World Bank, UNDP and the Global Environmental Facility (GEF), whilst liaising closely with related international initiatives such as the Global Water Partnership (GWP) and the World Water Council. Its charter would highlight the importance of transboundary water management as an international public good and would promote the principle of subsidiarity in the provisioning of such a good.

Regional economic groupings actively promoting regional public goods (such as SADC) should be encouraged and supported through the development of financing initiatives for basin-specific activities within these groupings. The EU could take the lead in organizing such an initiative within which the experience of the various councils could be exchanged and expanded upon.

The study also recommends that Consideration 47 in the recently adopted EU Water Framework Directive should be used to establish a more proactive role for the EU in shared river basins internationally; and, specifically, those immediately outside the EU. A brokerage role for the EU should be made more explicit and streamlined with EU development programmes in critical transboundary river basin regions. Member states such as Sweden could support this role under the umbrella of the ISWF.

Notes

1   This study focuses on UNDP, UNFPA and UNICEF.
2   It should be noted that the report entitled 'Transboundary Water Management as a Global Public Good' differs from the other studies in several respects. This is primarily because it deals with a specific and more limited issue, and functions more as a complement to the study on global public goods.

Annex B: Country Classification Scheme: Approach, Methodology and Results

Various options were explored to design a classification scheme linked directly to the capacity to mobilize external and domestic resources, which could help to better match financing instruments with types of countries. Two sets of variables were initially identified to calculate an index for the *external resource mobilization capacity* – FDI, ODA inflows, international reserves and exports – and another for the *internal resource mobilization capacity* – domestic savings, tax revenues, fiscal deficit, bank credit and gross fixed capital formation. For each of these sets, a principal components analysis was carried out in order to identify those that were highly correlated. As a result, FDI inflows and exports of goods and services remained the key indicators of the capacity to mobilize external financing, and internal savings and tax revenues as a percentage of the Gross Domestic Product remained as indicators of the capacity to mobilize domestic resources. A total of 132 developing countries for which 1990–2002 data was available were included in the sample, and the simple average of the annual values of each variable was calculated for the two periods under consideration, 1990–1996 and 1997–2002.

A first approach involved the construction of a composite index by rescaling the ranges, normalizing the variables in each set and calculating their averages. In addition to problems related to the availability and quality of the data, the aggregation of different indicators involves loss of information (countries whose indicators would have different values could have the same averages), and presents difficulties in deciding about the weights that should be assigned to each indicator. For these reasons, rather than calculating composite indexes it was decided to rank countries according to the values of each indicator and to use a two-step process for defining categories and the relative standing of countries within each category. In the first step, countries were classified according to their levels of FDI for external resource mobilization and of domestic savings for internal resource mobilization. In the second step, countries were ranked within each of these categories to determine their relative positions using their levels of exports for external resource mobilization and of tax revenues for domestic resource mobilization. This methodology, summarised in Table 3.3 in the text, has the advantage of avoiding the loss of information associated with the calculation of averages across indicators and, in contrast with the construction of indexes, the relative position of countries is not affected by absolute values, standard deviations and correlation effects.

A matrix to place countries was constructed by combining the external and domestic resource mobilization categories defined through this two-step process. Figure 3.1 shows the results of the combination of both rankings comprising data for the period 1997–2002. Four countries – China, Brazil, Mexico and Argentina – which have received very large amounts of foreign investment, were considered as 'outliers' and placed in a special category (category 0) along the external resources axis. The rest of countries were divided according to their rank into three groups (labelled 1, 2 and 3 for high, medium and low capacity), each with the same number of countries. A similar process was carried out along the domestic resource axis to divide countries according to their domestic savings rankings, placing them into three groups with an equal number of countries (labelled A, B and C for high, medium and low capacity, respectively). This leads to a matrix with 12 cells, even though some of these combinations (for example, low external resource mobilization capacity with low domestic mobilization capacity) led to apparently incongruous categories with few special-case countries in them.

In addition, comparisons were made between the categories defined using this methodology and those devised with other criteria such as income levels, debt service, governance, science and technology capacity and ODA inflows.

Some highlights are: most countries categorized as IDA-only, LICUS or Blend (receiving IDA and regular loans) by the World Bank are countries with a lower capacity to mobilize internal and external resources (Figure B1); most countries in sub-Saharan Africa are placed in the categories of low capacity to mobilize resources (Figure B2); a higher resource mobilization capacity is associated with higher per capita income (Figure B3); countries with higher debt/GDP ratios have a lower capacity to mobilize resources (Figure B4); and countries with a higher

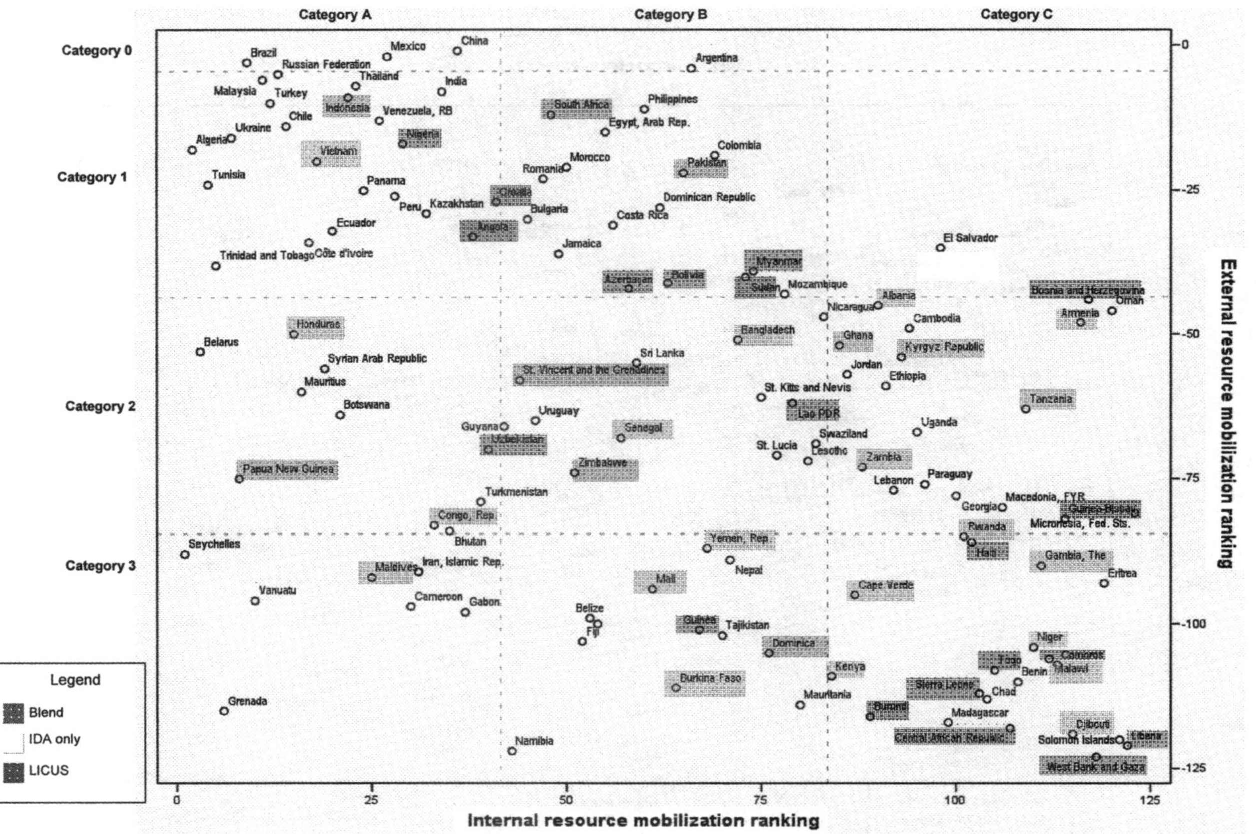

Figure B1   IDA-only, LICUS and Blend countries and resource mobilization capacities

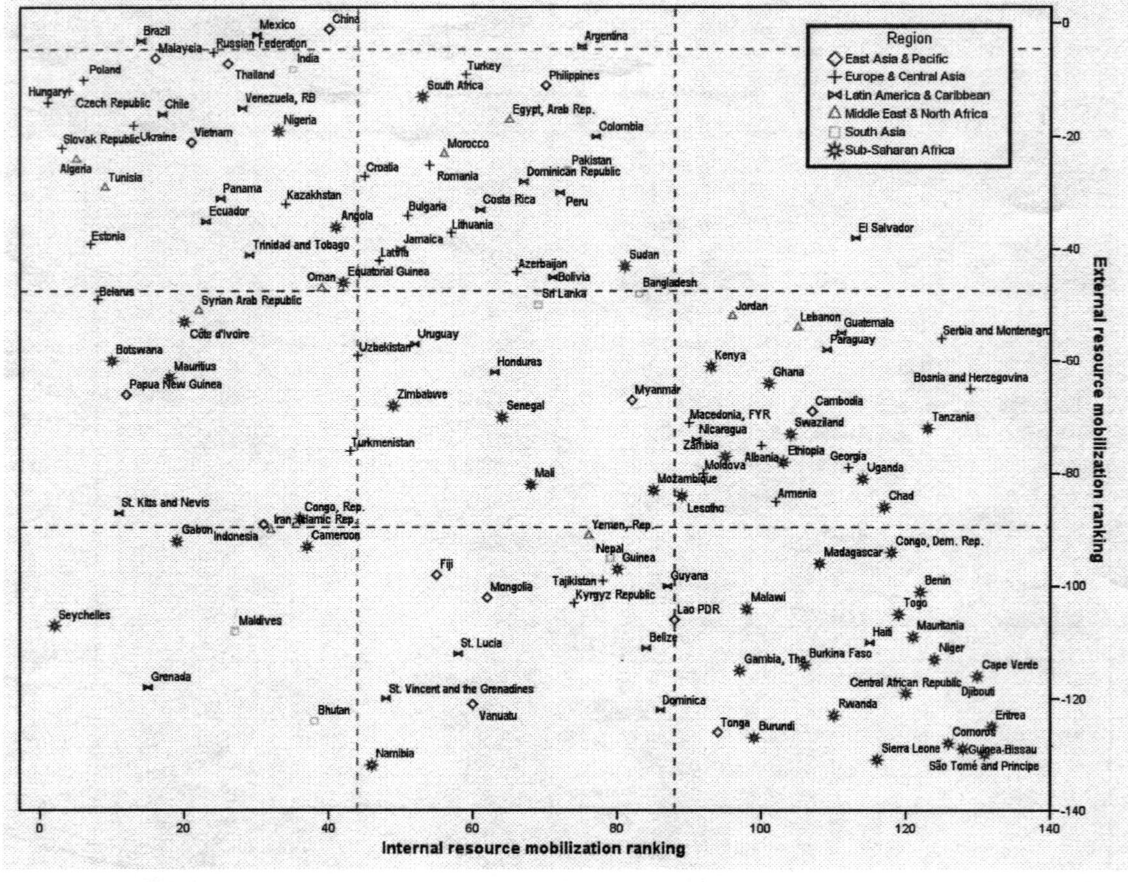

Figure B2   Regions and resource mobilization capacities

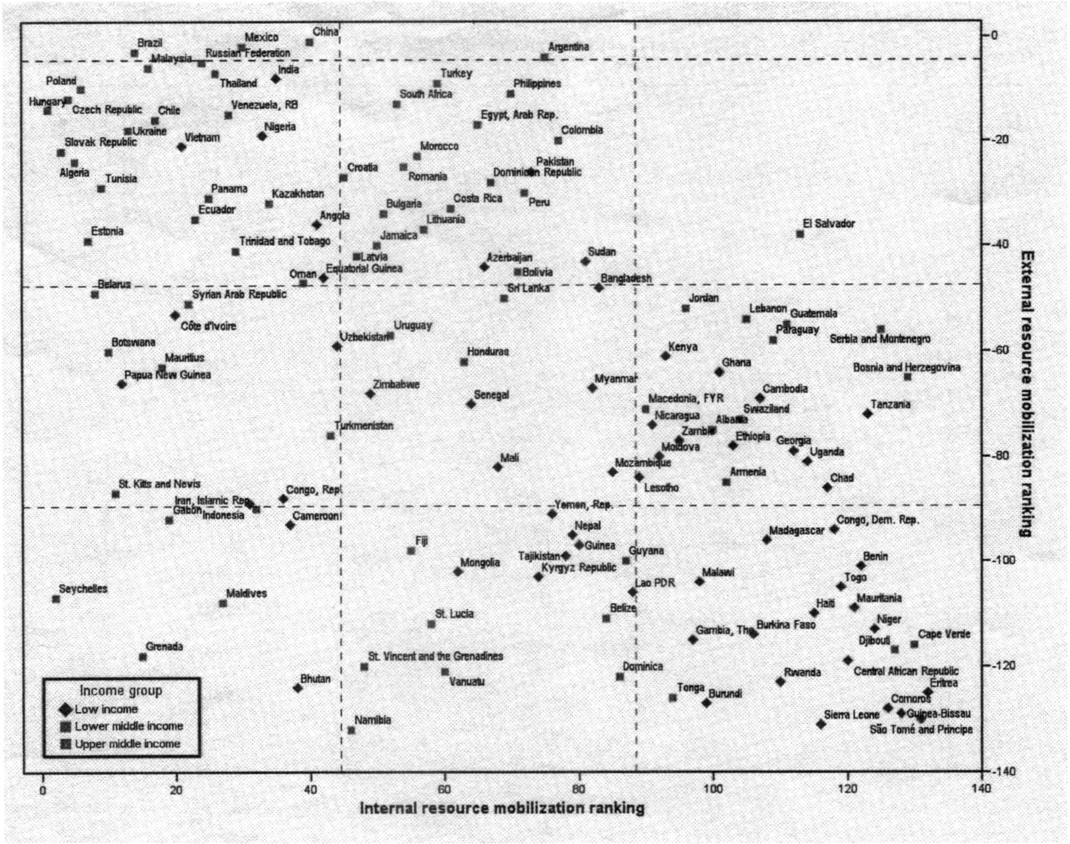

Figure B3   Income and resource mobilization capacities

226

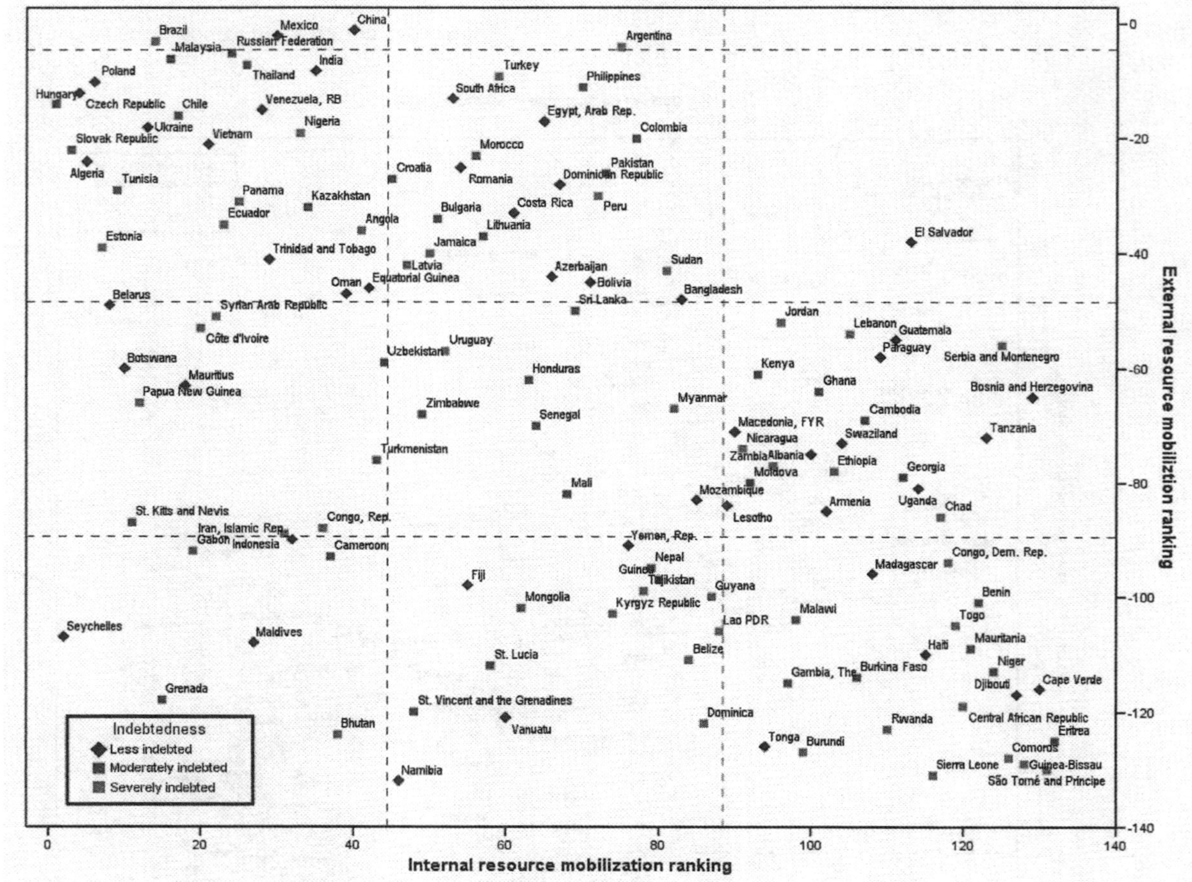

Figure B4   Indebtedness and resource mobilization capacities

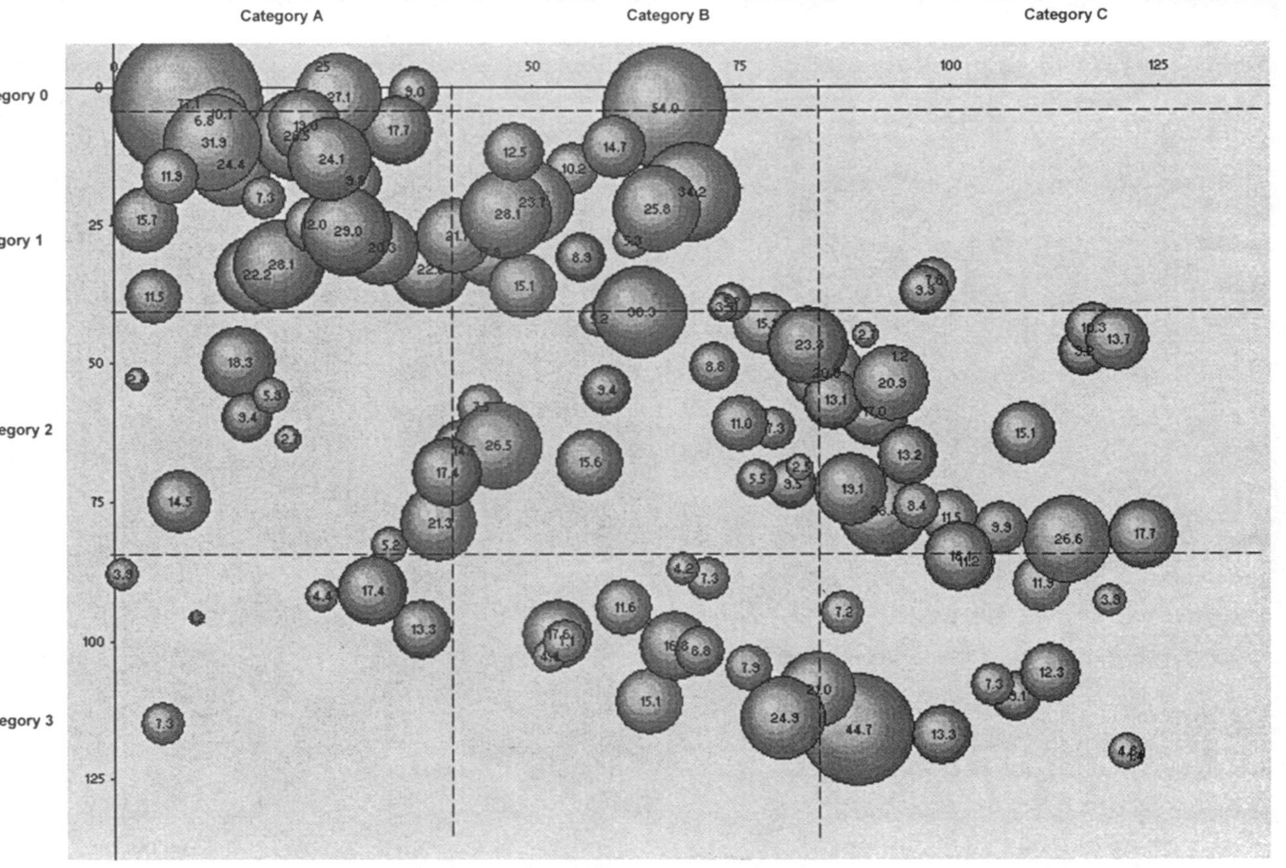

Figure B5 Debt service and resource mobilization capacities
Note: Each circle represents the country position in the ranking. The area of each circle corresponds to the value of the ratio Debt service/Exports (its value is indicated in the number).

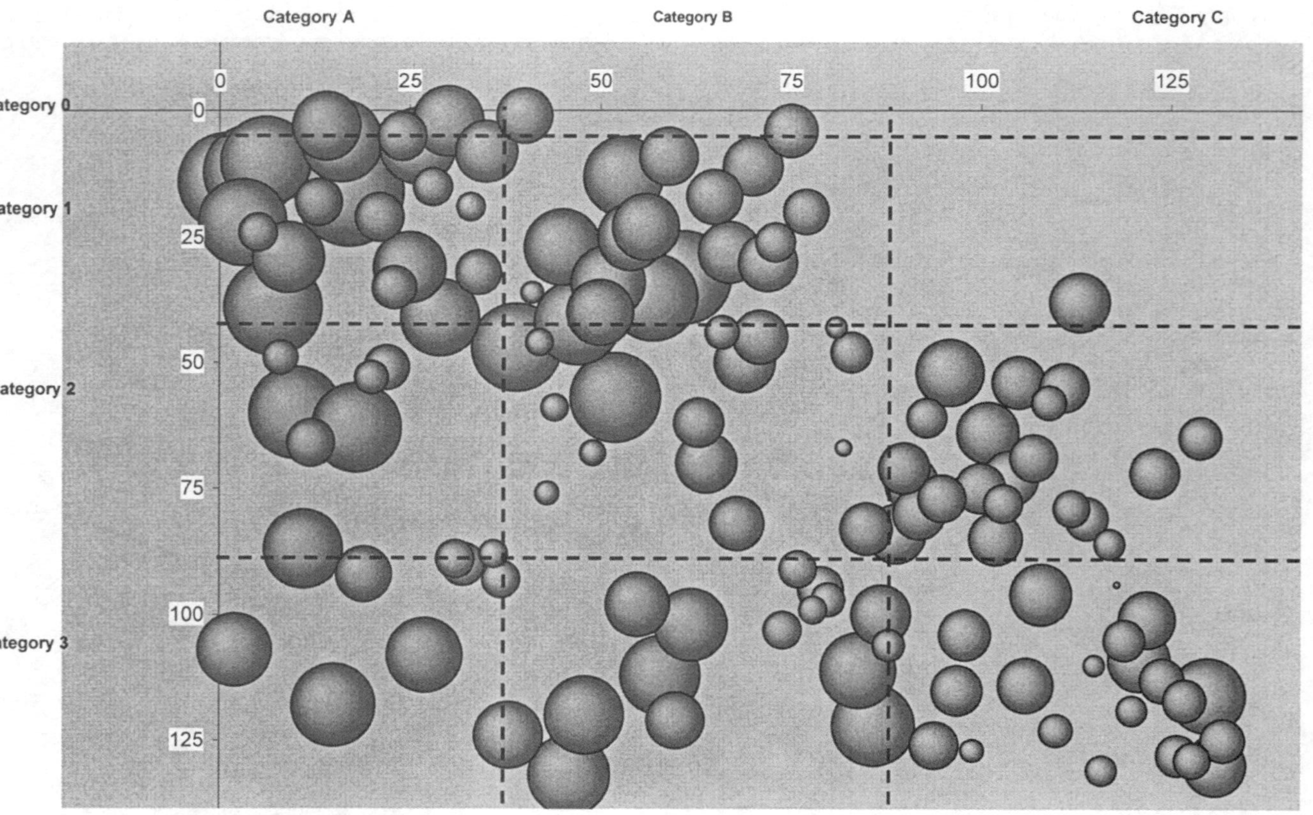

Figure B6 World Bank Governance Indicator and resource mobilization capacities
Note: Each circle represents the country position in the ranking. The area of each circle corresponds to the value of its governance indicator.

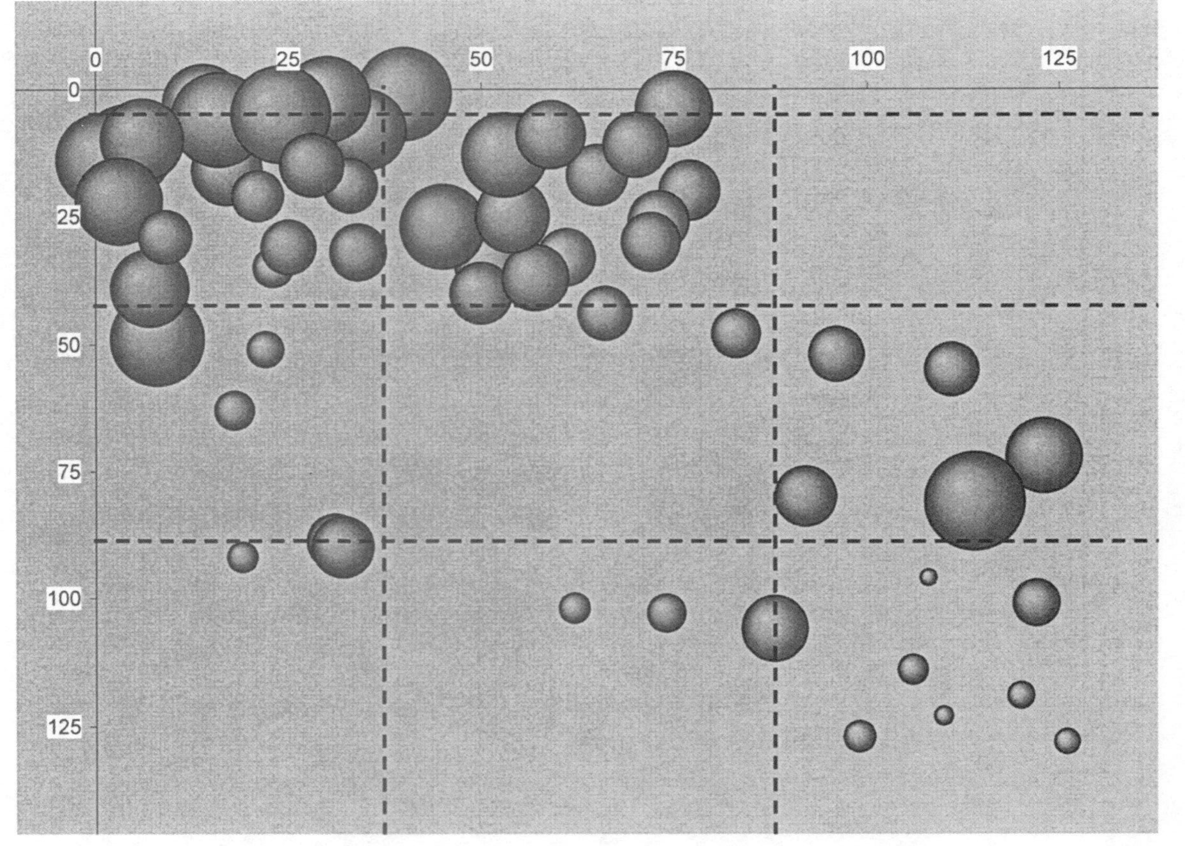

Figure B7 Science and Technology Index and resource mobilization capacities
Note: Each circle represents the country position in the ranking. The area of each circle corresponds to the value of its S&T index, which is not available for all countries.

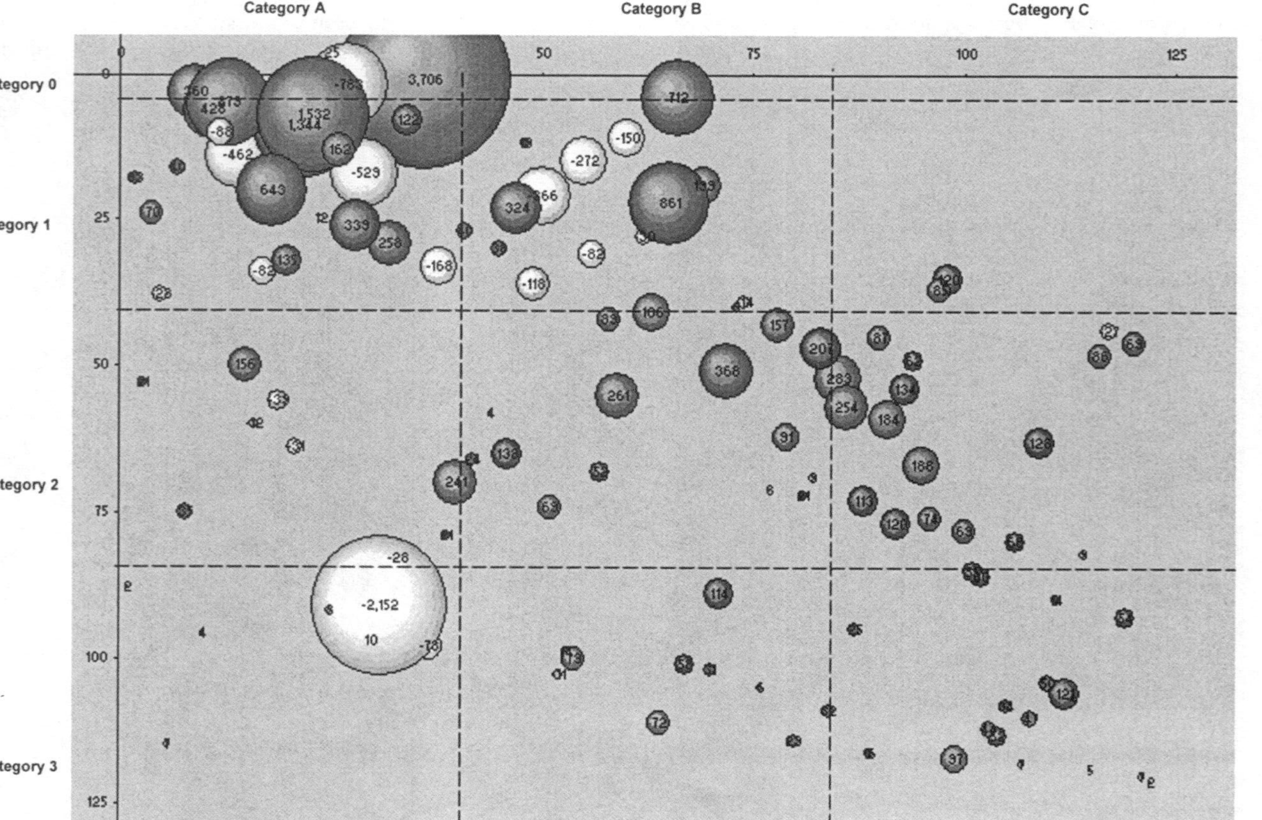

Figure B8 ODA net flows and resource mobilization capacities

Note: Each circle represents the country position in the ranking. The area of each circle corresponds to the value of net ODA flows in annual average for the period 1997–2002. White circles indicate negative ODA net flows.

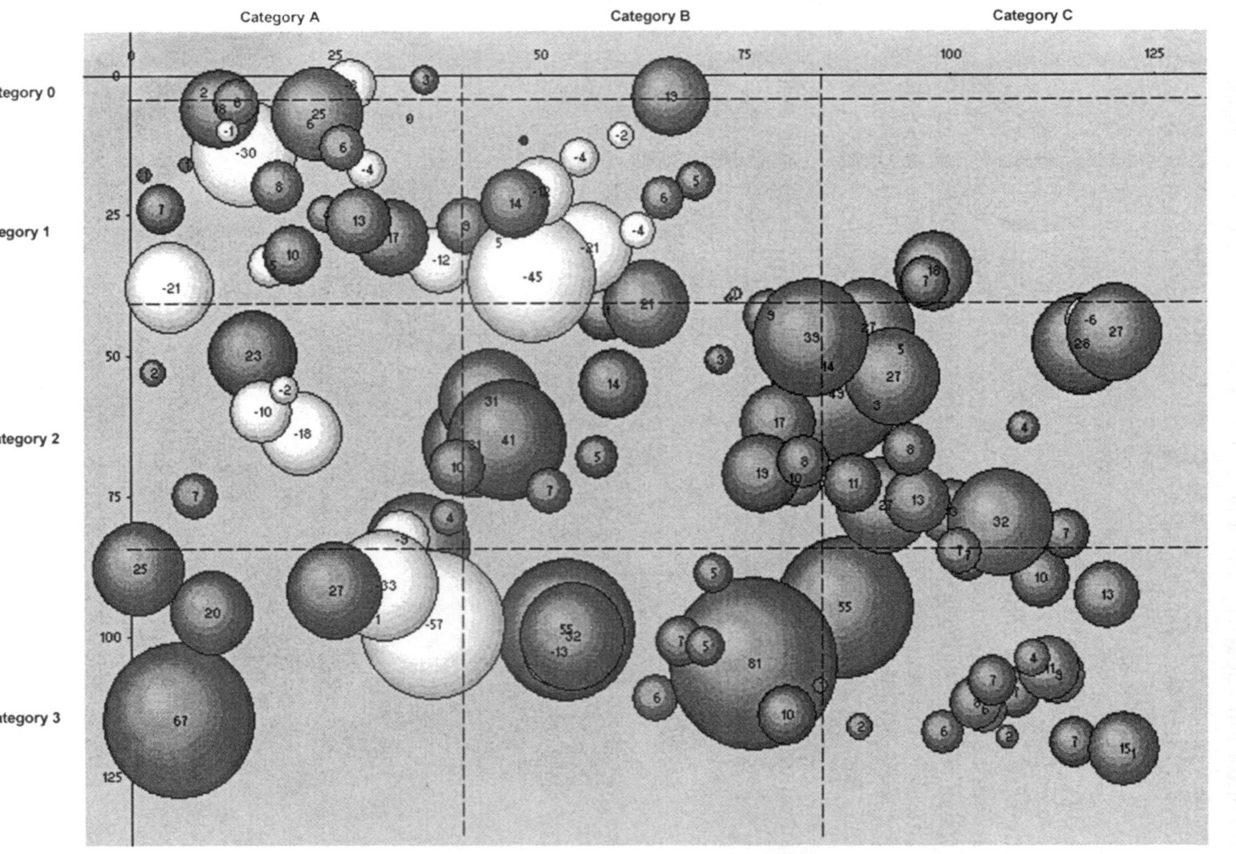

Figure E9   ODA net flows per capita and resource mobilization capacities
Note: Each circle represents the country position in the ranking. The area of each circle corresponds to the value of net ODA flows per capita in annual average for the period 1997–2002. White circles indicate negative ODA net flows.

mobilization capacity have higher levels of debt service over exports (which would imply they are able to withstand higher levels of debt service), and that some low-income countries have a smaller debt burden because of the HIPC initiative (Figure B5).

In addition, a comparison with the World Bank's composite governance indicator (Kaufmann, Kraay and Mastruzzi 2003) suggests that governance levels are not closely associated with the resource mobilization standing of a country (Figure B6), while a comparison of resource mobilization capacities with the Science and Technology Capacity Index (Sagasti 2004a) shows a strong positive relationship (Figure B7). Finally, countries with a higher capacity to mobilize internal and external resources receive more ODA inflows (Figure B8), and most countries that have negative ODA inflows have higher resource capacity mobilization, but when ODA per capita figures are used instead of absolute amounts, a higher concentration of ODA is found in countries with relatively lower capacities to mobilize external and domestic resources (Figure B9).

Index

isolationism   101
Italy, aid-giving   36

Japan   5
   aid policy   109–10
   aid-giving   36, 38–9

Kagan, Robert   105
Kennedy Compromise   6
Kyoto Protocol   87, 101, 170

Latin American Reserve Fund   74, 77
learning   54–5, 183
learning and innovation loans   75
lending windows   13
Lewis, W. Arthur   1
limited reforms   131, 133–7, 141–3,
   184, 186
liquidity provision   163
loans   79, 119, 122, 126
local/regional partnerships   172–3
lotteries   127
Luxembourg, aid-giving   36

McNamara, Robert   2, 5
major reforms   131, 133–7, 143–6,
   184, 186
market creation   129, 170–1
   annual revenue from   157
Marshall Plan   1
Matthew effect   53
Meltzer Report   160
Millennium Challenge Account   38,
   45, 69, 109
Millennium Development Goals   9,
   19, 31, 51, 52, 183
mission creep   111
mobilization of financial resources
   90–100
   country classification   98, 99
   developing countries   95–7
   external   93
   indicators of capacity   91–2
   internal   93
Monterrey Summit   9, 52, 89, 116,
   183
Moody's agency   85
multilateral debt reduction   161
Multilateral Development Banks
   160

Multilateral Investment Guarantee
   Agency   80
multilateralism   102
multipolarity   108

Nature Conservancy   81
net capital flows   10, 11
   developing countries   12
net equity flows   10, 11
net flows on debt   11
net official flows   10, 11
net private flows   11
Netherlands, aid-giving   37
New International Economic Order
   47
New Partnership for African
   Development   9, 15, 60, 64
New Zealand, aid-giving   37
non-core funding   159–60
non-governmental organizations   7,
   23, 113
North Atlantic Treaty Organization
   (NATO)   107
North Korea   109
Northeast Asian Development Bank
   162–3
Norway, aid-giving   37
Nurske, Ragnar   1

official capital flows   15–16
official development assistance   3, 5,
   8, 15, 50
   by country   36–40
   as percentage of GDP   15
   stagnation of   20
Organisation for Economic Cooperation and Development   9
   Economic Outlook   106

Partnership for Polio   89
Patten, Chris   40
performance-linked mechanisms   45
personal gifts   80
Pew Research Center, Global
   Attitudes Report   104
political economy   100–16
political viability   57, 100–16
Poor and Fitch-IBCA   85
portfolio equity flows   13
portfolio flows   127